P9-DHR-552

Rules of Engagement

To our parents, Pat and Morys and Hilary and Michael,
who with over ninety years of marriage between them
have given us a role model and set the foundation
for us to build on.

Katharine and Richard Hill

Rules of Engagement

HOW TO PLAN A
SUCCESSFUL WEDDING

—

HOW TO BUILD A
MARRIAGE THAT LASTS

NEWCASTLE REGION
LIBRARY

- - JAN 2010

LION

Copyright © 2009 Katharine and Richard Hill
Copyright © 2009 Care for the Family
Illustrations copyright © Kate Sheppard 2005

The authors assert the moral right
to be identified as the authors of this work

A Lion Book
an imprint of
Lion Hudson plc
Wilkinson House, Jordan Hill Road,
Oxford OX2 8DR, England
www.lionhudson.com

ISBN 978 0 7459 5505 6

First edition 2005
Revised second edition 2009
10 9 8 7 6 5 4 3 2 1 0

All rights reserved

Acknowledgments
pp. 19–24 Material provided by Simple Extravagance Wedding Services.
pp. 59, 83, 90–91, 117, 119 Extracts taken from *The Marriage Book* by Nicky
and Sila Lee published by Alpha International, 2002. Used by kind permission
of Alpha International.
pp. 63, 116, 138 Extracts taken from *The Marriage Preparation Course Manual*
by Nicky and Sila Lee published by Alpha International, 2003. Used by kind
permission of Alpha International.

This book has been printed on paper and board independently certified
as having been produced from sustainable forests.

A catalogue record for this book is available from the British Library

Typeset in 9/12 Photina MT

Printed and bound in Great Britain by J F Print Ltd., Sparkford, Somerset.

Contents

Appendices

Acknowledgments

Writing this book together has been both a huge challenge and enormous fun.

We are so grateful to Rob Parsons for his wisdom and support, and for writing the foreword and afterword. Thank you also to the team at Care for the Family, and especially to Becky Matyus, Lindsey Sisk and Jo Shepherd for their contributions to this updated edition and to Jenny Steele at Moochu Design for designing the cover.

We also owe a huge debt of gratitude to Nicky and Sila Lee. We 'caught' our passion for marriage and family life from them and are grateful for their continued inspiration, support and encouragement.

We are very grateful to those couples who have allowed us to use their stories. We have changed their names to protect their privacy. The depth of experience that they and many others have shared with us over the years has given us a vast reservoir to draw from.

Thank you to Ross Cobb, Director of Music at Christ Church Clifton, Bristol, who helped us compile the suggested list of music for weddings. Many thanks also to Rachel McWalter from Simple Extravagance wedding planning service for sharing her expertise with us.

Thank you also to all those who have read through parts of the drafts, and given their comments and suggestions, and especially to Gail Ferguson and the team at Lion Hudson.

Finally thank you to our children, George, Charlotte, Edward and Henry, for their encouragement and for making family life so much fun.

Foreword

Over the past twenty-five years or so, I have been privileged to speak to many thousands of people about marriage. Very often at the end of those seminars, queues of people wait to talk about their particular difficulties. I do my best, in the small amount of time available, to address their situation and point them in the direction of some longer-term help. They are sometimes in tears, but at the end of our conversation the couple take time to thank me for the marriage event they have just attended. And then every so often they pause and say, 'If only we'd heard some of this in the early years of our relationship.'

You are about to read this book because you are at the beginning of your relationship – a time for optimism, hope and the promise of good times ahead. But even if all your expectations are fulfilled, the truth is that you will go through some difficult times. In fact your love will never develop fully unless you face such times in your relationship and come through them together. When those times occur, it is important to realize that you are not alone: you are not the only couple in the world who are suddenly finding it hard to talk together, you are not the only ones in financial trouble and there are others who have found that a good sexual relationship sometimes take a little effort (someone once said, 'If a man wants a wild Friday night he had better begin working on it Monday morning!'). When we realize that it's not 'just us', it takes the pressure off and we can more easily find a way through. I love the way that *Rules of Engagement* enforces this truth; it's realistic, practical and down-to-earth.

Foundations are important and this book will help you lay firm ones for your marriage. Starting with the myriad of things that have to be considered for the actual event – which, having just experienced my daughter's wedding, I believe to be on a par with running a small country – it considers the issues that you will face in the early years of your relationship. I urge you to work through the whole book. So many people spend years planning the wedding, but hardly a single day considering the issues they may have to face in the years of marriage that lie ahead. But you are not in that category, for you are taking time to make sure you never have to say, 'If only we'd heard that earlier.'

Let me take this opportunity to congratulate you not just on your marriage, but on your wisdom in taking a little time at the start of your lives together to strengthen the foundations on which you will build that marriage: in short, taking seriously the rules of engagement.

Rob Parsons,
Executive Director, Care for the Family

Introduction

If you have just got engaged, congratulations!

You are about to begin an exciting and wonderful adventure, but one which is not without its challenges. Our purpose in writing this book is to help you meet those challenges as they come along, beginning with the first challenge: planning your wedding. While planning a wedding is great fun, it will almost certainly be hard work. The same can be said of building a marriage.

We have been married for nearly twenty-five years. We love being married and count our marriage as one of our greatest achievements. However, looking back, we don't take one moment of it for granted. Like any worthwhile achievement, building a marriage can be costly. Nevertheless, we believe that there is no greater investment that we can make.

When you became engaged, it is likely that your decision was based on your love for each other and your desire to spend the rest of your lives together. You may be glad to know, however, that there are some other benefits to being married.

Research indicates that not only are married people happier but they are also healthier and have better prospects of employment. Marriage gives companionship; it forms the basis of family life and provides a safe, secure and stable environment within which to bring up children. As you begin to build your marriage together, not only will it benefit you, individually and as a couple, but also the communities in which you live and, therefore, society as a whole.

As you may have already discovered, organizing a wedding requires the strategic know-how and precision planning of the most complex military campaign! We hope therefore that the first section of *Rules of Engagement* will be of value as you organize your wedding day. It will help you to decide on your priorities, set a budget and plan the details accordingly. Most importantly, we hope it will help you keep your wedding day in perspective against the rest of your lives together.

The second part of the book contains ten 'rules of engagement', these being ten principles upon which to build your marriage. They are not intended as a restrictive set of regulations to tie you down but as tools to enable you to set each other free to fulfil your potential and to equip you for a marriage that will be significant and benefit generations to come.

The principal task of engagement is learning how to move from being single to being a couple, to thinking 'us' rather than 'I'. Building a strong marriage is not just about marrying the right person, however much we love them. It involves choice and commitment. It means acquiring skills and developing habits that will lay strong foundations for the future.

At the end of each section, you will find some exercises to enable you to discuss what you have read and to apply it to your relationship. We recommend that you work through these exercises with your fiancé(e), or together perhaps with another married couple who have some experience of the everyday ups and downs of married life.

Our hope is that, as you read this book together, you will develop a vision for your marriage. Perhaps you will discover new things about each other. Most importantly, we hope you have a lot of fun as you prepare to ride the roller coaster of married life. And that you will still be there for each other twenty, thirty, forty and even fifty years on.

Part 1

Planning the Wedding

The Engagement

George Bernard Shaw is quoted as saying, 'Like fingerprints all marriages are different.' Similarly, all proposals are different. Some are very simple, low key affairs, whereas others are much more flamboyant.

Jed proposed to Lucie by checking the tide times, getting up early in the morning and digging the words 'Will you marry me?' into the sand, to the delight and entertainment of others on the coastal path that morning. Andy proposed to Julie by giving her a large present which became a game of pass the parcel, each layer containing an object that symbolized an aspect of their love for each other.

However your proposal has taken place, it is unique to you and marks the beginning of planning your new life together.

The ring

The custom of giving and receiving rings traditionally symbolizes promises made and goods bestowed. We have friends who were on a very limited budget when they got engaged. The engagement ring was initially a curtain ring, replaced when they eventually saved some money. Personal preference as well as budget will dictate your choice but look around and consider all your options before buying. You may want a modern setting. Or you could consider buying an older ring from an antique market. The size and shape of your hands should also be taken into account. Those with long fingers can wear large rings; those with shorter fingers are generally better with something smaller and simpler. Unless you want to keep your engagement ring for special occasions, it is advisable to avoid a ring with a setting which looks as though it may catch on clothes or become scratched with wear.

Announcement

At one time it was customary for the bridegroom to ask his future father-in-law formally for permission to take his daughter's hand in marriage. Although this is no longer a formal requirement, many future grooms still do so out of courtesy. In any event, the first people to hear the good news should be both sets of parents.

Some families still follow the tradition of placing a public announcement in the 'Forthcoming Marriages' column of a national or local newspaper. If you wish to do this, some newspapers still require the announcement to be submitted in writing and signed by one of the couple or a parent. Traditionally it is arranged and paid for by the bride's parents.

Engagement party

You might like to have a party to celebrate your engagement. This can be as formal or as informal as you wish, with friends, family or both. Some parents also like to host a party to celebrate. If they live some distance apart, they may even wish to organize separate celebrations.

Length of engagement

The length of an engagement is often dictated by practical considerations.

Luke and Ally were engaged for eighteen months to enable Ally to finish her course and complete her exams. Dave and Anna were married after an engagement of only four weeks because he was in the air force and given a posting abroad at short notice.

The availability of the church, register office or other approved venue, as well as the particular season of the year in which you want to marry, may also influence your choice. Currently, the average engagement is eighteen months, though anything between five months and two years is common. While you want to leave enough time to make the arrangements, too long an engagement can put a strain on your relationship.

Wedding Myths

We hope what follows will help you navigate your way through the weeks ahead as you tackle the practicalities of your wedding. Many magazines and websites will give you up-to-date information on what to buy and where to buy it, but we hope that the following pages will give you some general principles to bear in mind as you make plans together.

One of the delights of preparing couples for marriage is the number of weddings we are now invited to attend. Looking back, the most memorable weddings have been wonderful, not necessarily because of the great venue, grand reception or even the good food and drink. What has made them special has been the relaxed atmosphere and obvious love and enjoyment of the day by the bride and groom, encapsulated primarily in the way they say their vows to each other.

The following pages will help you to have a relaxed and memorable day and to keep the wedding arrangements in perspective against the backdrop of the rest of your lives together.

We want to begin by dispelling five myths that you may have been led to believe:

✖ MYTH 1
You can have a perfect wedding
Settle for a wonderful wedding involving imperfect people.

✖ MYTH 2
Your wedding day is for you and your fiancé(e)
Of course this is your special day but it is also an important day for at least two sets of parents and two or more families. If you can recognize this and learn to involve them in the arrangements, you will reap the benefits in the long term.

You are also hosting a celebration for your guests and it is a wonderful opportunity to show your appreciation for all they have done for you over the years. So when planning your day, give consideration to their needs as well as your own. (This is particularly important to bear in mind if your parents are contributing to the cost of the wedding.)

✖ MYTH 3
The wedding industry has only your interests at heart

Visit any wedding fair and you will be inundated with the latest must-haves for the perfect wedding, many of which will involve you parting with a considerable amount of cash. There are of course many honest bridal businesses who sell beautiful things at a fair price. Just be aware that the wedding business is what it says – a business.

✖ MYTH 4
Planning a wedding is glamorous and stress-free

If you plan carefully and stick to your budget, planning a wedding together can be fun. However, it is hard work and there will almost certainly be times when you have a difference of opinion either with each other or with your parents over the arrangements. Turn to *Rule 4, Find Joint Solutions* on p. 80. Be realistic about what can be achieved within the time and budget available.

✖ MYTH 5
You have to spend a fortune to have a fantastic wedding

It is quite possible to have a fantastic wedding on a limited budget. Be resourceful and use your common sense and initiative. Budget your time and money carefully and ask friends to help. (See p. 52 for suggestions for cutting the cost.) Search the internet to find discount prices. Do your homework and be creative.

There is no doubt that planning a wedding can be a stressful business. Looking back, many couples have commented on how getting engaged seems to have catapulted them overnight into the exciting but all-consuming world of wedding planning. One couple said, 'The moment we got engaged, it felt like we had stepped onto a treadmill that was gaining speed and momentum and over which we had no control. We didn't know how to get off.'

Rachel McWalter, who runs the wedding planning service Simple Extravagance, advises couples to begin by pressing the 'pause' button.

'So many couples are pressurized into making expensive decisions without taking time to sit down and think through the type of wedding that they really want.'

So, before committing yourselves to any expenditure, set time aside to discuss and agree your priorities for the day. In particular, discuss whether you would like a church wedding or a civil ceremony. Then decide on the style of the reception and the number of guests. Try to be sensitive to the wishes of your respective families.

We suggest you use the following as a basis for discussion:

Agree values

Think about and discuss together:

1. Why do you want to get married?

2. Would you like a civil ceremony or a church wedding and why?

3. What part of the day do you think will be most special to you and why?

4. What do your parents expect from the day?

5. Why do you want others to share your day with you?

6. Who are you thinking of inviting?

On the basis of the above, complete the following:

Our values

The things that matter most to us about our wedding are:

1...

2...

3...

4...

5...

6...

If you can press the 'pause' button and agree your priorities for the wedding day, you will find your other decision making will fall into place within the framework you have set.

Setting a Budget

Having discussed your values, the next task is to set an amount that is available for you to spend. If you are considering borrowing money, be realistic and only borrow what you can actually afford over a given period of time. Remember that your circumstances may well change and so will your needs. Of course you want your wedding day to be special but it might be wise to refrain from spending more money on that extra flower arrangement, chocolate fountain or stretch limousine if it means having insufficient money to buy a kitchen table or put a deposit on your first home.

Before committing yourselves to any expenditure, speak to family members about whether they would like to contribute to your wedding costs. If possible, determine when the money might be available. Then decide your overall budget for the wedding.

Having decided the amount that is available to spend, next consider setting a more detailed budget. As a rough guide, allocate:

50% to the reception	10% to photography
10% to attire	10% to stationery
10% to flowers	10% to extra items

Before you discuss actual figures, you may find it helpful first to establish what specific parts of your wedding to prioritize. This will provide you with guidelines for costing individual items of expenditure. In order to do this, turn to the Wedding Budget Planner (p. 23) and in the first column assign a rating of between 1 and 3 to each item, according to its importance to you both where

1 = Very important
2 = Important
3 = Not important

For example, if you feel that wedding photographs are very important and would make all the difference to the wedding day and afterwards, you would rate wedding photographs 1. However, if you feel that a vintage wedding car would not be of importance to you, you would rate it 3.

In thinking through the importance of each item, you might discover that something you originally considered a priority is in fact not as important to you both as you had thought.

The next step is to complete the budget column by allocating the amount of money you anticipate spending. There will obviously be wide variations in the cost of each item but the amount you decide to spend in relation to your overall budget will directly relate to the level of importance that you have given it. To continue the example above, if you have rated the wedding photographs 1, this will mean spending a higher percentage of your budget on them, probably employing a professional photographer. However, if you had graded photographs as 3 in importance, you would direct that money to other priorities which might mean asking a friend to take photographs for you.

Some expenditure will be non-negotiable (for example, money already spent or fees for the ceremony). For most items, however, choices will need to be made and it may be necessary to bear in mind the Chinese proverb, 'If you do this, then you can't do that!'

While completing the Budget Planner, bear in mind your overall values for the day. For example, the amount of money allocated for the reception may allow you *either* an expensive sit-down meal for 50 *or* a finger buffet for 200. If one priority for the day is to share the occasion with as many friends as possible, that priority will dictate your choice. You may need to go back to your list and revise it as time goes on. Be warned. The issue is often not the individual item that is way outside your price bracket but the add-on effect of several items that are just beyond what you can afford.

If you are having difficulty in making a decision, you may find completing something like the following chart helpful in weighing up alternatives. The example given here is where to stay on the first night of the honeymoon.

	Option 1 **Stay at reception venue**	Option 2 **Stay at a nearby B&B**	Option 3 **Stay at a good hotel nearby**
For	No need to travel	Local Reasonably priced	Very special − would mark the occasion
Against	No formal 'going away' Other guests may be staying there	Not very special	Expensive
Cost	££	£	£££

Wedding Budget Planner

	Grade (1–3)	Budget	Cost
The engagement			
Ring(s)	....	....	....
Party	....	....	....
Photographs	....	....	....
Hen party	....	....	....
Stag party	....	....	....
Wedding preparation			
Invitations	....	....	....
Ring(s)	....	....	....
Bridesmaids' / pageboys' presents	....	....	....
Best man's present	....	....	....
Ushers' presents	....	....	....
Parents' presents	....	....	....
Presents for each other	....	....	....
Wedding cake	....	....	....
Photographer	....	....	....
Video	....	....	....
Menus	....	....	....
Orders of service	....	....	....
Flowers for church	....	....	....
Flowers for reception	....	....	....
Bride's flowers	....	....	....
Bridesmaids' flowers	....	....	....
Outfits			
Bride	....	....	....
Groom	....	....	....
Best man / Ushers	....	....	....
Bridesmaids / pageboys	....	....	....
Father of the bride	....	....	....

	Grade (1–3)	Budget	Cost

The ceremony

	Grade (1–3)	Budget	Cost
Wedding venue hire	....	....	....
Fees for officiant	....	....	....
Organist / choir / bells	....	....	....
Other musicians	....	....	....
Heating	....	....	....
Guest book	....	....	....
Cars	....	....	....
Confetti	....	....	....

The main reception

Venue hire	....	....	....
Food	....	....	....
Drink	....	....	....
Entertainment	....	....	....

Party/evening reception

Venue hire	....	....	....
Food	....	....	....
Drink	....	....	....
Entertainment	....	....	....

Other

Honeymoon	....	....	....
Guest accommodation	....	....	....

Tips for Taking the Stress Out of Planning

1. Keep hitting the 'pause' button.

2. Don't feel pressurized into making decisions.

3. Remember your initial priorities – write them down and put them in a place where you will see them.

4. Keep the wedding in perspective.

5. Buy a wall planner and write down important dates.

6. Buy a folder with pockets to keep all the paperwork together.

7. Handle tasks in a sensible order. Focus on what needs doing, one step at a time.

8. Plan the ceremony. Then make the difficult and expensive decisions, e.g.

Reception + number of guests
Colour scheme/Tone for the day
Bridal outfit
Bridesmaids' dresses
Groom's outfit
Photography
Cars
Stationery
Flowers

9. Try to be sensitive to your families' wishes.

10. Build some planning-free zones into your diary, such as going

out for a meal with your fiancé(e) and agreeing not to mention the wedding.

11. Buy some fizz or party poppers to remind you that this is a celebration. Crack open the fizz and pull the party poppers if you're feeling stressed!

The Wedding Planner Calendar

Each November we buy a magazine which, as well as giving very impractical advice on how to make your own evergreen swags or individual Christmas puddings for twenty, also provides an easy-to-follow Christmas planner. As an aide-mémoire it is invaluable and prevents us from forgetting to ice the Christmas cake before 11.00 p.m. on Christmas Eve.

We hope that the following planner will be of similar use as a general guide. Please ignore the suggestions that are not relevant to you. Add your own ideas as well. Some individual subjects are dealt with in slightly more detail in the next section, 'The A–Z of Planning a Wedding'.

It is quite possible to arrange a wedding in a few weeks. We have used six months as the average starting point but you can adapt the timings to suit your individual circumstances.

At any stage remember to hit the 'pause' button.

At least six to three months before

1. Plan the type of wedding and number of guests.

2. Choose the date, time and place for the ceremony. (If you plan to invite guests who live abroad, send them a 'Save the Date' card to give them plenty of advance notice.)

3. Choose and book the venue for the reception.

4. Set a budget.

5. Arrange to see the minister or registrar.

6. Find out about and attend a marriage preparation course (check out www.prepareformarriage.org.uk or contact info@ncsn.org.uk for details of a course near you).

7. Organize the catering: either book professional caterers or arrange for friends to help.

8. Order your wedding cake, arrange for a friend to make it or plan to make your own.

9. If you want live music, book or arrange it now.

10. Order the wedding cars or arrange to borrow them from friends.

11. Choose and book a photographer.

12. Choose and book a florist or arrange for friends to help provide flowers.

13. Choose and invite attendants – bridesmaids, pageboys, best man and ushers. Invite anyone else you would like to take part in the service.

14. Bride: begin thinking about your wedding dress. Consider whether you want to buy, hire, borrow or have one made.

15. Groom: consider what you will wear and order it if necessary.

16. Choose and order (or arrange the making of) dresses, outfits and accessories for the attendants.

17. Decide where to go for your honeymoon and make reservations. (Arrange somewhere nearby for the first night at least.)

18. Order or design and make your wedding invitations (see Appendix 3).

Three to two months before

1. Discuss and plan your wedding music (see Appendix 10).

2. Discuss and plan the wedding service or ceremony, including appropriate readings (see Appendices 8 and 9).

3. Discuss the order of service with the minister or the ceremony with the registrar. Place an order for or make the orders of service (see Appendix 6).

4. Agree a date for the wedding rehearsal and notify all the people involved.

5. Order any additional stationery, e.g. place cards, cake boxes.

6. Discuss and agree menu with caterers if appropriate.

7. Discuss and arrange for the provision of any necessary road signs or extra parking facilities.

8. Choose and buy your wedding ring(s).

9. Plan and organize a list of wedding presents. (Most large department stores operate a wedding gift register.)

10. Make an appointment to see your doctor or family planning clinic if necessary.

11. If you are planning to go abroad for your honeymoon, arrange any necessary inoculations. Obtain any necessary visas.

12. Check your existing passports are in order. Organize a passport in the bride's new married name if you wish.

13. Buy any necessary clothes for going away and for your honeymoon. Buy or decide upon the shoes you will be wearing on the day.

14. Research accommodation options for those travelling to the wedding from a distance.

15. Book time off work for the wedding and honeymoon, including a few days before the wedding if possible.

16. Finalize your guest list and send out invitations. Include a date by which the guests should reply. Keep a record of replies.

Eight to six weeks before

1. Meet with the florist and select flowers.

2. Buy presents for the bridesmaids, best man and any other attendants.

3. Make arrangements for where any bridesmaids or pageboys will dress on the day of the wedding.

4. Check that all licences, banns and certificates are in order for the ceremony. Unless you are marrying in the Church of England, visit

your local register office to give notice of marriage and purchase a marriage licence.

5. If you are marrying in the Church of England (or the Church in Wales), go to hear your banns read.

6. If you plan to change your name, notify the relevant organizations (see Appendix 2).

7. Organize the stag night and the hen party.

Four weeks before

1. Bride: have a final fitting for your wedding dress, wearing the shoes you will wear for the ceremony. It is also a good idea to wear the shoes around the house so they are comfortable on the day.

2. Make a provisional seating plan for the reception if appropriate.

3. If you have a 'going away' outfit, check that there will be a room at the reception available for you to change.

4. Bride: discuss ideas for your hair with a hairdresser or find a friend who will help you. Try the style out beforehand. Try out your make-up.

5. Groom: begin to think about and write speech.

6. Make arrangements for the bride's and groom's families, if appropriate, for the night before the wedding.

Two weeks before

1. Confirm arrangements for photographs, flowers, cars and catering.

2. Assemble clothes and other items for honeymoon.

3. Check that any table decorations, linen and place cards are in order.

One week before

1. Give final numbers to caterer.

2. If required, send wedding announcement to newspaper.

3. Wrap gifts for attendants.

4. Bride: arrange a facial, manicure, pedicure or any other relaxing treatment if you wish.

5. Pack honeymoon luggage. Check tickets. Give tickets and spare car keys to best man.

6. Attend the wedding rehearsal if appropriate.

7. Make arrangements for your clothes to be taken home from the reception after the wedding. If you have hired suits, make arrangements for these to be returned.

The day before

1. Fill car with petrol. Check oil, water and tyres.

2. Pack going-away clothes and have suitcase(s) delivered to reception.

3. If there will not be time on the day, give presents to attendants.

4. Get a reasonably early night.

The day

Relax and enjoy!

Tips for enjoying the day

1. Allow yourselves plenty of time to get ready.

2. Don't 'sweat the small stuff' (i.e. don't let small issues spoil the day).

3. Be your own internal camera – make yourselves pause every so often to take in and remember each stage of the day.

The A–Z of Planning a Wedding

While you may want to read this section through, it is designed as a reference section for you to dip into and return to as necessary.

🏵 Accessories

The right accessories can beautifully enhance your wedding dress. Even if you are not wearing a veil, most brides choose to have flowers in their hair, either attached to a headdress or woven in singly. You may prefer to wear a hat to complete your outfit, especially if you are not wearing a traditional wedding dress. Shoes need to be comfortable and non-slip with a heel to suit your dress and height. The groom, best man, the father of the bride and the ushers may choose to wear coordinating ties or waistcoats.

🏵 Accommodation

It is helpful to research local hotels or bed and breakfasts for guests travelling any distance. You might include a list of options at varying prices with the invitations, giving websites or contact numbers.

🏵 Approved premises

It is possible to have the wedding ceremony and reception in approved premises such as a castle, mill, tithe barn or stately home. Your local register office will be able to give you a brochure listing the options available in your area. Select the venue where you wish to marry, check the availability of the registrar and book them together.

🏵 Attendants

The custom of having attendants at a wedding is a practical one. Traditionally, older bridesmaids were there to help prepare and dress the bride for her wedding day. Many bridal parties are now made up of one or two older bridesmaids, together with younger bridesmaids or pageboys.

A bride will often ask a sister, friend, nephew, niece or godchild to take part in this way. If you plan to involve very young children as attendants you may need to be flexible as to what they are able (or prepared) to do on the day itself.

🐝 Banns

If you decide to marry in the Church of England, you will need to have your banns read. Banns are the public announcement of your intention to marry. They are read out in the churches of the parish where each of you live for three consecutive weeks before the wedding and are valid for three months. There will be a small fee. Once they have been read out, the vicar will give you a banns certificate.

If you want to marry in a church other than your local parish church, you may need to obtain a common licence or, in exceptional circumstances, a special licence. See 'Church weddings' on p. 35 for more information.

🐝 Best man

The best man carries considerable responsibility for assisting the groom on the wedding day. Grooms generally choose a brother or a close friend. The best man helps the groom arrange the stag night. He looks after the ring(s) during the service and may also have custody of the honeymoon tickets and passports. He sits with the groom during the service and sees that everyone has transport to the reception. At the reception, it is the best man's role to make a speech and to reply on behalf of the bridesmaids.

🐝 Bridesmaids

Traditionally, bridesmaids are unmarried (a married bridesmaid is called a matron of honour). The bridesmaids follow the bride and, if appropriate, help with her train. We have been at weddings where the bride has (once in error and once planned) followed the bridesmaids into the church. The chief bridesmaid may look after any younger bridesmaids or pageboys and holds the bride's flowers during the ceremony, returning them to her usually during the signing of the register. Either she or the bride's mother may help the bride to change and may also look after the wedding dress if the reception is being held away from home. It is usual for the bride to choose the bridesmaids' dresses. The style will depend on that of the wedding and of the bride's dress in particular. If bridesmaids are of different ages, one option is to choose a particular fabric and have all the bridesmaids' dresses made in it to styles that suit the individuals. Although traditionally bridesmaids' dresses are paid for by the bridesmaids themselves, today the cost is often shared.

Cake

The wedding cake forms the centrepiece at the reception. Traditionally it is a rich fruit cake, iced and decorated, which may have two, three or four tiers. Some couples keep the top tier and use it as the christening cake for their first child. Although fruit cake is traditional, many couples choose a chocolate or plain sponge cake instead or as well. The bride and groom generally cut the first slice of cake before the toast and speeches. The rest of the cake is then sliced and served after the speeches. Many people like to send a slice of cake to anyone who has been unable to come to the wedding and cake boxes can be ordered for this purpose. You can order a cake from a professional baker, buy one from a supermarket to decorate, or arrange for a friend to make one for you.

Catering

The size, type and time of your reception (and of course your personal preference) will all influence your choice of food. If you are using professional caterers for your reception, go through the menu carefully with them and let them know of any special dietary requirements for your guests. If you are not using professional caterers and are holding a small reception, you might consider asking a friend to help or inviting close friends and family members to contribute dishes. It is advisable to choose simple dishes that you think most people will enjoy.

Ceremony

Take as much care over planning the wedding ceremony itself as you do in planning the rest of the day's activities, whether you are marrying in a church, register office or other approved venue. You might want to consider involving others in the service by asking them to take specific roles in the readings, prayers or music (see Appendices 8, 9 and 10 for suggested readings and music).

If you are marrying in a church where you are already part of the church family, the wedding service can be a great celebration of your individual lives being joined together in God.

If you choose to marry in a licensed venue, regulations stipulate that nothing with religious connotations can be incorporated into the ceremony.

Children

When compiling a guest list, many brides and grooms agonize over whether to include children in the invitation. You may want to include all close family members but most parents will understand if children are not invited. If you do decide to invite a number of young children, it is a good idea to provide some specific entertainment for them, such as a bouncy castle or DVD or games room which will ensure both they and their parents enjoy the day to the full.

Church weddings

If you decide to marry in church, the first thing you need to do is to arrange to see the vicar or parish priest and ask if they will conduct your wedding.

Marriage in the Church of England or Church in Wales: you will be able to marry in a church where you are on the electoral roll or where either or both of you live in the parish. You can also marry in a particular church:

i) if one of you was baptized or prepared for confirmation in the parish, or

ii) if you or one of your parents has lived in or attended church services in the parish for at least six months at any time, or

iii) if one of your parents or grandparents was married in the parish.

The vicar will arrange either for your banns to be called on three consecutive Sundays before the day of your wedding or for a common licence to be issued (see Banns). The marriage will also be registered by the vicar so there is no need to involve the superintendent registrar. A fee will need to be paid.

Marriage in any other church or religious building: A registrar's certificate or licence to marry needs to be obtained for every marriage according to any other denomination or faith other than the Church of England (see Civil ceremony). The church or religious building must normally be in the registration district where either or both of you live. If the church does not have its own registrar, you will need to arrange for the registrar to attend the service. There will be a prescribed fee for this.

🐝 Civil ceremony

You may decide on a civil ceremony, either in a register office or in another building approved for civil marriage. The ceremony in the register office will be much shorter and simpler than a church service and the number of guests you can invite will be limited by the space available. Ceremonies in approved premises can be personalized to suit you; again, the number of guests will be determined by the size of the premises. All marriages must be witnessed by at least two adults.

If you choose a civil ceremony, you may marry at any register office or approved premises that you choose. You need to:

i) contact the superintendent registrar of the district where you intend to marry;

ii) make arrangements at the venue in question (if not a register office);

iii) also give formal notice of marriage to the superintendent registrar of the district *where you live*.

Both of you must have lived in a registration district for at least seven days immediately before giving notice at the register office. If you both live in the same district, you should attend your local register office together to give your notices of marriage. There will be a fee for this, details of which can be obtained from the superintendent registrar. If you live in different registration districts, each of you will need to give notice in your own areas. After giving notice, there must be an interval of a further fifteen clear days before the registrar issues the certificate and the marriage can take place. (For example, if notice is given on 1 April, the marriage may take place on or after 17 April.)

The notice of marriage is valid for one year. If you have a long engagement, many register offices run a provisional booking system which means that you can book more than a year in advance if you wish. You can then go ahead and book the reception and simply give your legal notice of marriage at the appropriate time to confirm the booking.

Because the notice is a legal statement, you must give notice in person. A relative or friend may not give notice on your behalf, nor may it be done by telephone. Most register offices have an appointment system. When giving notice of marriage, you will need to produce proof of your identity and nationality (for example, birth certificate and passport). If you are divorced, you will need to show a decree absolute bearing the court's official stamp. If you have been widowed, you will need to bring a certified copy of your spouse's death certificate. Also, if you have changed your name, the relevant documentation will need to be shown. Additionally, if either of you is under eighteen, the registrar will need proof that a parent or guardian consents to the marriage.

If either of you is divorced, you may choose to have a civil ceremony followed by a church service of blessing (see Appendix 4). Whether you can marry in church in these circumstances depends on the policy of the church in question. Most ministers like to talk to you about the past to help you make a new start (see *Rule 6*).

🌾 Confetti

Many churches or register offices will have guidelines about where it is possible to throw confetti. They may make an announcement about this before the arrival of the bride. Flower petals or crushed lavender make an attractive alternative.

🗡 Dress

Bride: choosing a dress can be very easy or very difficult, depending on how precise an idea you have of the style you want. The traditional wedding dress is white and floor-length but you can choose whatever style you like. Remember that during the service it is the back of the dress that will be seen. It is a good idea to have a detachable train, designed so it can be hooked up for the reception. You may prefer to wear a shorter wedding dress or a suit. You can buy your dress ready-made or have it made for you, either professionally or by a friend. Alternatively, if you are gifted in this area, you may be able to make your own dress. If you are on a limited budget, consider buying an end-of-line sample, hiring or buying a second-hand dress off the internet. It's also worth finding out whether there are any second-hand bridal wear shops in your area. Arrange a fitting wearing the shoes that you plan to wear on the day.

Groom: for a formal wedding, a groom will often wear traditional morning dress or, for a late afternoon wedding, a dinner jacket, both of which may be hired. Alternatively, an ordinary suit is fine. The important thing with dress is to check the expectations of each family.

The best man and other close family members usually take their lead from the groom. If you are in the armed services, you may wear your uniform. Plain black, lace-up shoes look good with most suits. If you buy new shoes, remember to wear them in so that they are comfortable on the day.

🗡 Drink

Champagne and sparkling wine are the traditional drinks to serve at a wedding. For receptions with a sit-down meal, consider serving red or white wine with the food and a non-alcoholic alternative. A glass of champagne or sparkling wine may be given to guests on arrival and also before the toasts. If you are doing your own catering, many retailers provide free glass hire if you buy the wine from them. If the venue allows you to provide your own drink, consider a sale-or-return arrangement and take into account any corkage charges.

Where professional caterers are supplying the wine, make sure that you agree a price and taste it beforehand. Alternatively, you can just serve soft drinks, in which case a fruit punch, such as elderflower cordial with mint and slices of lemon, can make a good alternative. If you have a limited budget, you might consider a paying bar in the evening.

🐝 Entertainment

If your reception is in the evening, you may want to organize music and dancing. This can be live or recorded music. A barn dance or ceilidh is also great fun and ensures that most guests can participate.

🐝 Evening reception

If you have friends that you have been unable to include in the main reception, consider inviting them to the service and then to a later evening reception after the main reception has finished. Another way of including more friends is to invite everyone to the speeches and cake cutting immediately after the ceremony. A selection of guests then moves on to a smaller reception. In this case, separate invitations need to be issued (see Appendix 5).

🐝 Flowers

When choosing flowers, think carefully about where they will be most noticed and appreciated by your guests. It is surprisingly easy to overrun your budget in this area. If you are using a florist, ask to see photographs of their work or find one who comes with a personal recommendation. When you meet the florist, take along swatches and a sketch of your dress plus a small piece of material or ribbon from the bridesmaids' dresses. If a friend is arranging your flowers for you, discuss with them in detail what you would like. The style and shape of the bride's bouquet will be partly dependent on the design and style of her dress. Similarly, consider size – a petite bride would be dwarfed by an enormous bouquet while a tall bride may look odd with a very small posy. Small posies of fresh flowers are also suitable for young children to carry.

As well as the bride's bouquet and headdress, you will need to consider flowers for the bridesmaids, buttonholes for the groom, father

of the bride, best man and ushers, flowers for the church and flowers for the reception. Potted plants can sometimes be hired for the day from local nurseries and marquees can be decorated with hanging baskets. If you are getting married in a season when flowers are more expensive, consider using artificial flowers mixed with real foliage and the occasional spray of fresh flowers. If you use real flowers, consult the table in Appendix 7 and try to obtain flowers that are in season. Whatever flowers you decide on, ensure your arrangements are in keeping with the venue and style of the day.

Gift list

Wedding guests very much appreciate having a wedding list from which to choose a gift. Most department stores operate a wedding register where gifts can be bought in person, on the telephone or online. There are also dedicated wedding-list companies. Alternatively, it is possible to produce your own list. Compiling a list is quite time-consuming but it ensures that people give you what you really need and avoids duplication. If possible, choose gifts in the widest possible price range and keep a note of all you receive so you can write thank-you letters. If gifts are brought to the reception, arrange for the best man or bride's mother to be responsible for them.

✻ Hen party

A hen party is generally organized by close friends of the bride. It should take place at least two weeks before the wedding and can take any form from a day at a spa or health farm to an afternoon shopping followed by a pizza and DVD. It is often arranged to take place at the same time as the groom's stag party. The costs are generally divided between the group.

✻ Homecoming

It is worth some planning and some help from friends to ensure that when you arrive back from your honeymoon not only is the electricity and water connected but there is some food in the fridge and sheets on the bed. When you are tired from travelling, this can make all the difference.

✻ Honeymoon

Remember that you will be tired after the wedding so it is sensible to stay somewhere locally for the first couple of nights in order to recover and then travel further afield if you plan to do so. An energetic water sports holiday or a trek across the foothills of the Himalayas may not be the best honeymoon choice. If you want to have the trip of a lifetime, plan it a year or so into marriage. Decide whether to honeymoon in this country or abroad and whether you want a hotel or self-catering accommodation. The more you find out about your destination, the less chance of your being disappointed. Book ahead where possible, as leaving too much to chance can be stressful. Where possible, a personal recommendation is invaluable.

Remember to specify that you want a double bed; it is worth saying when you book that it is for your honeymoon. Most hotels will try to give you a good room and some will even offer flowers or sparkling wine. Remember also to allow some spending money in your budget. If travelling abroad, you may need to order currency. Take out insurance and check that your passports and any visas are in order. If the bride would like to change her name on her passport, a form can be obtained in advance from the post office for this purpose. Of course you want your honeymoon to be wonderful but do be realistic and don't let small imperfections spoil your time together.

Insurance

As with most areas of life, it is possible to insure a wedding. This will cover eventualities such as theft, cancellation of the reception due to illness or double-booking of the venue. Consider also taking out travel insurance for the honeymoon.

Invitations

The invitations should be sent two to three months before the wedding. Formal invitations are usually printed. Printers, department stores and large stationers hold sample books of designs to suit all tastes and budgets. It is also possible to buy packs of preprinted invitations to be completed as appropriate after purchase.

It is increasingly common for a couple to design their own invitations. An informal invitation needs to contain the same information as a formal invitation but there is more choice, both in what may be said and how to say it, as well as in the appearance of the invitation in terms of colour and illustration. (For appropriate wording, see Appendices 3, 4 and 5.)

Along with the invitations, you may wish to enclose a response card, a map and directions to the ceremony, details of accommodation and the gift list.

Jewellery

It is worth considering in advance what jewellery the bride and bridesmaids will wear that will complement their dresses.

Legal matters

The definition of a legal marriage is the union of one man with one woman, voluntarily entered into for life to the exclusion of all others.

You must be over eighteen, or over sixteen with your parents' written consent, and legally free to marry. A marriage may take place on any day at any time between 8 a.m. and 6 p.m. in a registered place of worship, a register office or other approved premises. Civil or ecclesiastical preliminaries (banns, licence or superintendent registrar's certificate) must precede every marriage.

⚘ Make-up

It is a good idea for brides to practise applying their make-up before the day itself. It might be wise to put make-up on after putting on the dress, perhaps protecting the dress with a scarf.

⚘ Marriage preparation

By attending a marriage preparation course during the months leading up to your wedding, you will be ensuring that you are preparing not just for the wedding day but for your future together. If the registrar or minister does not offer you marriage preparation, contact The National Couple Support Network at Care for the Family, Garth House, Leon Avenue, Cardiff, CF15 7RG, tel: (029) 2081 0800. Alternatively, email info@ncsn.org.uk who will try to put you in touch with a course in your area. Visit www.prepareformarriage.org.uk to find out more about different ways in which you can prepare for marriage together.

⚘ Music

Church wedding: if you are getting married in church, it is worth spending time and care choosing the music for the service. You should discuss your choice with the minister. Depending on the church's tradition, there are usually a number of options, such as a formal choir, organ music or a band. It is worth choosing hymns and songs that most people know. You will also need to choose music for the entrance of the bride and for when you both leave the church, as well as music to play during the signing of the register. (Some suggestions are contained in Appendix 10.)

Civil ceremony: music for a civil ceremony must not contain any religious reference. Either modern or classical music may be played (live or recorded) when entering and leaving the marriage room. Both the selection of music and where it is to be played should be agreed in advance with the superintendent registrar. It would also be wise to check that suitable equipment to play music is available.

🦋 New name

At the end of the ceremony, the bride signs her maiden name in the register. Taking a new name is optional and some women choose to retain their maiden name for a number of purposes. The acquisition of a new name is one of the most visible signs of a new marital status. If you are changing your name, you'll need to inform the relevant organizations. These are listed in Appendix 2.

🦋 Order of service

This can be printed professionally or produced by yourselves at home. The style of the wedding invitation may be replicated in the order of service. It is customary to include the names of everyone taking part in the service, not only the minister but also those of friends or family who are giving readings or leading prayers. If you would like to invite another minister to take part, you should ask the resident minister's consent.

Hymns can be printed in full but you need to check whether you need permission for the copyright. Ask the minister if there is a specific music copyright licence number: if so, include the completed phrase 'All music is covered by CCL no. ...' at the bottom of the page.

Otherwise the appropriate address to write to for this information generally appears in the acknowledgments in the front of the hymn book. In many cases no fee is required, provided you print an acknowledgment in the order of service.

Remember to order one order of service per person plus some spare copies as you might like to send a copy to anyone unable to be there on the day.

🦋 Photography

The cost of the photography at your wedding can constitute a large part of the wedding budget and it is worth taking time and care considering

Ideally, get a personal recommendation, ask to meet the photographer and look at their work. In the absence of a personal recommendation, you can check whether they are a qualified member of the MPA (Master Photographers Association), BIPP (British Institute of Professional Photographers) or Guild of Wedding Photographers. Most wedding photographers will have a website on which you can see examples of their work. Discuss beforehand in detail what you want from the photographer. You may wish to have a reportage style documentary of your day or more formal photographs. Either way, ensure that all key family members are included.

Check exactly what the photographer is offering in the way of prints, albums or online ordering. Find out the cost of extra prints and reprints. Remember that whatever price you agree with the photographer, you will almost certainly want to order more prints than you anticipated. Check that the photographer you meet will be the one who turns up on the day and that they have insurance and back-up equipment. Also check with the minister or registrar whether any pictures may be taken during the ceremony. The majority of photographs will almost certainly be taken after the ceremony and at the reception. Consider also whether you would like the photographer to come to the house to photograph the bride getting ready.

If the majority of photographs are taken on arrival at the reception, do consider the needs of your guests and offer them a drink while other photographs are being taken. Similarly, remember to offer the photographer refreshment if they are there all day. If your budget does not run to an official photographer, consider choosing a friend or friends with some experience and make sure they know what is expected of them. Do bear in mind, however, that it is quite a responsibility to be asked to take photographs at a friend's wedding. Another idea is to put disposable cameras on each table for guests to use during the reception and leave behind for you to develop.

Pictures taken on your honeymoon are also an important part of the record of your wedding, so remember to pack a camera and a couple of memory cards.

🏵 Post-wedding blues

After all the excitement and build up to the wedding, it is not uncommon
to feel let down on return from honeymoon and to struggle to readjust
to normal life. 'I got married last October and I'm confronting wedding
withdrawal. It's been hard to kick the high of the bridal habit and to

put away my wedding dress and veil for ever. But what goes up must
come down. It's the law of fiancé(e) physics.' (*Wedding Day Magazine*,
February/March 2004)

Adjusting to married life and building foundations for the future is
fun but can be hard work. Work through the Rules in the second half
of this book and understand how to build a relationship that will last a
lifetime. Try to understand and meet each other's needs, make special
time together and seek help if you need it. Use the memories of your
wedding day as a springboard to the future (and brides don't have to put
their wedding dress and veil away immediately).

Quantities

The type of reception you are having will influence both your choice of food and drink and the quantity you will require.

For an informal buffet, allow between ten and fifteen finger food items per head. There should be a variety of food. If the guest list numbers between 50 and 100, allow a choice of eight to ten different dishes. If the guests number 250 or more, provide about twenty different sorts of food.

As a general rule, you should allow half to three-quarters of a bottle per head of wine, sparkling wine or champagne. A litre will provide six glasses of soft drink, and remember that guests will drink more on a hot day.

Receiving line

Where there is a formal receiving line, the bride and groom line up with both sets of parents to greet the guests individually as they arrive at the reception. Alternatively, you may decide that only the bride and groom receive the guests or you may opt for no receiving line at all.

Reception

The choice of location for your reception will depend on the number of guests, the atmosphere you wish to create and whether it is to be a formal or informal occasion. You may wish to hold the reception in your own home or, if you have the space, in a marquee in your garden. A rough estimate of space required is 1 square metre per person. A church or village hall is often a good choice and lends a community feel to the celebration. Most large hotels are available for wedding receptions or you may wish to consider somewhere more unusual, perhaps a canal boat or a castle or other historic building. Visit the places you are considering and obtain written estimates to enable you to compare costs and make up your mind.

Rehearsal

The minister, or whoever is conducting your service, may suggest a date for a wedding rehearsal in the week prior to the wedding. This is a good opportunity to go through the ceremony and clarify any queries you may have. You need only wear casual clothes for this. Practise walking up the aisle *slowly*: many people walk too fast because they are nervous.

🦋 Rings

The exchange of engagement and wedding rings continues a tradition that began thousands of years ago. Engraved betrothal rings existed in medieval times. Gold is the traditional metal for engagement and wedding rings. It is mixed with other metals to give it strength and is classified according to the quantity of pure gold in the ring. The purest is 22 carat; 18 carat is less expensive and more hardwearing; and 9 carat contains the least gold. Platinum is another hardwearing metal that is suitable for a wedding ring. White gold is also a popular option, and is cheaper than platinum.

Have your ring size measured properly at any jewellers. Remember that brides will wear their engagement and wedding rings together so choose rings of the same metal and try them on together to make sure that they fit well and do not rub. The groom often chooses a wedding ring to match the bride's or occasionally a signet ring instead. It is a good idea to order your rings eight to ten weeks before the wedding in case they need alteration. You may also wish to have them engraved on the inside with the wedding date, your initials or a personal message.

🦋 Seating

The seating arrangements again reflect the formality of the occasion. If you are serving cake or canapés, guests may stand throughout. At an informal buffet, guests may wish to choose where they sit in groups at small tables. A sit-down reception requires a seating plan and place names. This will involve a considerable amount of work and probably cannot be finalized until the day before the wedding. Take care to put guests at a table with at least some people that they know, as it will add to their enjoyment of the day. Nowadays many brides and grooms choose to sit among their guests. However, if you have a top table, the conventional arrangement is to sit the wedding party facing the guests and next to each other as follows:

Bridesmaid
Groom's father
Bride's mother
Groom
Bride
Bride's father
Groom's mother
Best man

Depending on your family circumstances, the order may need to be adapted. It may be more appropriate to arrange for each parent to host a table of their own.

✹ Speeches

There is a traditional order to speeches at the reception. These are normally given at the end of the meal, although it is quite feasible to have them before the meal begins. The bride's father or a family friend makes the first speech and proposes a toast to the bride and groom. The groom then replies and thanks the bride's parents for the wedding and for their daughter. He can also thank his own parents and all others who have contributed to the special day. He then proposes a toast to the bridesmaids. The best man then replies on behalf of the bridesmaids. There are many books on the market giving advice on speech-making. A golden rule is to remember the range of guests and to be careful to avoid giving offence when using humour.

✹ Stag night

The stag night is generally organized by the best man and groom and is a chance for the groom's male friends to give him a good send-off. The stag night should take place at least two weeks before the wedding and might in fact be simply a night out or an entire weekend of sport and entertainment. As with the hen night, the cost is generally shared among the group.

✹ Table decorations

Depending on the style of the reception, tables can be decorated to follow a theme. Where the budget is limited, a single flower or a candle looks attractive. If you plan to have something more elaborate, keep any decorative arrangement on the table either low or very high so your guests can speak to each other without having to peer through hedges of foliage. Be imaginative: we recently attended a wedding with a seaside theme where the tables were decorated with buckets and spades filled with sand and sticks of rock with the bride and groom's names on them.

🐝 Transport

There is a wide range of special transport that can be hired for a wedding, including vintage cars and horse-drawn carriages. A larger, chauffeur-driven car has the advantage of being roomy inside so the bride can arrive at the ceremony with her dress uncreased. If spending money

in this area is not one of your priorities, consider asking friends to put ribbons on their cars and to help with transport. Alternatively, if it is a sunny day and the reception is nearby, the bride and groom might like to walk, although it would be advisable to have a wet-weather contingency plan. The bride and her father generally travel from the house to the ceremony together as do the bride's mother and the bridesmaids. After the wedding, the bride and groom can leave for the reception in one car and the bride's parents and bridesmaids in the other. Whatever the arrangement, it is the responsibility of the best man to ensure that no one is left at the church and that all the guests have transport to the reception.

❋ Video

Most of the advice on choosing a photographer also applies to choosing a company to make a video recording of your wedding. Personal recommendation is always helpful in this area. Alternatively, you might consider asking a friend to do the job for you, although the result will obviously be different. If you are having a professional film made, remember to discuss the choice of music that you would like on any soundtrack. If you plan to video the ceremony, remember to ask permission from the minister or registrar first.

❋ Vows

Your vows are probably the most important promises you will ever make to another person. The making of the vows can be the most special and moving part of the day. Talk to your minister or whoever is conducting the ceremony about the wording used and make sure that you both fully understand and are happy with what you are promising. Although some couples learn their vows by heart, most take the safer option of repeating them phrase by phrase after the minister or registrar. The standard wedding vows beautifully embody all that it means to give yourselves to each other 'till death do you part'. However, if you marry in a civil ceremony, you have the opportunity to write your own vows.

❋ Wills

The act of marriage revokes any previous will you may have made. Although possibly not top on your list of priorities at the moment, you do need to consider making new wills, or making a will for the first time. It is not the case as is generally assumed that in the event of your death everything will automatically go to your spouse and it will be easier for those left behind if they know your wishes.

Ten Tips for Cutting Costs

✍ **1. Weekday wedding:** consider having your wedding on a weekday as venues may be cheaper. Honeymoon travel may also be cheaper midweek.

✍ **2. Dress:** consider buying an end-of-line sample, buying off the internet or hiring. You can also buy from a second-hand bridal wear shop, buy from the high street, or borrow a dress. If you or a friend can sew well, consider making your own. Leave the reception in your wedding clothes rather than buying new outfits. Buy or make dresses for bridesmaids that can be worn again.

✍ **3. Reception:** restrict the main reception to close family and friends. Invite others to a less formal reception before or after the ceremony. Alternatively, invite them just for cake and speeches.

✍ **4. Drink:** if the venue allows, bring your own wine (but check corkage charges). Serve a cheaper sparkling wine instead of champagne. Provide a paying bar for an evening reception. Alternatively, serve soft drinks only, for example, fruit punch or elderflower cordial with sparkling water.

✍ **5. Food:** ask family and friends to bring a dish or ask a friend to do the catering.

✍ **6. Cake:** ask a friend to make it or buy it ready made from any large supermarket or store, and then ice it yourself.

✍ **7. Flowers:** choose flowers that are in season (see Appendix 7). Ask a friend to arrange the flowers for you. Have a single flower (e.g. a gerbera) in a bottle on each table. Carry an informal bunch of flowers rather than a grand bouquet.

✍ **8. Transport:** ask friends with suitable cars to put ribbons on them and act as chauffeurs.

✍ **9. Music:** make a playlist for a CD or MP3 player to play at the reception rather than hiring a band.

✍ **10. Photographs:** ask friends to take photographs and give you a CD of their digital photos. Put disposable cameras on each table for guests to use. Alternatively, use a photographer with a smaller business who does not need to charge VAT.

Part 2

Rules of Engagement

Will You Marry Me?

'It's just beautiful,' she whispered, gazing down at the ring on her finger. The diamond sparkled in the sunlight. Sarah and Jonathan were standing on a headland overlooking the harbour. What a difference a few hours made. She had left her small, dark, London flat that morning, glad it was the weekend, glad that she would be seeing Jonathan again but wondering where their relationship was heading and how long they could maintain it at such a distance. He had met her at the station and, as they walked to the harbour after lunch, he had proposed. It had taken her completely by surprise. She had dreamt of that moment since she was a little girl and now it had happened. She was going to be married and there was a wedding to plan. Thoughts of the next few months crowded into her head. Her train of thought was interrupted as a cloud passed over the sun...

'Will you really love me for ever?' she said, dragging her eyes from the ring on her left hand and looking up at him.

He paused before replying and his mind wandered back to his childhood – the family holidays and Christmases when they were all together. He looked away from Sarah and across the harbour to the horizon. His brow furrowed slightly as he remembered that grey February morning when all the colour had drained from his world. His father had spoken to him without looking up. 'I am sorry,' he had said, 'but I need to move away. Your mother and I are getting divorced.' He could still remember his head reeling and the feeling of helplessness. He realized at that moment that life would never be the same again.

He looked back at Sarah. When his parents got engaged did they feel like this? What had gone wrong? The questions were teeming in his brain.

'Jonathan...?' Sarah's voice brought him back to the present.

'Yes,' he stammered. 'Yes, of course I love you, Sarah. Sorry. It just suddenly felt like a really big step that we were taking.'

We are all too familiar with the consequences of family breakdown in our society but the good news is that most marriages last a lifetime. However, there are probably few engaged couples who at some time during their engagement do not step back and wonder, if only for a moment, what the future will bring and what the secret is to being part of a marriage that lasts 'till death us do part'.

The truth is that there is no secret.

There are, however, skills you can learn, choices you can make, habits you can put in place and rules you can follow which will ensure that together you build a marriage that lasts a lifetime.

Rule 1

Build Strong Foundations

Katharine: Several years ago we spent five very wet but wonderful days in Venice. The website that we used to book our accommodation recommended our hotel for 'location, location, location'. There was no doubt about it, we were well placed for sightseeing. However, what the wonders of technology failed to inform us was that major rebuilding work was taking place directly underneath our bedroom window.

With the exception of the pneumatic drill heralding a new day at 6.30 a.m., Richard was in paradise. Each day gave him the opportunity to study the unique methods of the Italian construction industry before moving on to enjoy the Renaissance art that was at the top of my agenda. He questioned the local residents and discovered that work on the foundations had been in progress for many months. Thousands of wooden piles were being painstakingly sunk into the mud to form a solid base upon which building could begin. We were assured that such time and effort was spent on strengthening the foundations to ensure that the building would stand the test of time and the elements.

A strong marriage needs strong foundations. There are things that we can do together to build those foundations. It will take time and effort but the result will be that we will have marriages that will stand both the test of time and external pressures.

These foundations are:

1. Building a friendship

Richard: We met at college, class R, sitting in specifically allocated seats for all lectures. Katharine was given seat 1 and I had seat 15 (directly behind seat 1). Halfway through the first term, the class went out for a meal together. Katharine has absolutely no sense of direction and, as the evening drew on, became anxious as to how she would be able to navigate her car home through the city centre. Resourceful to the end, she realized that I lived nearby and so asked if she could follow me home.

I completely mistook Katharine's intention and, on impulse, jumped out of my car at some red traffic lights, raced back to her car and invited her back for coffee.

That evening was the beginning of our building a strong friendship. Although we began to discover some of our differences, friendship was an essential part of the strong foundation for our marriage.

Friendship will continue to grow when the initial feeling of 'falling in love' has died away. Whether, like us, you have got to know each other gradually or whether you have had a whirlwind romance, a strong friendship undergirding your relationship will enable it to withstand the test of time. Building a friendship of necessity involves spending time together.

2. Spending time together

When you are engaged or newly married, you probably need no encouragement to spend time together.

Katharine: In the months before we were engaged, Richard was working in Birmingham and I lived in Bristol, so we conducted our relationship via the M5. I would leave work on a Friday on the stroke of 5.00 p.m. and travel to Birmingham. It didn't seem to matter that I spent most of the weekend either watching Richard play hockey or helping him build a kit car, as it was just being together that was important. On one occasion, I inadvertently left my bag behind and thought nothing of driving the 180-mile round trip to retrieve it the following evening, just so we could spend more time together.

In *The Marriage Book*, Nicky and Sila Lee stress the importance and value of spending time together:

> We are convinced that married couples need to continue planning special time for each other... If in marriage we continue to make time for each other, the romance will be kept alive, we shall have the chance to communicate effectively and our understanding of each

other will deepen. The regularity and nature of this time together will create the fabric of our relationship over a lifetime.

Richard: Every marriage will benefit from putting this principle into practice. Katharine and I arrange to meet together at lunchtime once a week. Katharine knows that I have written this appointment into my work diary for six months ahead, and I will endeavour to schedule my work commitments around our arrangement. We have learnt to plan, to protect and to prioritize that time together, and looking back we are very glad we have. Time together will keep a relationship growing, prevent us from slipping into living parallel lives and give us a foundation upon which to build a marriage.

As well as having a weekly time together, our marriage has also benefited from planning a weekend away together once a year. We did not do this when first married and on reflection realize what we missed! Planning a weekend away becomes much more difficult if there are children but the long-term benefits it gives to the relationship far outweigh the (not inconsiderable) stress of organizing childcare.

Although time together is crucial to building a relationship, one of the tasks of engagement and early years of marriage will be learning to balance time – time together and time apart. Both are needed. Time apart (sometimes alone and sometimes with others) can cause us to value and appreciate the time we have together, so neither partner feels 'smothered'. Talk honestly together about how to achieve the right balance in your relationship.

Richard: Another practical consideration is adjusting from one diary to two. For years, we operated three diaries: my work diary, Katharine's diary and the kitchen calendar. We learnt the hard way. Years of double-bookings or committing each other to impossible arrangements has meant that we now work from one diary (the kitchen calendar). We also ensure that we regularly copy everything into our personal diaries. Find a system that works for you.

3. Recognizing your differences

Katharine: We are writing this chapter while staying in a beautiful cottage with outstanding views over Exmoor National Park. It is springtime and the field directly outside the window is full of newborn lambs taking their faltering first steps or skipping along in the spring sunshine, a reminder of new life and new beginnings.

We married in late spring and our first home together was a basement flat with a small patio courtyard. We remember our surprise a year later at the discovery of spring bulbs pushing their way through the soil in barrels outside the back door. Unknown to us, the bulbs had been lying dormant beneath the soil throughout the autumn and winter months.

The expectancy and enjoyment that heralds the arrival of spring can greet you as you begin your relationship together. It is a season of adventure and discovery. Like the bulbs under the soil, hidden aspects of each other's character may come to light but as time goes on you may not always enjoy everything you discover about each other. In the early days of marriage you may find some aspects of your fiancé(e)'s character that you initially found attractive begin to irritate you. As one man commented: 'When we were first engaged, I loved my fiancée's

carefree and relaxed attitude to life. However, now we are married, I find it intensely irritating that she won't make a decision...'

After we had been married for six months, I gave Richard a card showing a man dropping his clothes onto the floor with the caption 'Dirty clothes on the floor... clean clothes in the cupboard... AMAZING!' When living with his parents, Richard's clothes seemed miraculously to find their way from bedroom floor to cupboard, being washed and ironed in transit. He had subconsciously assumed that I would adopt the same role as his mother. It took time for him to realize that he hadn't married his mother and that I had very different expectations on this issue.

We are all different. One of the challenges of engagement and the early years of marriage is to learn to work together to manage differences creatively. Far from being a negative force, our differences can complement each other and strengthen our marriage.

4. Meeting each other's needs

In order to manage your differences and to build a strong marriage, you need to try to meet each other's needs. The key to achieving this is in your attitude to each other.

Richard: No amount of comment from Katharine in those first months of marriage about the state of the bedroom floor had made any difference. It was only when I understood that, in putting the laundry into the basket, I was meeting Katharine's need for value and support that I started to change the habit of a lifetime.

Another difference that came to light shortly after we were married concerned our attitude to television. Katharine watches very little television whereas, to her great irritation, I will flick it on as soon as I come into the room. This became a source of potential conflict until Katharine realized that I watch television as a means of unwinding at the end of the day. I also then appreciated Katharine's need for the occasional television-free zone. This is an issue that occasionally still comes up for renegotiation...

Take a break

Exercises

Consider together how you will put in place strong foundations for your marriage.

1. Friendship

Think back over the period of time that you have known each other. Each list five things that you enjoy doing together, e.g. going to the cinema, having a meal together, walking, DIY, sport.

1...

2...

3...

4...

5...

Talk about how you can keep building your friendship when you have been married for five, ten, fifteen years.

ADAPTED FROM *THE MARRIAGE PREPARATION COURSE MANUAL*, ALPHA INTERNATIONAL PUBLICATIONS

2. Spending time together

Think about how you can prioritize time together.

Plan a regular time when you can spend time together (doing something you both enjoy, other than planning the wedding, e.g. each Wednesday evening 8.30 p.m. – 10.30 p.m.).

This week...

In the weeks before the wedding..

After the wedding ....

3. Recognizing your differences

Talk together about anything new you have discovered about each other.

4. Managing your expectations and meeting your needs

Each consider the following statements. On a rating of 1 to 10, score how each matches your expectations (where 1 = strongly disagree and 10 = strongly agree). The object is to understand each other's expectations in these areas, many of which will be dealt with in more detail in subsequent chapters. (e.g. I expect to have the television/music on most of the time: K 2, R 8)

I expect to save money each month.

I expect to make important decisions together.

I expect a period of time on my own each day.

I expect we will go out with friends most weekends.

I expect we will share the household chores.

If we are able to conceive, I expect to have children.

I expect we will have a holiday each year.

I expect I will be relaxed if our home is untidy.

I expect only one of us will work full time.

I expect to have the television/music on most of the time.

I expect my fiancé(e) to meet my emotional needs.

I expect us both to take the initiative in lovemaking.

If either of us has a faith, I expect we will support each other in it.

I expect to see our families regularly.

I expect that we will always plan ahead.

Talk together about anything new you have discovered about each other. Think about areas where you need to change and areas where you need to accept one another's differences.

Rule 2

Choose to Love Each Other

Tom received the following letter from his fiancée, Jo, shortly after they were engaged:

> 'My darling,
> Thank you for agreeing to be my husband. I don't deserve you and I must be the luckiest woman in the world. I can't wait to be with you for ever. I think of you every moment of the day and dream of you at night. I will love you like this for eternity. Nothing will ever change.'

But of course ten years later things have changed. Tom and Jo remain happily married, but life has moved on for them as it will for each of us.

Being newly in love is a wonderful experience. Your emotions are heightened and you may think of each other every minute of the day and night. It is a special time and you need to enjoy it while it lasts.

However, it is important to realize that no one can live at that intensity of emotion indefinitely. Psychologists suggest that such feelings generally last about two years. After that, the nature of your love for each other will change. If your love is to deepen and grow, you must begin to use your will and not just rely on how you feel. In fact you must *choose* to love each other.

Katharine: Last week, while vacuuming the bathroom floor, I inadvertently hoovered up a sports sock that had been tossed vaguely towards the laundry basket by its owner and left to rest where it had fallen. The machine shuddered to a halt with a simultaneous emission of black smoke and a smell of burning rubber. First we took it apart ourselves to no avail. A local repairer, after a cursory glance, confirmed that it would be very difficult to fix. Resigned to further expenditure, we simply left it for disposal and purchased a new one. It was much easier to buy a new model rather than repair the old.

The sociologist Alvin Toffler, writes that 'People today have a throwaway mentality. They not only have throwaway products but they make throwaway friends and this mentality produces throwaway marriages.' Like the vacuum cleaner, marriages are often cast aside when they no longer seem to be working.

The key to building a marriage that lasts is your attitude to the relationship. You need to choose to work at your relationship together and not simply to discard it when you hit difficult times. You need to 'begin with the end in mind' from your engagement day onwards.

Participants in a research project commissioned by Care for the Family attributed the secret of lasting marriage to the commitment they made to each other and to the marriage itself. This was described as the 'glue' of the relationship. DIY enthusiasts may be familiar with the type of glue that is bought in two separate tubes. The adhesive and the hardener need to be mixed together before being used. The two substances then work together to form a bond that cannot easily be broken. In the same way, both the public and the private work together to form the bond

of marriage. Forces that are internal (your love for each other) and
external (the public ceremony and status) work together to form the
commitment that is the glue of the relationship.

If you are in a position to buy a house or flat together, you will need to
sign a contract binding you legally to fulfil your obligation to complete
the purchase. Marriage, however, is much more than a legal contract. It
is based on trust and commitment between two people who are choosing
to promise to love each other for a lifetime.

Whether you are planning a large, formal occasion or a small, family
affair, whether your wedding is to be in a church, at the register office or
another venue of your choice, the most important part of the ceremony
will certainly be when you publicly make your promises to each other.

You may like to use the traditional wording:

> I [Name] take you to be my husband/wife
> to have and to hold
> from this day forward,
> for better, for worse,
> for richer, for poorer,
> in sickness and in health,
> to love and to cherish,
> till death us do part
> according to God's holy law,
> and this is my solemn vow.

Another way of saying this would be:

> I *choose* to love you
> whatever happens,
> however I feel,
> whoever I meet,
> whenever we have problems,
> whether or not I feel in love.

*Steve and Jane were married in March and had planned a honeymoon
in Scotland. Jane had enjoyed family holidays there as a child and was
looking forward to rediscovering old haunts with Steve. They spent
the first few days sightseeing and then planned to go walking in the*

Choose to Love Each Other

Highlands. At the beginning of the second week when out walking, Jane found she had to stop to rest more frequently and, towards the end of the fortnight, she found she was having some difficulty breathing. She put it down to exhaustion after the stress of the wedding and tried not to dwell on it. However, a visit to the doctor on their return revealed that she had a small tumour on her lung.

Steve writes, 'When the doctor told us the news, we felt as if the bottom had fallen out of our world. I felt numb. All our hopes and plans were suddenly thrown into the air. We were faced with a very different future than that we had planned. In fact we didn't know if we had a future. A month ago I had promised to love Jane in sickness and in health. One night as I considered the prospect of the months that lay ahead I suddenly realized the enormity of what I had promised. The simple fact that we had promised to love each other whatever the circumstances was what kept us going. Our love for each other grew stronger despite her illness. Jane died two and a half years later. They were a very special two and a half years.'

Continuing to love each other is a choice. The reality is that none of us knows what the future will bring. When you promise to love your husband or wife for better or for worse, you are choosing to put their needs before yours whatever the circumstances and however you feel. You are committing yourselves to them, to seek always what is best for them. This runs counter-culture in today's 'me'-centred society but it is the only way to work together to create a marriage that lasts a lifetime.

Actress Meryl Streep has been married to sculptor Don Gummer for over thirty years. In a memorable interview for a magazine a few years ago, Streep expressed an unswerving commitment to her marriage and family life, despite the pressures of the world they live in. She was quoted as saying, 'Our marriage and our children and their future well-being inform all the decisions that we make.'

Just as we choose to marry each other, we also choose to stay married. 'The "till death us do part" aspect of marriage is not an untouchable ideal but a living reality that is insured by an unswerving commitment – a wilful agreement to keep love alive' (*When Bad Things Happen to Good Marriages*, Drs Les and Leslie Parrott).

Take a break

Exercises

1. Why did you decide to get married?

....

....

....

....

....

....

2. Discuss the vows you will say to each other at your wedding. Which phrase do you find most challenging? Discuss why with your fiancé(e).

Rule **3**

Keep Talking

Katharine: It was a Saturday in early autumn five months after we became engaged. We had spent the day visiting a castle in Devon, and struggled back shoe-horned into a Mini with a beautiful lemon tree in an enormous terracotta pot. During the past few months we had spent many happy hours reading glossy magazines with full-colour pages depicting what a first home could look like. One picture that had caught our eye was of a bare apartment that was transformed into a dream home by strategically placed houseplants, in particular a blossoming lemon tree.

We were thrilled with our purchase, which later took pride of place in our first home, and lovingly cared for it, watering it daily. It flourished and we looked forward to the harvest. Weeks and months went by and we settled into married life. The plant got pushed behind a chair and watered at weekends, when and if we remembered. Slowly, without anyone noticing, the leaves began to curl at the edges, turning from green to yellow to brown, until only the twig-like branches remained.

As one woman friend realized, looking back on her marriage: 'Our lack of communication killed our love – it began to wither and one day finally died – like a plant without water.'

Katharine: During my time as a family law solicitor, I saw many people who had entered married life with the same hope, excitement and enthusiasm with which we had bought that lemon tree, but who were now sitting in the waiting room, facing the stark reality that their early hopes and expectations had not been met.

Linda was one such client. She came in, her two-year-old in a buggy, and sat down, fighting back the tears. She told us about her marriage. 'The first couple of years of our relationship seemed great. We had fun and were both busy with our careers. Then Amy was born and I stayed at home to look after her. Simon was promoted and had to work long hours. I made a life for Amy and myself at home. Simon and I didn't have much time together and, looking back, I think we began to live parallel lives. I feel we don't know each other any more. We have stopped communicating about things that matter.'

Sadly, Linda's story is not unusual. Lack of communication can make two people who love and commit to each other on their wedding day eventually feel like complete strangers.

Just as the lemon tree needs water to thrive, your marriage will need good channels of communication from day one if it is to blossom and grow.

There are steps you can take to improve communication:

1. Recognize your differences

Family background

How your respective families communicated as you were growing up will have a significant impact on how you have learnt to communicate as adults. One of you may have come from a family where factual information was exchanged but feelings never openly discussed. On the other hand, your fiancé(e)'s family may be loud and gregarious, everyone and everything brought into the open, talked about and laughed or cried about.

Recognizing that your family background affects how you communicate as an adult is a vital part of learning the necessary skills to communicate with each other, especially during the early years of marriage.

Personality

Your individual personalities, whether you are natural extroverts or introverts, logical or intuitive, undoubtedly affect how you communicate.

Jon is a logical introvert and married Alex, an intuitive extrovert. Jon will think carefully about what he is going to say and his first words are usually his last on the subject. Alex, however, thinks as she speaks. She works out her opinions by talking them through. Her first words are just that and she will generally go through a raft of options before she arrives at her final conclusion. Recognizing their personality differences has helped them enormously to learn to communicate better as they start out in marriage.

2. Make connections

Richard: We had optimistically agreed to take on the task of telephoning and reserving tickets for a concert for three entire families. The booking lines opened at 8.30 a.m. on Saturday morning. At that time we would be on a train to Oxford so had put credit on the mobile phone the previous day and charged the battery overnight. Doubtless to the extreme annoyance of others travelling in the same carriage, we began ringing at 8.31 a.m. and pressed the redial button every two minutes. Each time we were greeted by the increasingly familiar and annoying pre-recorded message, assuring us that they valued our call but that all operators were busy. Finally, at 9.23 a.m., we made a connection. Credit card to hand, we set about booking the tickets and were just giving the details when the train entered a tunnel and the signal was lost. No signal, no message. Shouting louder or speaking more slowly made no difference at all. We were just steeling ourselves for the unenviable task of conveying the news to our disappointed friends when we emerged from the tunnel. Network coverage was resumed and the signal restored. By the time we reached our destination, we had made the connection, communication had taken place and we had successfully purchased the tickets.

To begin to build a lifelong marriage together, you need to learn from the outset how to be good senders and receivers of messages, making sure there is no interference with the signal. You need to learn how to express yourselves honestly and how in turn to listen, recognizing those factors that may distort the message or prevent its being heard.

It is much easier to learn such skills while engaged than several years into marriage when bad habits may have set in. There are exercises at the end of this chapter which will help you learn to talk to and listen to each other better. Ensuing discussions about how you each might feel about certain aspects of the wedding arrangements will give you much opportunity for practice!

3. Talk honestly

If you are to build a strong relationship together, you need to develop honesty in your communication and learn to talk together about how you feel. From your engagement onwards, your aim should be to move from independence to interdependence. This includes resolving to have no secrets and to share your thoughts and feelings, your hopes and your dreams. In doing this you make yourselves vulnerable. It takes courage. Be gentle with each other and go at your own pace. You have a lifetime ahead of you.

4. Listen well

We have probably all had the experience of not being listened to, of being ignored. It can make you feel angry, frustrated and insignificant. However, when someone pays you the compliment of really listening and giving you their undivided attention, the opposite can be true: you feel valued, special and loved.

Paul Tillich writes: 'The first duty of love is to listen.' Just by listening, you have the potential to make your fiancé(e) know that you love and value them. This is a skill you can learn now and continue to use once you are married. Many people are poor listeners. It is easy to slip into the habit of letting your mind wander, not really giving your partner your full attention. It is surprisingly easy to allow another agenda to run in your head or to think about what to say next while someone is speaking to you.

In order to communicate well, there are other things you need to do:

i) Be aware of your tone of voice and body language
Thirty-five per cent of our communication is tone of voice. An amazing 55 per cent is body language. Imagine one of you is upset. The question 'What's the matter now?' spoken with the emphasis on now and with hands on hips can have quite a different meaning from exactly the same words spoken in a gentle tone and with eye contact.

ii) Recognize interference
In the mobile phone story, the interference in the tunnel meant that no message could be communicated. No booking could be made.

Sarah and Ian have been married for five weeks. Since they got back from their honeymoon, Sarah has been very busy at work. Ian has invited some friends over for the evening. He knows that she is under pressure and wants to try to help. She knows that the last meal she cooked for his friends was a complete disaster.

He says, 'Don't worry about cooking tonight. We'll get a takeaway', meaning 'That will take some pressure off you.'

She hears, 'I'll get a takeaway because I don't want you to cook another disastrous meal for my friends.'

She says, 'Don't you think I can be trusted to cook, then?'

It is easy to see how the conversation could spiral downwards unless they are together able to recognize how the past has interfered with the present and distorted what Sarah heard. Playing the children's game Chinese whispers, is fun expressly because the original message becomes distorted as it is passed from one person to another. However, the same distortion can occur to a message that you want to communicate to your fiancé(e). Your separate experiences of life, your memories and attitudes, prejudices and assumptions, can all distort the message being conveyed. If you can learn to recognize any distortion in the message, you can take a step back and reconnect before any misunderstanding occurs.

iii) Choose the right time
Choose a time that suits you both.

Mike and Susannah were engaged for eight months and have recently married. He comes to life at 10.30 p.m. at night but struggles to have a conversation much before 9.00 a.m. in the morning. Susannah's body clock is the reverse. They have had to work hard to find a time to talk together when they are both at their best.

Recognizing this and each making the effort to accommodate the other has been crucial for them in learning to communicate.

iv) Find the right place

Katharine: It can be helpful to choose not only the best time but also the best place for you both. We know for example that it is difficult for us to communicate when sport is on the television. So choose a physical environment where you both find it easy to give each other undivided attention without distraction. If necessary, turn off the television and ignore the telephone. If you can take positive action to address this issue now, you will be starting off your married life with good habits in place that can be valuable for the future.

Lizzie and Jeremy have been married for five years. During the first few years of marriage, they took it in turns to cook in the evenings and ate together at the kitchen table. When their first child was born, they moved the table out of the kitchen and replaced it with a sofa so that Lizzie could sit comfortably and feed the baby. They then found it was easier to have meals sitting on the sofa, side by side, in front of the television. Three years later they have realized that the sofa has actually become a barrier to communication in their marriage. The sofa is now out and the table is back in. They have meals together at the table again, facing each other and continuing the conversations they began five years ago.

Meal times are a great opportunity to talk to each other. Eat together when you are engaged and continue the habit into marriage.

5. Understand how we communicate

Katharine: We spent the first two nights of our honeymoon in a small hotel in the Cotswolds. Our enduring memory of breakfast on the first morning was being surrounded by couples at nearby tables with the newspapers raised between them, blocking eye contact and any conversation, other than the occasional request for more coffee and toast. We were excited about the previous day and full of memories of the wedding which we wanted to talk about. Soon we became aware that we were the only ones speaking and it felt as if our conversation was resounding around the room.

It was no effort then but the challenge is to make the effort to keep talking to each other years on into marriage (even if the sports page does look inviting).

'Communication is the meeting of meaning. When your meaning meets my meaning across the bridge of words, tones, acts and deeds, when understanding occurs, then we know that we have communicated.'

CHERISHABLE LOVE AND MARRIAGE, DAVID W. AUGSBURGER

Communication is about connecting with each other. In your day-to-day relationships, you communicate with different people on different levels. When you first meet and are attracted to another person, you may begin speaking at the level of clichés and light conversation – for instance, 'How are you?' 'Fine, thanks.' As you get to know more about each other, you begin to relate more deeply. You exchange information and make stronger connections.

The diagram opposite shows different possible levels of communication.

Communication Ladder

A healthy, developing relationship will move up the rungs of the communication ladder. As it does so, you will share thoughts and opinions, communicate more detail about things, in the process making yourselves vulnerable to each other. Taking an interest in each other's world is the first rung of the ladder. This may mean developing an interest in a fiancé(e)'s hobby or sport, solely for the sake of sharing it with them.

Richard: When we first got engaged, we found we did not need any encouragement to be interested in each other's lives. As well as doing things together that we both enjoyed, Katharine became an expert in building a kit car and I took a new and lively interest in art galleries.

If you can be interested in how your fiancé(e) spends the day, whether at work or at home, your friendship can be strengthened as you share the highs and lows together. The challenge is to keep being involved in each other's lives and to build new interests together. Valuing each other's beliefs and opinions, even when they are different from your own, can trigger talking about and listening to how each of you feels in a climate of total honesty.

To be able to communicate with honesty requires trust. You need to know that when you express your hopes and fears, your fiancé(e) will listen and value what you are saying and not respond with rejection or ridicule. As you climb the ladder of communication together, you will find that trust and intimacy will grow too. Moving from one rung to the next is not difficult but, as with any climb, it requires encouragement and effort. And it gets easier with practice.

Take Libby Purves' advice: 'The only real essential is to continue the conversation you started when you first met' (*Nature's Masterpiece: A Family Survival Book*, Libby Purves).

Katharine: And what about the lemon tree? It was too precious to throw away so we pruned it to get rid of the dead wood and soaked it in a bucket of water. We made time to water it regularly, gave it some sunlight and it continues to thrive…

So don't worry if your communication runs into some difficult times. Deal with the issues and your relationship will continue to grow.

Take a break

Exercises

The aim of the first exercise is to help you begin to identify and talk about how you feel.

1. Think about your wedding plans. Each write for two minutes about how you feel (e.g. I feel anxious that the wedding is only eight weeks away and we haven't yet ordered the invitations. I feel excited about having all our family and friends together to share our day.)

Exchange the paragraphs that you have written and talk to each other about how you feel.

2. Listen/Talk

a. Choose a good time to talk when you have time to sit down together with no distractions.

b. Choose one issue to talk about. It may be something from Exercise 1 above.

c. Decide who is going to speak first.

d. That person is allowed to speak without interruption for a specified period of time (if you find it helpful, the speaker could hold something in their hand as a visual reminder of whose turn it is to speak).

e. When the speaker has finished, the listener must recap what they understood the speaker to have said, including the feelings expressed. Sometimes this is called 'reflecting back' what you have heard. Then ask, 'Is that what you said?'

f. If they have got it right, the speaker will agree. If not, the speaker can have more time to explain what they mean and how they feel.

g. Speaking and repeating back can be continued until the speaker is sure the listener has understood.

h. When step (g) is complete the listener should ask whether there is anything that the speaker would like them to do to progress the matter further.

i. Now the listener in turn follows steps (d) to (h).

j. Use this structure to continue the discussion until you are both sure that you understand what the other wanted to communicate. It may seem contrived at first but this exercise can prove a very powerful tool in helping us communicate with one another.

Rule **4**

Find Joint Solutions

When you first meet and fall in love, you may find it difficult to imagine ever arguing.

Tom and Helen had been engaged for six months and the wedding was now only eight weeks away. They were paying for a large part of the wedding themselves and Helen was budgeting carefully, having just repaid her student loans. Tom noticed with pleasure that Helen had bought a notebook which she was using to keep account of their expenditure. Although they had agreed that they wanted a special wedding, neither wanted to begin their new life together with debts they were unable to pay. Tom considered he was lucky to be marrying someone with whom he seemed to agree on everything. As he finished addressing the last invitation, he sat back and reflected with pleasure that all seemed to be going to plan. They had booked the church and the reception. Arrangements were progressing well and so far they had kept to budget.

He was brought back from his thoughts by a ring at the door, heralding the arrival of two parcels addressed to him. He opened them eagerly.

Perfect. They had arrived just in time for his stag night. He had used eBay to source two 'Star Wars' light sabres, blue and red. They were expensive, but he had reasoned at the time that they were just what he wanted and would provide hours of fun and entertainment. Helen came in and looked at the open parcels in disbelief. 'How much did they cost?' she asked. 'I thought we were saving money for the wedding!'

If Helen and Tom had not argued before, they now began in style. The purchase of the light sabres became the focus of a quarrel that continued well into the evening. Helen even questioned whether they should postpone the wedding.

Conflict is inevitable

Even if you are able to negotiate the minefield of wedding arrangements without disagreement, conflict is inevitably part of every marriage. We all find it difficult to set aside our own agenda and accommodate another.

Katharine: We honeymooned in Crete and thought a romantic idea would be to hire a bicycle together, side by side under a canopy, and pedal into the sunset. The only problem was that we failed to appreciate our different expectations about what a day in the saddle would be like. Richard anticipated some energetic cycling up and down the surrounding hills and set off at a blistering pace, hoping to find a secluded beach on the far side of the island.

I had an entirely different expectation: a gentle pedal along a flat terrain with time taken to enjoy the surrounding countryside. Putting my head down and cycling for the Tour de France was certainly not on my agenda, so I took my feet off the pedals and left Richard to it, simply applying the brake at necessary intervals.

We had both wanted to conduct the bike ride in the way we envisaged and neither of us made any allowance for the other which, in the heat of the midday sun, did not produce a harmonious state of affairs.

In the cool of evening, we were able to look back and reflect on the disappointment and frustration of a day which had fallen spectacularly short of our individual expectations. And the following day we resolved the issue by hiring a motorbike for the rest of the week.

Becoming engaged and then building a marriage can be like learning to share a bicycle with someone. It takes time and effort to work together and to understand each other's expectations for the journey ahead and you may at times be forgiven for wanting to pedal on your own or take your feet off the pedals altogether. The journey will certainly take you up some steep hills and over some rough terrain but, if you are prepared to find the best way forward, you can journey far.

John Gottman observes that 'Lasting marriage results from a couple's ability to resolve the conflicts that are inevitable in any relationship' (*Why Marriages Succeed or Fail*). If disagreements are inevitable in marriage, the good news is that there are steps (as outlined below) that you can learn to take to bring you together.

1. Recognize your differences

How you react to conflict depends on a number of factors, including your experiences as you were growing up and your different personalities. Understanding those differences can be the first step in helping you deal constructively with conflict when it does arise.

Family background

Recognizing how your different family backgrounds dictate your initial response to conflict is important to help you understand each other and negotiate together.

Daniel felt the colour rising on the back of his neck. He kept his eyes trained firmly on the small portion of pizza left on his plate. Carrie's parents had taken them out for a meal and it had been a perfect evening. Perfect, that is, until her father had mentioned the wedding arrangements. It seemed to him that World War III had just been declared. He dared not look up but could imagine other diners looking at their table in amazement. All three were at each other, hammer and tongs, hardly stopping to draw breath and, what was more, they almost seemed to be enjoying themselves. He couldn't remember a family argument like this at home. When his parents had a disagreement, there would be a stony silence for hours, sometimes days. But not this.

It is vital to understand that feeling anger is not wrong in itself. It is simply a sign that something is wrong. Different personalities react differently when angry. The key to resolving conflict together is to learn how to handle anger appropriately.

In *The Marriage Book*, Nicky and Sila Lee suggest that, when angry, people are likely to behave like one of two animals. You may be a thick-skinned rhino that, once angered, charges at speed, demolishing anything or anyone in its path. Or, alternatively, you may act like a hedgehog which, when threatened, curls up into a ball and sticks out its spikes. The task of marriage is to build intimacy and closeness as the years go by. It is clearly impossible to get close to a charging rhino or a prickly hedgehog.

Katharine: When we were first married, we used to think that, as only one of us behaved like a rhino when angry, only one of us had a problem. That was until one summer evening a year into marriage. It began as a trivial discussion but, as the issue widened, we both became angry and upset and I resorted to my favourite tactic of putting up an impenetrable barrier of non-communication. Richard, already annoyed because of the disagreement and faced with the frustration of a wall of silence, banged his fist hard on the bedroom door, causing substantial damage to both.

That particular evening was a catalyst for us in recognizing that internalized 'hedgehog' anger communicated by withdrawal can be just as harmful to a relationship as the 'charging rhino' approach.

We are still working at handling anger appropriately. But several years on, Richard has repaired the bedroom door.

2. Find the best time

Louise and Robert seldom argued – that is, until they got engaged. Issue after issue seemed to come between them. Disagreements over the wedding – about the timing, the music, the table plan and the budget – widened into disagreements about everyday issues that previously they had been able to agree on. Six months into marriage, Louise reflected, 'I think the pressure of the wedding arrangements caused us to argue more. It was a huge relief to go on our honeymoon and find that we could get along fine without arguing about every small detail of life.'

The times that people argue are usually those when they are most stretched. It could be just before an important occasion or when they are under pressure. Often these will be late at night. If you find yourselves engaged in a heated debate late at night, call a halt and postpone the discussion until a better time. The important thing is that the issue is deliberately deferred, not swept under the carpet or forgotten. Some friends, Pete and Nikki, told us that, having pressed the 'pause' button on a discussion that was taking place at 11.00 p.m., they set their alarm clock for 5.30 a.m. the following morning so they could attempt to resolve the issue before going to work.

Although there is almost never an easy time to resolve differences (and 5.30 a.m. may not be your preferred time to do so, particularly if you are not a 'morning person'), avoid discussions late at night. Tiredness causes issues to get out of perspective. So:

Don't try to resolve an issue late at night or just before an important occasion.

Do find the best time for both of you.

3. Don't attack each other

Jim and Pippa had agreed to open a joint account after they were engaged. Jim now looked in disbelief at the bank statement. They were overdrawn – again. He could have suggested that they methodically go through the box of receipts to see where the money has gone. Instead, he turned the attack on Pippa.

'I can't believe we are overdrawn. You are just so useless.'

A year into marriage Pippa still has an almost total recall of Jim's words and of how they made her feel.

When engaged in a heated discussion, it is important not to confuse the issue with the person. Avoid at all costs the phrases 'You always...' and 'You never...'. Instead, aim for 'I' statements to explain the issue overdrawn again.'

If you can learn to do this, it will explain why each of you is feeling angry and help focus on the issue between you.

4. Don't widen the issue

It is so easy in the heat of the moment to use counter-attack as a first line of defence by simply widening the issue under discussion. So 'You are so useless' is followed by 'I bet you haven't even paid the deposit for the band yet.' This is then countered with 'Anyone would think I was the only person involved in planning this wedding. I'm having to do everything. You are so selfish.' In three swift moves, the issue has widened from Pippa being overdrawn at the bank to the unrelated topic of Jim's perceived selfishness in not pulling his weight with the wedding arrangements. To resolve conflict effectively, focus on the issue rather than on attacking each other.

5. Learn the third way

After they were married, David and Jo began renovating their new property. They ripped out the fireplace which now lay in pieces in the skip and set off together to choose a new one. Four hours later, having visited every reclamation yard and grate shop in the area, they sat in a coffee shop, unable to agree. The afternoon they had been looking forward to had turned into a focus for conflict and disagreement.

Jo wanted an antique fireplace with decorated tiles. David wanted a modern one with a plain surround. Jo wanted a real fire. David wanted gas. And so on.

They found themselves getting more and more frustrated and annoyed with each other as the afternoon wore on. They sat staring into the half empty coffee cups, a wilting flower and the crumpled shopping list between them. He wished they had left the fireplace as it was. At least they agreed that they disliked it. They both felt strongly but if neither was prepared to give in, they would return home empty-handed and would have to live with a hole in the wall. Perhaps he should give in, but he couldn't bear to live with those tiles...

He took a pen from his pocket. Slowly and deliberately, he smoothed out the shopping list and began to draw. They ordered more coffee. Forty minutes later they had designed a new fireplace between them. It was completely different from either of their original ideas but they had designed it together.

Resolving conflict effectively means taking the issue that is between you and putting it right out in the open. Then together find a third way forward.

It is easy to think that when there is an issue to be resolved, it is about either winning or losing. Establishing a pattern where one of you always gets their own way and the other always gives in will not help you build a marriage where you value and respect each other. Learn to negotiate and find a third way forward on the small issues and you will know how to deal with the big issues as and when they arise. And if your first solution doesn't work, go back and try again, and again.

So Tom and Helen and the light sabres? They have resolved to use them every few weeks to remind themselves that, if handled correctly, conflict can strengthen a marriage. May the force be with them!

Take a break

Exercises

1. Talk to your fiancé(e) about how you each saw conflict resolution modelled while you were growing up.

2. What things cause you to be angry with each other?

3. How do you each react when you are angry?

4. How might you help each other react better?

5. Discuss how you could resolve conflict more constructively in the future.

Rule 5

Keep Short Accounts

'... But even if we deal with conflict well there are some situations where the only solution lies a little deeper than technique...'
THE SIXTY MINUTE MARRIAGE, ROB PARSONS

Katharine: My parents used to live in a property with a central gutter which, during autumn and winter months, would gradually fill up with dead leaves from nearby trees. At the same time every year, Richard would receive a telephone call asking him if he would make the somewhat hazardous journey onto the roof to remove the debris from the channel.

Despite this annual expedition, we failed to learn from my parents' example. After we had been married for a couple of years, we moved to a house with a flat roof. One Christmas Day, just as the turkey was ready to come out of the oven, we heard the ominous sound of running water, coming not from the bathroom but from the spare bedroom. We had failed to keep the gutter clear of leaves and inevitably a blockage had occurred, resulting in water descending through the bedroom ceiling. Seasonal festivities were put on hold whilst Richard climbed onto the roof in the torrential rain to clear the gutter (wearing swimming trunks, despite the temperature). The effect of clearing the drain was immediate. With a tremendous sucking noise, the trapped water shot down the drain and away from the house.

In the same way that a build up of leaves can cause a blockage in a gutter, a build up of misunderstanding and hurt can, over time, cause a blockage in a relationship. It is an inevitable fact of life that, intentionally or not, you will hurt each other, however much you may feel in love. If left unresolved that hurt can create a distance between you. In order to build intimacy, the hurt needs to be identified and forgiven and the channel of communication needs to be kept clear.

Some friends were recently given tips for married life at their wedding service. To their surprise, top of the list was the suggestion that they return the king-size bed to the department store. The advice was based on some words from the Bible that had been read earlier in the service: 'Don't let the sun go down while you are angry.' The reasoning given was the smaller the bed, the less chance of being able to cling on to the edge with a barrier of hurt and unforgiveness between you.

Participants in a recent survey commissioned by Care for the Family confirmed this advice. Those interviewed unanimously agreed that one of the factors that had kept their marriage going over the years was their resolve 'never to go to bed on an argument'. Accordingly, if a curfew has been called into play (see p. 84) and a potentially heated discussion postponed to a better time, deal with the immediate hurt caused to each other whilst putting the issue itself on hold.

It is important to keep short accounts with each other from the very outset of your relationship. This will involve acknowledging when you have been hurt and then apologizing and forgiving.

1. Identify the hurt

Katharine: Friday night is 'family night' for us when we try to stay in and spend an evening together as a family. If the children choose what to do, the evening usually involves eating pizza and watching a DVD together. On one recent Friday, we visited the DVD shop. After lengthy negotiation and discussion, a film was selected and, armed with the statutory bag of popcorn, we queued to pay. On reaching the front of the queue we were horrified to find that a previous DVD we had hired was overdue. We owed four weeks of rental (a not inconsiderable sum of money). We later discovered that the DVD in question had been inadvertently knocked under a cushion at home and forgotten about. Had we known it was there, we could have taken action to return it immediately. However, until we spoke to the sales assistant, we had been unaware of the fact that the outstanding balance had continued to accumulate.

In the same way it is vital for each of you to begin your engagement and to build your marriage by being prepared to tell each other when there is a problem between you and when you feel hurt, so there is no possibility of building up an accumulation of grievances. This process is made much easier if you can begin by explaining how you feel, for example, 'I felt hurt when you didn't take my views into account this morning...'

2. Apologize

Once the issue has been explained it is out in the open, and the 'gutter' can be cleared, first by apologizing for any hurt caused and then by forgiving in return.

Richard: There have been many times when we have felt hurt or annoyed by something that the other has said or done. Neither of us finds it easy to admit we are wrong and to apologize as it involves swallowing our pride and choosing not to seek to justify our behaviour. However, as soon as one of us has taken the initiative and apologized, we find any irritation melts away and it is much easier to take the next step to deal with the hurt. This is to forgive.

3. Learn to forgive each other

Forgiveness is not brushing the hurt under the carpet and pretending it doesn't matter. It involves confronting the ways you may have hurt each other, bringing them out into the open and then, for the sake of the relationship, choosing to let go. Forgiveness is often costly and may require courage. Where the hurt is deep, healing may take some time.

Rob Parsons writes in *The Sixty Minute Marriage*:

'Forgiveness feels the pain but doesn't hoard it; it allows tomorrow to break free of yesterday. It is always hard, sometimes foolish and, at its heart, God-like.

There is no hope for us without it.'

The following story, adapted from *The Marriage Book*, shows how the process of apologizing and forgiving was key in enabling Deborah and Miles to deal with hurt brought with them into their marriage from just before their wedding day.

Two weeks before the wedding, Deborah went to have the final fitting for her dress. She was going from her office in a taxi at Christmas time, so London was very busy. She was in a traffic jam, feeling very excited, when she saw a couple walking away from her with their arms around each other. As the taxi drew nearer, she was shocked to see that it was her fiancé, Miles, with his arm around another woman. Moreover, she knew that the woman in question was his previous girlfriend.

Deborah said, 'It was like a horror movie. My taxi was going very slowly so I watched them for a bit longer, thinking "What shall I do? Shall I jump out of the taxi?" My heart was beating like mad. I couldn't believe my eyes. Then I saw them arrive outside her office. They said goodbye and kissed each other. It wasn't a passionate kiss, but it was enough of a kiss. At that moment my taxi picked up speed and I arrived for my fitting. I was so upset that I couldn't even cry. During the fitting I kept on asking them to hurry up. All I wanted to do was to get on the telephone.'

The truth of the situation was that Miles had been meeting his former girlfriend for lunch to apologize for his failure to end their relationship properly. As far as he was concerned, his intentions were completely honourable. He never said sorry to Deborah because he didn't feel the need to. For her the issue remained unresolved. In fact after the wedding, to add insult to injury, the story kept coming up at parties as a joke.

Several years later Miles and Deborah went on The Marriage Course (a course designed to give any married couple tools to build a healthy marriage). It was only then that they were finally able to talk honestly together about what had happened. Miles for the first time understood how Deborah had felt. He was able to apologize and Deborah was then able to forgive and, finally, let go. It was an important moment in their relationship.

To build a strong relationship together through engagement and into marriage, resolve to deal with hurt as it arises and keep short accounts with one another, first by choosing to identify and deal with hurt or misunderstanding and then by apologizing and forgiving each other on a daily basis.

Take a break

Exercise

1. Ask each other whether there is any unresolved hurt between you. (Try to explain what the hurt is and how it makes you feel.)

2. Say sorry and forgive each other.

3. Resolve to do this on a daily basis.

Rule 6

Unpack Your Baggage

Part One

Richard: We both have the same memories of our eighteenth birthdays. We each remember the excitement and anticipation of the large present torn open to reveal a suitcase, which was then opened to reveal another suitcase and then another, until there was a complete set. On reflection, the suitcases were perhaps a symbolic gift. At eighteen, we were free to pack our bags, leave home and move on.

One or both of you may have packed and moved on many years ago. For others, getting married will be the first time you have physically moved away from your childhood home. In either case, becoming engaged and getting married means you need to move away not only physically but also emotionally.

Whatever your situation, your engagement means that you and your fiancé(e) are setting out on a journey together. You will each begin the journey with two invisible suitcases. The first is a new suitcase, which is empty, just waiting to be packed. Together you can choose what to put in it. The second is a larger, well-worn suitcase which is already full to bursting. Packed inside is your past. Like it or not, you bring it with you into marriage. You cannot travel without it. It contains your memories, your successes and failures, the joy and the laughter, the heartache and pain that you have encountered on your journey so far.

Everyone begins engagement with a different set of luggage. As we have said, one of the tasks of marriage is to do some unpacking. It is only as you begin to understand what is in each other's suitcase that you can travel on together.

Family background

However diverse your cultural backgrounds, the influence of your parental figures and the homes you grew up in will take up a great deal of room in the suitcase. Within the context of the family, you will have observed your role models adopting methods of communication and conflict resolution, as well as demonstrating physical intimacy and forgiveness. These have moulded the preconceptions that you bring with you into marriage.

Laura and Ian called to see us six months after they were married. Ian came from a family where conflict between his parents had been loud and angry for many years. They eventually separated with some bitterness when he was a teenager. Painful years of angry words had taught Ian to avoid conflict at all costs. Laura's family had never resolved an issue without a good robust debate, but they were close to each other and loved nothing better than to get an issue out into the open. They hotly debated every matter from which colour they should paint the front door to the latest government policy on education. Laura and Ian sat at our kitchen table and showed us their wedding photographs. As the evening went on, the issue that they really wanted to talk about bubbled to the surface. Whenever a subject was disputed and Laura raised her voice, Ian's instinctive reaction was to turn and run for cover until the perceived storm had passed. This left Laura feeling hurt and rejected. She also felt a deep frustration that issues were not being resolved.

When asked how he felt when Laura raised her voice, Ian's reply was illuminating.

'I think she doesn't love me, and I am frightened that she will leave me.'

'Why do you think you feel that way?'

'I've been thinking a lot about that. I think it goes back to my parents because they shouted at each other until I was a teenager, when my Dad left. He left my Mum and he left me and I still wonder if it was my fault. Raised voices trigger memories and past hurt that I can't face so I run away to hide.'

Laura later wrote: 'In talking this issue through, we were able to unpack the way in which our backgrounds are influencing how we see things. I understand now how Ian feels when I raise my voice and I know why he reacts like he does. Just knowing this helps.'

Once you recognize past influences, you have a choice. You each have positive things from the past to value as well as negative things to be aware of. As you pack a new suitcase together, you can choose areas on which to model your relationship. Equally, you can choose the areas in which to act differently.

Family traditions

Richard: In our suitcases will also be presumptions about family occasions. The first Christmas after we were married brought to light our very different notions of what we each perceived as the correct procedure on Christmas Day. Our family traditions had differed in almost every aspect of the day: whether we attended church at midnight or in the morning, whether we opened presents before or after lunch, whether we took a hearty walk or watched television and even whether we served brandy butter or custard (we now have both!).

Roles and responsibilities

How we regard everyday roles and responsibilities around the home can also be influenced by our upbringing. In any given situation, you need to work out what is best for you and for your marriage. Unless you discuss this together, you may find that you simply take on the roles you have observed your parents or step-parents fulfilling as you grew up.

Katharine: My mother is good at map-reading and always sat in the passenger seat to map-read on family excursions. Richard's mother has never taken a driving test and his father always drove. When we were engaged, we both reverted to our parents' role. Much angst, many U-turns and one memorable trip from the Isle of Arran (off the west coast of Scotland) to Bristol (south-west) via Hull (east coast) which, while providing panoramic views of the Pennines, could easily have been avoided if we had realized that for our marriage the best combination is for Richard to map-read while I drive. Now if Richard is driving and there is doubt over the route, he will simply pull over and, without even discussing the issue, we swap places.

Each of you has strengths and weaknesses. You need to play to your individual strengths, to pull together where you have corresponding weaknesses and work towards building an equal partnership.

While you are engaged, it is worth discussing how you think you are going to make decisions. It is obviously not practical to consult on every small detail, so agree between you which routine decisions you will each make (for example, who organizes payment of which bill) and which big decisions you need to make together.

In preparing to build your new relationship, you need to be certain that you have grasped these two key elements of marriage: first, leaving behind your parents and, second, uniting to begin a new life together. If you marry in church, this may be reflected in the words of the service: 'For this reason a man will leave his father and mother and be united to his wife and the two will become one flesh.'

For the sake of your marriage, it is important that you do both; that you leave and then unite, psychologically, emotionally and physically. As you begin married life, you need to relate in a new way to your parents and parental figures with whom you have had a close relationship. While you are young, you are dependent on your parents providing for your physical and emotional needs. As the years go by you learn to become increasingly independent. Your marriage signals the completion of that process. You set up home with your spouse and from then on you need to look to each other for mutual support. Naturally we value greatly our parents' continued love and support but we need to recognize that our loyalties have changed.

Richard: We were at a wedding recently where the question, 'Who gives this woman to be married to this man?', was answered by both parents together: 'We do.' It was a moving moment in the service, symbolizing the end of one stage of life and the beginning of something new.

It was their first Christmas together. All the family had been invited. Anxious to make a good impression on Nick's family, Kate had found a recipe for the Christmas pudding. The turkey had been delicious and no one seemed to have noticed that the sprouts were slightly overdone. All was going well. She felt a small sense of pride as she served the pudding. Nick's sister tasted it and confirmed that it was delicious but added, as an afterthought, that it was possibly not quite as good as the recipe her mother used to use. Left at that, the damage might have been limited. As it was, Nick readily agreed with his sister's verdict. Digging himself in deeper, he then went on to offer to obtain the recipe from his mother so Kate could make it for everyone the following year.

Not surprisingly, Kate has never made Christmas pudding since.

With the benefit of hindsight Nick realized his mistake in supporting his mother and sister in public in preference to his new wife. He later also understood how undervalued that had made her feel and vowed never to let that happen again.

This change in loyalties is likely to be as much of an adjustment for your parents as it is for you. You will also need to build a relationship with your new parents-in-law. You need to resist firmly but gently any unhelpful outside interference and establish a new independence together. While you will be grateful for your parents' advice and support, you must be sure to make your own decisions on issues that affect you both, such as where you live, what china you use or even where you hang the pictures. You can help your parents adjust to this change in loyalties by taking the initiative in maintaining contact with them and discussing issues such as the timing of family holidays, visits and phone calls.

The heated crucible of the wedding arrangements may well provide an early opportunity for negotiating with parents and future parents-in-law. The wedding itself may also provide a specific opportunity to thank your parents for all they have done for you over the years, either in a speech or perhaps in a letter. The aim of this change in dependency is to seek to build a mutually supportive relationship. In families where relationships have been difficult in the past, the marriage can herald a new beginning and may in time itself be a vehicle for healing and forgiveness.

Past relationships

You may find another significant item in your invisible suitcase that you bring with you will be the influence and memory of past relationships. Particularly if you have been married before, it is important that during engagement and the early years of marriage these issues are unpacked and recognized. Many of the issues relating to preparing for a further marriage are dealt with in the second part of this chapter.

Open your suitcases during your engagement, and continue to unpack over the years ahead. Choose together what to bring from the past and pack it in your new suitcase together.

Take a break

Exercises

Try working through the following questions individually and then exchange your answers with your fiancé(e). Consider carefully what he or she has written. Then discuss the significant issues. Pay particular attention to understanding an issue that only one of you has highlighted. You may need to adjust some of your own answers as a result. In the questions we have referred to parents and parents-in-law but the exercise could equally be applied to any other significant relationship.

1. Each make a list of the four main items in your suitcase (influences from the past that you recognize you are bringing into marriage), e.g.

I never saw my parents argue and so I find conflict difficult.

My parents were physically very affectionate to each other and to us as children.

My mother died when I was nine and I grew up with my brothers in an all-male household.

My father did all the decision making in my parents' marriage.

Discuss your lists together.

2. Does a parent (seek to) control or interfere in your decisions and the direction of your lives? If so, agree how to establish boundaries.

3. Identify any issues relating to your parents and/or parents-in-law that might lead to tension or arguments between you. How can these be resolved?

4. In what ways could you support your fiancé(e) with regard to your parents and parents-in-law?

5. How can you show your support and gratitude to your parents and parents-in-law?

6. How can you best keep in touch with your parents and parents-in-law?

7. Discuss possible Christmas and holiday arrangements.

[This section seeks to put some guidelines in place for those considering remarriage. However, do seek help if you are struggling with issues from the past which you are finding difficult to deal with alone. You can find out more about Care for the Family's initiative for those parenting in a stepfamily, 'Life in a Stepfamily', at www.careforthefamily.org.uk/stepfamily. Care for the Family's 'A Different Journey' initiative supports people who have been widowed at a young age. Visit www.careforthefamily.org.uk/adj to find out more. And please call (029) 2081 0800 if you would like to speak to someone about either of these initiatives, or any other area of Care for the Family's work.]

For those marrying for a further time the suitcase will be a little larger and may take a little more time to unpack. Whether your previous marriage ended in divorce or because of the death of your spouse, the experience of being married will not only have shaped you as a person but will also have influenced your expectations of any future marriage. At the time of engagement, past experience will complicate your emotions.

Where your previous marriage has ended in divorce

After her first marriage ended in divorce, Julie found herself amazed that someone might want to build a new relationship with her. The broken marriage had left her struggling with low self-esteem. As she later wrote, 'I knew my friendship with David had deepened, and every part of me longed for the friendship and security that he offered. However, at the back of my mind lurked fear, fear that I might be hurt again and fear of a new commitment. The last few years had been tough and I had reached the stage where I found it difficult to believe anything good could ever happen to me again.' She also found to her surprise that she had to relearn dating skills as she experienced again the wonder and excitement of beginning a new relationship.

If either partner has had a difficult relationship in the past, there may be issues of trust and commitment that surface when considering engagement and remarriage. These need to be addressed together sensitively.

Lauren's first husband's inability to tell the truth had taught her not to trust anyone again. She was now engaged to Rob and it was to be his first marriage. They both knew that if their relationship was going to grow, Lauren would need to take a risk and learn to trust again.

Rob wrote: 'I realized that I also had a part to play in helping Lauren to leave the past behind and to help her trust me. In the first months of our marriage, my work often took me away and so I would make the effort to telephone every night just to reassure her, to help her to begin to trust again.'

In order for their relationship to grow, Rob needed to recognize the issues that Lauren faced. The challenge was to be as understanding and tolerant as possible about this. On the other hand, Lauren needed to help the relationship by letting go of her past and trying to give Rob undivided attention.

If you are engaged and both of you have been married before, you need to be aware of each other's issues and to endeavour to support each other in dealing with them. This may be a long and often demanding task but one that will get easier as your relationship deepens.

Part of choosing to love our fiancé(e) will be choosing to let go of the past.

Pip had been married to Tim for two months. It was a second marriage for both of them. Pip always said that her first husband, Tony, 'had a thing about timekeeping'. Her memories of the marriage were of angry scenes if any member of the family was more than a few minutes late.

One particular evening, Pip had said she would be home by 7.30 p.m., but became stuck in a traffic jam. She had no way of contacting Tim and grew increasingly anxious as the minutes ticked by. The traffic crawled along as five minutes became ten, fifteen and then twenty. When she eventually arrived home, it was after 8.00 p.m. She burst in, apologizing profusely and, without even stopping to take off her coat, began to prepare the evening meal. Tim stood by the open door, looking at her in complete astonishment.

Even though some issues from the past may surface during engagement, others may not come to the fore until the early years of marriage. The important thing is to recognize them, face them and resolve to move on together.

Eileen found that her sexual inexperience in her first marriage had damaged her self-esteem. This in turn threatened her new relationship: 'My former husband once told me I was "frigid". He had hurt me deeply at the time, but I tried to forget and bury it under the trauma of separation. I remarried several years later, and that word came back to haunt me in the context of my sexual relationship in my new marriage. The belief that my new husband too might think I was frigid troubled me greatly. It was only when I faced the issue and talked to a friend that the power that the word had over me was broken.'

If either of you has been unhappily married before, the crucial question to ask is: 'What is it about *this* relationship that means things will be different this time?' As another woman explains: 'If I had realized that I was just swapping one set of problems for another, I would have thought more carefully before getting married again. I thought the problem was my husband. I have now discovered that part of the problem lay a little closer to home.'

The truth is you must first turn the spotlight on yourselves. It is as you acknowledge what your part may have been in the breakdown of a previous relationship that you will be able to see how you can be part of building a different future.

Where you have been widowed

Becoming engaged after one is widowed, particularly if widowed young, may cause different but equally complex emotions to surface. For some, bereavement may result in a loss of confidence and reluctance to risk being hurt again. For many, the role of husband or wife will be intrinsically bound up with the person who has died. The new fiancé(e) is of course a different person and the task will be to endeavour to avoid comparisons. People need to treasure the past. Memories of the deceased are very precious and are inevitably brought into a new marriage. You should not expect a fiancé(e) to replace a spouse who has died.

A bereaved spouse considering remarriage may still have feelings of loyalty to the partner who died. One woman struggling with this issue explains: 'I felt that I was being disloyal in forming a new relationship. Talking with a friend who had been widowed herself helped me. I realized that I had promised to be faithful "till death us do part". Death had now parted us, and I was free to move on. I also knew that my husband would have wanted the best for me and deep down I knew that this was the best...'

It can be liberating to discover that you can have two wonderful marriages. You can love your fiancé(e) without in any way denying the feelings you still have for your first husband or wife.

Richard: A friend of ours who was widowed and has now remarried wrote of his experience: 'It is probably inevitable that one makes comparisons. However, they are very dangerous, both because every marriage is different and also because of the danger of hurting your partner's feelings. This is doubly so because if one's first marriage was very happy, the power of nostalgia can sometimes make it seem even better than it was. When you feel that your second marriage is not absolutely fantastic (as inevitably you will from time to time), the tendency can be to turn to overly rosy memories of your first marriage.'

Our best man married a widow who had three young children. The wedding day was very special. While not denying there was some heartache, it was a great celebration that valued the past while marking the beginning of a new future for a new family.

If you are engaged to marry someone who has been bereaved, remember that grieving does not have a clearly defined ending. Moments of grief are to be expected. These will often come without warning. Be prepared to recognize the signs and to give your partner time alone when they need it. It will be helpful also to be particularly aware of birthdays and anniversaries such as that of the date the spouse died. The most difficult and unexpected memories may be triggered by a piece of music, a fragment of verse, or even the sight of an elderly couple in each other's company. They can induce grief without warning.

Richard: Our friend's letter continued: 'The wound of bereavement cuts deep but, over time, it begins to heal. Remarriage can be part of the healing process. Whilst the scar has faded, it will never go away completely. It is thirteen years since Caroline died, and yet a couple of weeks ago I heard a piece of music that tore the scar tissue away and left me in tears. With it came the sense of disloyalty to my (new) wife, but also the comfort of a burden shared. It will probably never go away, although undoubtedly will become less a feature of life.'

If your fiancé(e) has been widowed, it is vital to grasp that it is possible for them to grieve for their first spouse while also loving you and looking forward to your marriage. The fact that they may miss their first husband or wife does not mean that they love you any less. Keep talking about how each of you feels and seek to move forward together. Talk about the spouse who has died and, particularly if there are children, listen to family memories. This will be part of moving on together and will avoid the possibility of such memories becoming taboo.

Deborah married a widower with children: 'In the early days of marriage, I did not share things I had experienced that had caused me pain as they seemed trivial in comparison with (my husband's) pain. I am sure now that it would have been better for our relationship had I done so.'

As your relationship deepens, your fiancé(e) needs the security of knowing that you are committed to building a relationship together for the future and are not seeking to bring back the past.

Practical matters

Whether you are divorced or widowed, there will be practical matters to consider in a new relationship. In marriage, the giving and receiving of a ring is a symbolic act. If you have been widowed, your first wedding ring may be very precious to you but at the same time feel very threatening to your fiancé(e). Some couples put the first ring away. Others continue to wear it but on a different hand. Be gentle and understanding with each other and ensure that you are both happy with whatever is agreed.

Many couples marrying for the first time will plan to buy or rent a property together that will be their joint new home. If either of you has been married before, the chances are that one or both of you may already have your own property and you will need to decide where you will live. Your engagement is the time to discuss practical steps that you can take to make the property feel that it is your joint home. Simple changes, such as redecorating the bedroom or putting up different pictures, may help the spouse who is moving in to feel that they belong.

Another point of concern may be photographs. Where there are children from a previous marriage, it may be appropriate to have a photograph of the absent natural parent in the children's bedroom or in albums, although probably not in the main rooms of the house.

Whatever you decide about this and other issues, the important thing is that each of you is able to talk honestly about how you feel and to move forward together, celebrating the past but not letting it cast a shadow over the present.

Where there are children

Rachel and Andrew had just arrived back from their honeymoon and eagerly opened the folder to see the photographs of their wedding day. They had both been married before and had six children between them. It had been a very special day, with both families celebrating together. However, as they looked through the photographs, it struck them that there wasn't a single photograph of them on their own. Each photograph included a picture of one or more of their six children – an indication, possibly, of the years ahead.

Where there are children involved, you will need to apply all the advice on building a relationship from other sections of this book but now it has to accommodate the children as well. Inevitably, you are taking on a complex set of relationships, often without the luxury of time and space to explore them. If you are engaged to be married and either or both of you have children, make every effort to build your friendship and guard your special time alone together.

One couple who are newly married with four teenage children find the only time they are alone together is early on Saturday morning when two children are in bed and the other two have a paper delivery round. If there are children, where possible be imaginative and seize every opportunity to be alone together.

Your engagement is the time to discuss and agree on parenting styles.
Plan how you can support each other in setting boundaries and in areas of discipline. Talk through arrangements for special family occasions such as birthdays, Christmas, holidays and so on. If you can agree a way forward at an early stage, it will ensure that expectations are managed and understood.

Just as building a relationship with your fiancé(e) takes time, so does building a relationship with your stepchildren. If one of you has been used to having sole responsibility for the children, another adult joining the family will change the dynamics and require adjustment on everyone's part. When you become engaged, it is as if you open an account with your fiancé(e)'s child. The balance in the account is nil. If the children feel resentful about the new relationship, the account quickly becomes overdrawn. You will need to make many deposits of unconditional love, care, compassion and kindness before you can begin to make any withdrawals.

A parent and child have a shared history and a strong bond between

them. The task of engagement is to form a strong bond between yourself and your fiancé(e). Loving their natural parent is probably the best thing you can do for your stepchild. The weakest relationship in a new family is likely always to be that between stepchild and step-parent. They have no shared history. Their bond has to be carefully nurtured over time.

Step-parenting gives responsibility but no rights. Before committing to marriage, ensure that you have understood the full responsibility that you are taking on. If you find your fiancé(e)'s children difficult now, marriage will probably not change how you feel.

If you are engaged and marrying into a family where the natural parent has died, you might want to consider adopting the children. This will give you all the rights of a natural parent. This is obviously not a step to take without understanding its full implications. It may be something that you need to discuss with your fiancé(e) and other family members now and return to a year or so into marriage.

However eager you are to remarry, remember that any children involved may need more time to adjust to the idea. They have not had any choice about the situation that they find themselves in and may need time for their concerns to be addressed. Take account of their needs when planning the wedding and be imaginative in involving them in arrangements. Depending on their age, they could help with decisions about flowers, the colour scheme, the music, table plan and so on. It will be an investment worth making if they can be made to feel that they are part of this new family from the beginning.

For couples marrying a second time, practising the 'rules of engagement' is complicated by the effects of the past. Keep good lines of communication open between you. Unpack and deal with the past and use it to launch your future together.

Take a break

Exercises

1. Where your previous marriage ended in divorce
i) From the list below:
Put a tick where your needs were met in your first marriage. Put an X where your needs were not met.

Affection

Appreciation

Approval

Attention

Comfort

Encouragement

Respect

Security

Support

Talk about the issues raised.

ii) Each now choose three needs.

Discuss practical ways that you can meet those needs in your new marriage (e.g. I will meet your need for appreciation by remembering to thank you when you have done something for me).

2. Where a previous spouse has died

i) Each write down five things you love and appreciate about your fiancé(e). Exchange lists.

ii) Use the listen/talk exercise from pp. 78–79.

If your previous spouse died, choose a particular memory from the past that impacts on the present and tell your fiancé(e) about it. In particular talk about your feelings.

If you are engaged to someone whose previous spouse died, listen and try to understand how your fiancé(e) feels.

Tell your fiancé(e) if there is anything from the past you find threatening and why.

3. Practical matters

i) Identify any practical considerations you need to take into account as a consequence of one or both of you having been married before (e.g. the need to make your fiancé(e)'s property your joint home).

ii) Use the listen/talk exercise from pp. 78–79 to help you understand how you each feel.

iii) Find a joint solution (*Rule 4*), e.g. rearrange the kitchen cupboards and redecorate the bedroom or hang new pictures, chosen together.

4. Where there are children

In a stepfamily, the first and strongest bond is between the biological parent and their child. It is emotional, it has history, and there are legal and blood ties. This parent then meets a new partner. This chosen bond is emotional and may become legal too. The weakest bond in a stepfamily is between the step-parent and the stepchild. They do not have a shared history, and there are no legal or blood ties. Therefore, the emotional bond between them will take time and effort to develop.

The following diagram shows different possible relationships in a new stepfamily.

David proposed to Joanna. He has two children, Laura and Annie. Joanna has two children, Guy and Sarah.

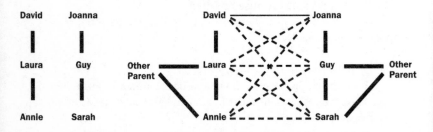

DIAGRAM BY KIND PERMISSION OF CHRISTINE TUFNELL

Draw a similar diagram for your new family, based on the model
opposite.

Strong bond - emotional, legal and blood ties. ▬▬▬▬▬▬

Less strong bond - emotional, and may be legal. ─────────

Weakest bond - no legal or blood ties and emotional ─ ─ ─ ─ ─ ─
bonds will take time to develop.

Discuss practical ways of strengthening each of the bonds, e.g.

David ─────── Joanna: We will book a babysitter on Wednesday evenings
so we can spend time together.

David - - - - - Guy: I will watch Guy play football on Saturday mornings.

Rule 7

Say 'I Love You'

Nothing compares with the euphoria of being in love. You feel you are walking on air; you imagine that this feeling will never end. The popular music culture repeats the refrain. It is easy to say to your fiancé(e), 'I love you', because that is how you feel.

Real love goes way beyond such feelings. It requires polishing and, like a diamond, is multifaceted and shaped over time. In Louis de Bernières's novel, *Captain Corelli's Mandolin*, Dr Iannis describes the nature of real love to his daughter:

> 'Love is not breathlessness, it is not excitement, it is not the promulgation of promises of eternal passion, it is not the desire to mate every second minute of the day, it is not lying awake at night imagining that he is kissing every cranny of your body. No, don't blush. I am telling you some truths. That is just being "in love", which any fool can do. Love itself is what is left over when being in love has burned away... Your mother and I had it, we had roots that grew towards each other underground, and when all the pretty blossom had fallen from our branches we found that we were one tree and not two.'

Katharine: There is a cherry tree near our home. For eleven and a half months of the year, it is no different from any other cherry tree. Then in April it comes into flower: half white blossom and half pink from one trunk. Two trees have been grafted together; over the years, the two have grown as one.

Mutual attraction is usually what first brings people together. As this inevitably fades a little, there is a need to cultivate love over the years so that your roots entwine and you become one. Learning how to tell your fiancé(e) that you love them again and again in a way they understand will be part of this process.

Anna pulled the duvet tightly around her and sighed. She had just been drifting off to sleep when the noise of drilling downstairs had woken her. They had moved into the house two months ago, just after they had returned from their honeymoon. Jon had said it would need a lot of work doing to it, but she had no idea what that really meant. A new kitchen and bathroom perhaps and a quick lick of paint. The drilling was replaced by hammer blows which pounded through her head. She hated the house: the mess, the new electrical wiring, the half-finished pipe work, the central heating still to be installed – she had never wanted to change the kitchen anyway. But more than all that, she hated them because they took him away from her.

Jon was determined to make his marriage work. He wanted to show Anna how much he loved her and wanted to provide for her by building their dream home. This would be the symbol of his undying love. Each night he would come in from work and, barely taking time to grab some food, he would give Anna a passing hug and set to, often working late into the night and over the weekend. And when a little extra cash was needed to pay for the next stage, he would show his sacrifice to Anna by staying late at work to earn the extra money needed to finish the house.

Jon was pleased with the progress he was making, two months on, still within budget and scheduled to finish by Christmas in six months' time. He stepped back to admire his progress for a moment. As usual it was a solitary experience. No Anna. Jon could not understand it; the more effort he put into their home, the more distant and remote she seemed to become. She rarely helped and seldom showed the excitement that had been there when they first moved in.

Richard: Last summer, I stood at the checkout of the large French hypermarket, my trolley laden with enough supplies for a school camp. There seemed to be a problem. My schoolboy French was not making any headway with an increasingly frustrated and agitated sales assistant. I resorted to speaking English to her, slowly and loudly, accompanied by some excellent and clearly understandable arm signals, but to no effect.

As the queue reached the back of the shop, Katharine returned. A quick exchange in French resulted in a transformation in the situation and in the sales assistant herself. She now graciously took payment from a card that apparently was acceptable, rather than the one I had proffered.

In order to communicate effectively, we have to speak a common language. Gary Chapman, in his book *The Five Love Languages*, lists five ways in which people communicate love to one another. These could be described as:

1. Words

2. Actions

3. Time

4. Gifts

5. Physical touch

He uses the metaphor of language to examine the different ways in which we each give and receive love. He explains that, just as we all have a mother tongue which we find easy to speak and understand, so we

All five of these languages are important, but for each of us there will
be at least one in which we are fluent. As Chapman explains: 'In order
for us to feel loved by our partner, we must be "loved" in our favourite
language more than any other.'

Words

Words are a powerful tool. Kind words build up; harsh words cut down
and destroy. If your fiancé(e)'s primary love language is words, you can
show them how much you love them simply through the words that you
say. When a relationship is new, it is easy to compliment and encourage
each other. The challenge is to continue that over a lifetime together.

Actions

For others, actions convey love in a very special way. The possibilities
for expressing love in the language of action are endless. It could be
filling the car up with petrol, organizing that surprise, going to watch
your fiancé(e)'s team playing on a cold, wet afternoon or perhaps even
setting aside an evening to address all the wedding invitations. Simply
by performing these actions, your fiancé(e) hears that you have thought
about them and care for them, and knows that you love them.

Time

If your primary love language is time, then this means time with your
fiancé(e), so taking them out with a group of friends will probably not
be enough. What does matter is both the quality *and* quantity of time
together. It may be travelling together in the car; it may be a special date.
If your love language is time, it will not matter greatly if you are both
out walking and it rains, or out for a meal and the food is disappointing.
It is just the single fact of being exclusively together that conveys the
message that you are loved.

Gifts

Giving and receiving gifts is very important to some people. The action
of procuring and presenting a gift conveys the message of love. The gift

is a visual symbol; its monetary value is often less significant. If this is your fiancé(e)'s love language, a gift of a single flower or a favourite bar of chocolate can convey love in the same way as a more expensive present. The gift is a visual reminder that the giver has thought about and cares for the receiver.

Physical touch

This can be anything from brushing past each other to touch of a more intimate nature. If someone who senses love through touch receives it, they will feel all the same emotions that go with being told in words that they are loved. If that is your fiancé(e)'s language, you will need to use touch deliberately to show that you love them. As Gary Chapman describes it: 'To touch my body is to touch me. To withdraw from my body is to distance yourself from me.'

You need to make the effort to learn to say 'I love you' to your fiancé(e) in a language that they can understand. Just as in the French supermarket, the effects can be far-reaching. In fact, what often happens is that you try to communicate love to your fiancé(e) in the way you understand it. However, if this is not their primary love language, it will be like speaking a foreign language to them.

Jon was working supremely hard to build a home for Anna. Every hole drilled and hammer blow said 'I love you' but it was falling on deaf ears. Anna's language was time – time together.

Katharine: When we were first married, I would scour the shops for a birthday present for Richard, or occasionally buy him a present for no apparent reason other than to say 'I love you'. I was repeatedly disappointed when the gift was opened and simply put to one side with, at best, a grunt of thanks. Conversely, Richard's apparent incapacity to commit any time to shopping when my birthday or Christmas was on the horizon would also give me the impression that Richard did not love me.

One of Richard's primary ways of feeling and expressing love is through action. On many occasions he has spent hours tidying the house and then felt disappointed when I have sailed in, apparently oblivious to the transformation. He also loves arranging surprises. During our engagement and first years of marriage, he went to great effort to arrange many (beginning with the honeymoon) as a way of showing his love. It was not until several years later that I told Richard just how much I hate surprises. All his effort had completely missed the mark.

Over the years, understanding our differences and learning to show our love in a different language has transformed our relationship and enabled us to say 'I love you' in a way that we each hear and understand. On a good day, I receive the flowers and Richard the surprises.

When Jon and Anna heard about the concept of love languages, Jon said: 'It was like a light coming on. I suddenly grasped what was happening in our relationship. The hours I was spending on the house meant far less to Anna than they did to me. In fact, the investment of time in the building was having a negative effect because I discovered that Anna's primary way of feeling loved was through the time I spent with her, not the time I spent on the house. I was saying "I love you" through the action of building a home; what Anna wanted from me was some of that same time. I am now trying to give Anna the time that she needs.'

Anna said: 'I understood for the first time that Jon was saying he loved me by spending time on the house. I had only heard he loved the house more than me. It made sense of all the work and effort he was putting in, so I have had to learn to adjust and do some of the work with him. Jon then feels loved by me as I speak his language, and in that way I also get some extra time with him.'

Just as it takes years for the roots to entwine and for two trees to become one, so learning each other's love language and putting it into practice takes time and effort. It is an investment, however, that will realize a return that will last a lifetime.

Take a break

Exercises

Write down up to six occasions when you have been especially aware of your fiancé(e)'s love for you, e.g.

1. I know you love me when you come to watch me play football.

2. I know you love me when we go out for coffee together.

Then write down up to six occasions when you believe you have shown your fiancé(e) that you love them, e.g.

1. I have shown you that I loved you by cooking a meal for you.

2. I have shown you that I loved you by putting my arm around you at the cinema.

Taking into account what you have written, try to put the five languages of love in order of importance for you, assigning the most important to number 1. Then write down the list for your fiancé(e). When you have finished, compare what each of you has written. Resolve to use your fiancé(e)'s top two love languages this week.

ADAPTED FROM *THE MARRIAGE PREPARATION COURSE MANUAL* (ALPHA INTERNATIONAL)

Rule 8

Develop Intimacy

Richard: I took the tin out of the oven and looked in disbelief at the flat pancake that I had intended to serve with the joint. The recipe had said plain flour but there was none in the cupboard. I had substituted self-raising flour instead, reasoning that it would result in a slightly more elevated Yorkshire pudding which would be sure to impress...

In every recipe there are certain ingredients that must be included to ensure culinary success. The same principle can be applied to a marriage. Your relationship will not stand or fall on the quality or quantity of its lovemaking alone, but developing a fulfilling sexual relationship is an important part of a successful marriage. Nicky and Sila Lee write: 'Both need to recognize that their sexual relationship is not the icing on the cake of their marriage but an essential ingredient of the cake itself.'

As already discussed, the task of engagement is to prepare for a relationship of growing intimacy as you share your life together. Just as in other areas of your relationship, there are things you can learn which will help you develop intimacy in the way that you communicate and relate to each other physically. As one man said: 'I imagined that when we were married we would make love every night, and didn't think that there was much to learn. We now realize to enjoy sex we need to work at it, as with every other area of our marriage.'

This very intimate act of making love requires you to be completely vulnerable with each other in a place of safety, trust and honesty.

In marriage you promise to give yourselves unreservedly to each other and it is that commitment that forms the foundation of the marriage relationship. Giving yourselves to each other as you make love together, within the safety of the marriage vows, can be seen as the natural carrying out of that commitment.

Developing a sexual relationship should be one of the most pleasurable tasks of marriage which can continue well past childbearing years.

'In a good marriage, sex and love are inseparable. Sex serves a very serious function in maintaining both the quality and stability of the relationship, replenishing emotional reserves and strengthening the marital bond' (*The Good Marriage*, Judith Wallerstein).

The consequences of making love go far beyond the moment. Each time you make love together, your marriage is strengthened. While one purpose of sex is obviously to have children, sex is also for your enjoyment throughout your married life together. It will be no surprise to realize that in this area, as in every other, people come to engagement with different experiences and attitudes. The following might influence your expectations of your sexual relationship.

Family background

Your expectations will be moulded partly by the attitude to sex and physical intimacy that you saw modelled as you were growing up. Recognizing these influences on you will give you a starting point for working at your relationship together.

Hannah went to boarding school when she was eleven. Although she knew that her parents loved her, they did not show their affection for her physically. She reached adulthood believing that sex was a taboo subject and an optional extra in a relationship. Her inhibitions were deepened by an incident in her teens that left her frightened of physical intimacy. Her fiancé persuaded her to seek counselling and, helped by his patience and gentleness, they were able to begin to build a fulfilling sexual relationship in their marriage.

It's always absolutely fabulous

Sex in the media is nearly always portrayed as absolutely fabulous and divorced from any committed and long-term relationship. As you prepare for marriage, you would do well to understand that, even though the sexual relationship is indeed an integral part of the marriage relationship, it is unlikely to be always absolutely fabulous.

In *The Sixty Minute Marriage*, Rob Parsons writes:

'If we are going to have a good sexual relationship, one of the prerequisites is that we stop taking ourselves so seriously and quit imagining that our sex lives are going to impress Hollywood. In that

particular suburb of Los Angeles, it seems that the sex is always wonderful. The beds are always made, the women look fantastic and seem to have an insatiable appetite for lovemaking. The men are animal-like and yet tender, rough yet smooth, and never fall asleep straight afterwards. The real world is a little different. In the real world, there are periods and mind-numbing tiredness. Enjoy the films but don't compare your love life to them.'

Knowing your differences

Just as you need to understand the expectations that you bring with you, you also need to come to marriage aware of the differences between you and your fiancé(e).

It is generally held that men and women are different from each other in their approach to sex. In *The Marriage Book*, Nicky and Sila Lee write:

'Men can't get enough sex; women can't get enough romance. Men are thinking about the destination; women are thinking about the road. Men are like gas cookers: they heat up instantly and cool down rapidly. Women are like electric cookers: they take time to heat up but stay hot much longer.'

Such generalizations are just that – they do not apply to every man and every woman. It is important to interpret them for your own relationship. However, it is not uncommon for one partner to be more interested in sex and more easily aroused than the other. The key is to understand your sexual differences as individuals. The following may help (but be wary of generalizations).

Understanding what arouses you

In most cases, arousal is more complex for a woman than for a man. For many women, their attitude to sexual intercourse is inextricably linked with the quality of the relationship as a whole. To be able to give herself intimately to her husband, a woman usually needs to feel valued and secure.

Rob Parsons writes in his book *Loving Against the Odds*:

'A wife wants to know that she is wanted – not just for sex but to *talk with; loved enough to be the recipient of displays of affection which are unrelated to sexual intercourse – and loved enough to be wooed. If a man is uncommunicative and is more interested in the sports page than discussing issues that matter to her, then he had better take the sports page to bed – he's going to have plenty of time to read it. That's why the old advice is true: "If a man wants a wild Friday night, he had better begin working on it Monday morning…"'*

It is as a husband meets his wife's emotional needs that he will create the climate of trust for her to be able to give herself to him. Walter Trobisch puts it like this: 'A woman's greatest erogenous zone is her heart. And nothing touches her heart more than loving, affirming words.'

On the other hand, arousal for men is often less complex and more immediate. Men can be aroused simply by the physical proximity of their partner. A conversation in the film *The Story of Us* comments on the perceived differences between men and women: 'After an argument, men need to make love in order to make up, whereas women need to make up before making love.'

Whatever our differences, it is vital that we communicate about this deeply intimate area of our relationship.

Knowing the importance of romance

Romance may be more important to one of you than to the other. Often, romance plays a significant part in lovemaking for women. You need to take time to find out what things your fiancé(e) finds romantic. Romance can draw us together and give us feelings of closeness, intimacy and security. It can alleviate the routine of work and chores, paying bills and solving problems. Romantic acts need not incur great cost. They may simply involve doing something that is outside routine and which may require a little care and planning.

Planning ahead

As you learn about each other, you can discover how to unlock the pleasures of physical and emotional union. Each of you should take some responsibility for your part in that.

Cathy has been married to Greg for nine months. She says: 'Despite my

high expectations, our sexual relationship didn't get off to a very good start. We both had demanding jobs and evening commitments and so didn't get to bed until late, by which time I just wanted to go to sleep. I never initiated sex because I assumed that should be the man's role.'

Greg continues: 'Being married was great, but my one disappointment was with sex. Cathy would turn over and go straight to sleep and I would be left feeling frustrated. One evening, we met up with a couple from our marriage preparation course. It was so good to be able to talk about how I felt. As a result, we resolved to plan times to make love and Cathy agreed to take some responsibility for taking the initiative. We are still working at it but it is no longer the source of hurt and frustration that it was rapidly becoming.'

Cathy agrees: 'It was good to be able to talk and for me to realize just how Greg felt. I also found it helpful to realize that I had an important part to play. I could choose to take the initiative in making love, and that choice could override feelings of tiredness. We still have a long way to go but that evening was a real breakthrough.'

Although planning a time to make love may sound clinical, it does not rule out spontaneity as well and does ensure that this important part of your relationship does not become the casualty of your busy lives. Future circumstances, such as the birth of children or stress at work, may mean that either one of you may lose your desire for sex for a period of time. When this happens, as it surely will, keep an open channel of communication about how each of you feels so as to prevent hurt and misunderstanding.

It is important to begin to communicate about your physical relationship while you are engaged and to agree any boundaries that you may wish to put in place.

Putting the past behind you

Your sexual relationship can only develop and grow in a climate of trust and honesty. You may come to marriage with previous experiences of sexual relationships. It is important that while you are engaged you bring into the open and deal with any issues that could cause guilt, jealousy or mistrust so that they do not cast a shadow over the present.

Judy had been in previous long-term relationships before she met Steve. Steve was a virgin until he married Judy.

Steve explains: 'When we got engaged we wanted to make a new start together. I knew that Judy had had sexual experiences in the past and I was worried that she would always be making comparisons with me. I didn't know how to bring the subject up.'

Judy continues: 'I knew this was an issue we needed to talk about, but I didn't know how. I was worried that when Steve knew all about my past he might think that I wasn't good enough for him. A friend recommended that we did a marriage preparation course which involved completing a questionnaire and using it as a basis for discussion with another couple about our expectations of marriage. It was such a relief when the subject of sex came up. It was quite hard to talk about it but we were both able to say how we felt and to explain our hopes and fears. Just being open with Steve about the past was very healing. We have dealt with it now and have resolved to move on. I have also thrown away my box of photographs and letters so we can really make a new start.'

Being open with each other

If either of you has issues from the past relating to matters such as pornography, abortion or sexual abuse, it would be advisable to seek outside help during your engagement so that these issues can begin to be addressed. Working through the past can be painful but it has been demonstrated that marriage can be a vehicle for healing, forgiveness and a new start.

A person's sexuality is a deeply personal part of their life. You may initially find it difficult and embarrassing to talk openly about it to each other. Do persevere. It is much easier to develop a fulfilling sex life if you are able to talk together about what each of you finds pleasurable. You may find it helpful to read a good book about sex together and to use it as a basis for discussion during your engagement.

Children

A possible outcome of marriage that it is vital to discuss during your engagement is whether or not you plan to have children and how you each might feel if that were not possible.

Maria looked back on her marriage to Carl. 'Carl had been married before and had children from his previous marriage. He told me that he didn't want any more children, but I thought that once we were married I would be able to persuade him to change his mind. It's hard letting go of your dreams.'

If you have not done so already, and it is appropriate, it is also important to discuss and agree on methods of contraception.

Honeymoon expectations

Katharine: On our honeymoon, we spent the first two nights in the Cotswolds and then went to Crete. Here, the hotel rooms were individual small stone buildings set amid beautiful gardens.

We arrived in the early afternoon and carried our cases (still dropping confetti) through an avenue of bougainvillea to our room. It was a beautiful setting and the sea was glistening in the distance beyond. All was going to plan.

Other couples had told us not to expect too much. But this was our honeymoon and we knew our experience would be different. Two minutes later reality crashed in upon us as we stood on the threshold open-mouthed at the sight of two rock-hard single beds, each built into the stone wall and at least 10 metres apart!

Although for some sex on the honeymoon is wonderful, it is certainly not unusual to experience difficulty and for initial expectations not to be met.

Phil pushed out the boat and booked a five-star country hotel. They had planned the rest of the honeymoon together but the first night had been his responsibility alone. They arrived at the hotel tired and much later than anticipated but flowers and champagne were waiting for them in their room. Jenny was delighted. They opened the champagne and talked about the day. Phil then went to shower, leaving Jenny to relax. Twenty minutes later he came out of the bathroom to find Jenny lying across the bed – fast asleep. He decided not to wake her but nonetheless spent the rest of the night hugely disappointed. He had put so much effort into planning everything and felt badly let down. Although things improved slightly during the fortnight, both agreed that lovemaking on their honeymoon never reached the heights of passion that they had anticipated.

Have realistic expectations of sex on your honeymoon and talk about them to each other. You will have had a wonderful but exhausting day and your wedding night may not be the best time to anticipate a great sexual experience. You have a lifetime ahead of you to develop a sexual relationship that deepens in intimacy over the years.

Take a break

Exercise

Read the following statements on your own and then use them as a basis for discussion. Persevere even if you find it embarrassing. Honest discussion will give you a basis for a fulfilling sexual relationship. What do you believe?

Real intimacy can only be expressed through sexual intercourse.

The husband should take the lead in making love.

The husband should be the one most knowledgeable about sex.

Sex is for the bedroom – under the duvet with the lights off.

Sex is only for last thing at night.

Contraception should be the wife's responsibility.

One partner should never deny the other.

'Sexy' nightwear is important.

A couple must always agree their form of sexual activity.

An orgasm must be achieved for sex to be successful.

Tenderness is more important than technique.

Sex should not be practised when the wife is having a period or is pregnant.

There are no bounds to sexual activity within marriage.

ADAPTED FROM *LOVING AGAINST THE ODDS*, ROB PARSONS

Rule 9

Spend What You Can Afford

Leyla got in from work before Phil that evening. As she put the kettle on, the phone rang. The brief conversation that followed left her head spinning.

'Can I speak to Mr West please?'

'No, sorry. He won't be in for another half an hour. This is his wife. Can I ask who's calling?'

'The bank.'

Leyla's heart sank.

She and Phil had taken out a credit card just before they were married to pay for their contribution to the wedding. They had kept good account of expenditure at the time and were paying off the debt at an agreed monthly rate. However, two months ago, Phil's parents had come for the weekend. Leyla had wanted to make a good impression so she had bought extras in the weekly shop that she knew they couldn't afford. In the supermarket queue, she had looked at the trolley and decided on impulse to use the credit card. Phil would never notice. That had been the beginning. Over the next few weeks, she had slipped other items on the card that she needed – some new clothes for work, a birthday present for Phil, another supermarket shop. Using a plastic card didn't feel like she was spending real money and, as long as she got to the post before he did in the morning, he would never know...

Every day letters arrive offering more and more credit to 'take the waiting out of wanting'. Finance lenders come in all shapes and sizes and are now prepared to offer sums several times higher than a couple's income. Some even allow self-certification of earnings and there is no longer any requirement to demonstrate a regular pattern of saving. This has opened wide the door of opportunity for newly married couples to purchase a home. At the same time, it has greatly increased the pressure of debt. Borrow money, but borrow wisely and for items that you need –

Katharine: During my time as a family law solicitor, conflict over
finance figured high on the list of reasons cited as contributing to the
breakdown of marriage. I learnt then that debt is no respecter of person,
status or income. Whatever you are earning, the temptation is always to
spend that little bit more than you can afford. We live in a society that
pushes the use of credit but offers little guidance in managing debt. It
is unfortunately often true that the more people earn, the larger their
debt.

The casualties of debt sat in the waiting room outside my office. The
director of the pharmaceutical company, the newly qualified surveyor
and the check-out assistant experienced at first hand the crushing worry
that debt can bring and the fatal blow that it can deal relationships if
not handled properly. Each had used money foolishly and then, feeling
the weight of guilt, had retreated behind a wall of silence and secrecy
which ultimately proved too hard to scale.

Healthy marriages that last a lifetime need trust and honesty. This is just
as important in the area of finance as it is elsewhere in the marriage.

Family background

In the management of money, as in other areas, you need to begin
your engagement by understanding your differences and sharing your
financial expectations. It will be the attitude to money, and not the
relative standard of living in the homes you have been brought up in,
which will have influenced how you manage your finances.

Richard: Our respective families have very different levels of income but
both are generous and both have always lived well within their means.
Nonetheless, although we did not have excessive debts, our different
backgrounds did mean that we brought into marriage different spending
priorities which we needed to reconcile. In the early days of marriage,
we often had differences of opinion over our individual classification
of 'essential' and 'luxury' items. Discussions frequently centred on the
contents of the supermarket trolley, the focus of debate being the

purchase of items such as fresh orange juice and ground coffee.

When you are engaged, you need to recognize and understand the different attitudes to money that you are each bringing into marriage from your family backgrounds.

Personality

Some people get pleasure out of spending their money and others get enjoyment out of saving and seeing their reserves grow. As in every other area, the important thing is to recognize your differences and plan your approach to money together accordingly. If you don't already know, you need to discover if you are marrying a spender or a saver.

Spender/Saver Test

1. Do you know exactly how much is in your bank account at any given time?

2. Do you have a regular pattern of saving?

3. Do you generally compare prices before buying?

4. If you are employed, do you have any of your pay left by the time your next pay cheque arrives?

5. Do you only buy essential items?

If you have answered 'Yes' to most of these questions, you are probably a saver.

If a spender marries a saver, there is obvious potential for conflict. However, when budgeting, it is an advantage to have both character traits represented. The challenge throughout marriage is not to allow conflict over money to become an issue between you. Whatever your personality, communication is critical.

Katharine: We remember one occasion when we had a sum of money in a joint savings account. One Saturday afternoon, we were shopping separately and failed to discuss our intentions in any detail. Between 2.05 p.m. and 2.30 p.m., we each independently spent the (not inconsiderable) sum of money on entirely different items in different shops. Not only did we have to negotiate with each other but also with the bank as to the terms of repayment.

Managing your money together

Whatever the exact wording of your wedding vows, it is likely that you will promise to share all you have with your fiancé(e).

Richard: The promise we made to each other was: 'All that I am I give to you, and all that I have I share with you, within the love of God.'

The fact that we share everything is the starting point when we discuss together how we manage our money. When we were engaged, opening a joint bank account seemed to us a natural way of expressing the fact that we were moving from two separate lives to one joint one. I made the appropriate arrangements at the bank but three months into marriage was perplexed to find that the account seemed to be permanently overdrawn. Further investigation resolved the mystery. It transpired that only one of us had got round to arranging to pay our salary into the account. After more discussion, we both agreed to pay a proportion of our salaries into the joint account with an agreed amount being left for us to save or spend individually.

Our financial circumstances have changed more than once over the years. While we were training, we managed with very little money. After a few years of marriage, we both qualified as solicitors and moved from a flat to a house. Our standard of living rose substantially. Then, it seemed overnight, things changed again. Our first child was born. Katharine stopped work and I took a planned year out of law with a corresponding cut in salary. During that time, although we had to curb our expenditure, it is true to say we were no less happy than when we were living off two incomes.

Once you have decided whether you are a spender or a saver, agree how much, if any, money you intend to give to charity. If you share the same beliefs and value system, this may not be difficult. However, if you differ in your approach, learn to respect each other's views and to agree a way forward that you are both happy with.

Working out a budget

The very process of working out a budget together has a number of benefits. In particular, it will give you a clear picture of your joint financial position and be a catalyst for frank discussion.

It is recommended that you open a joint account. This reflects the fact that everything you have is shared. Agree an amount you are happy for each of you to spend individually without consulting the other.

Whatever your financial situation, the following steps will help you communicate about your finances from day one and prevent money becoming a source of tension between you.

While you are engaged, discuss:

1. your individual financial positions. If you are in debt, agree your plans for repayment

2. whether you will have a joint account/separate accounts/both

3. how much each of you may spend without consulting the other

4. who will manage your finances – husband/wife/jointly

After you are married:

1. Complete the spreadsheet at the end of this chapter. This will help you see exactly what money you have available and what your known future expenditure will be.

2. If your expenditure exceeds your income, the solution usually is to reduce your expenditure. First, check that you are claiming all benefits to which you are entitled. Then define essentials and luxuries. Cut down on luxuries until the figures balance.

3. Set aside a regular time each week to review your financial position. Go through bank statements, bills, cheque book stubs and debit receipts until you have an accurate picture.

Finally, if you find managing money difficult:

1. Buy a notebook and write down all the money you spend (include everything).

2. Cut up your credit card.

4. Seek further help if you need it, for example from Credit Action, a national money education charity (www.creditaction.com); independent financial advisers; debt counselling agencies such as Consumer Credit Counselling Service (helpline: 0800 138 1111; website: www.cccs.co.uk); or a friend you know and trust. We also recommend *The Sixty Minute Debt Buster*, by Katie Clarke with Rob Parsons.

Budgeting for the wedding

This is dealt with in detail in the first part of this book (p. 23). Whatever the arrangements for paying for the wedding, financial decisions will need to be taken. Working to a budget with your fiancé(e) will be good practice for budgeting together in your married life.

Income and expenditure calculator

Income (monthly)   £

Salary/pay
(including overtime)   ....
Tax credits   ....
Income support   ....
Child benefit   ....
Maintenance/CSA   ....
Housing benefit   ....
Council tax benefit   ....
Disability benefit   ....
Other benefits   ....
Other income
(e.g. return on investments)   ....

Income total   £.........

Expenditure 1: Formal commitments (monthly)   £

Mortgage   ....
Rent   ....
Council tax   ....
Maintenance   ....
Water rates   ....
Sewage rates   ....
Electricity   ....
Gas   ....
Oil   ....
Telephone   ....
Mobile phone   ....
Internet   ....
TV licence   ....
Cable/satellite TV   ....
Car MOT   ....
Car loans   ....
Car tax   ....
Car insurance   ....
Personal insurance   ....
Private pension   ....
BUPA   ....
Dentist   ....
House/house contents
insurance   ....
Personal loan
repayments   ....
Credit card
repayments   ....
Charity   ....
Catalogues   ....

Expenditure 1 total   £.........

Expenditure 2:
Regular spending
(multiply to monthly) £

Food ....

Petrol ....

Public transport ....

Entertainment ....

Drink ....

Pets ....

Launderette ....

Children's pocket money ....

Childminder/babysitter ....

School lunches ....

Chemist ....

Cigarettes ....

Expenditure 2
total   £.........

Expenditure 3:
Occasional costs
(divide to monthly) £

Christmas ....

Clothing ....

Holiday ....

House repairs ....

Car repairs ....

Veterinary bills ....

Redecoration ....

Birthdays ....

Optician ....

Dentist ....

Travel ....

Replacing household
(e.g. washing machine,
furniture) ....

Expenditure 3
total   £.........

Total Monthly Expenditure

Total 1 + Total 2 + Total 3

Grand total   £...............

Balance

Total income   £...............

Total expenditure   £...............

Monthly surplus/
shortfall   £.........

ADAPTED FROM *A FAMILY'S GUIDE TO BETTER MONEY MANAGEMENT*
(CREDIT ACTION)

Rule 10

Keep on Building

Richard: We have a colourful and somewhat eccentric friend called Jim who calls round to mow our lawn in exchange for sandwiches, telephone usage and various other small favours. Jim's favourite occupation in life is making a bonfire and he can make a bonfire unlike any other. On 5 November, our attempts usually only result in clouds of smoke which eventually peter out and serve only to upset the neighbours. On one occasion, in desperation, we doused the bonfire with a can of petrol and stood back as the flames leapt up impressively, only to see them die away in minutes.

Jim's bonfires, by contrast, last for days. One day, when asked the secret, his reply was simple: 'Build a good base and keep it well fuelled.'

You could use this principle in your marriage. Build a good base: use your engagement to prepare not only for the wedding day but also for the years ahead. Work through the exercises in this book together. Consider taking part in a marriage preparation course where you can learn effective skills to help you build your relationship. (For details of a marriage preparation course in your area, visit www.prepareformarriage.org.uk or contact The National Couple Support Network – info@ncsn.org.uk.)

Then keep your marriage fuelled. Use the skills on a daily basis. Spend time together, have fun together and learn to say 'I love you' again and again.

Katharine: Last week one of our children gave us a wedding anniversary card. The message inside read: 'Mum and Dad. Congratulations on your wedding anniversary. Keep it up!' Good advice indeed from an eleven-year-old.

If you have considered attending a marriage preparation course, you may have been offered a link with a support couple who can act as mentors as you begin this adventure together. If not, consider finding a couple you know who have been married for at least five years and ask if both of you can meet with them from time to time to talk to them about their experience of the ups and downs of married life.

Two years into marriage, consider working through a course, such as 'The Marriage Course' or Care for the Family's '21st Century Marriage', in order to refresh and refuel your relationship.

Richard and Katharine: James Jones, now Bishop of Liverpool, gave us a valuable piece of advice at our wedding: 'A marriage that works is a marriage that works for others.' We have found that to be true. There have been seasons when we felt that it was as much as we could do to keep our heads above water. However, what has strengthened our marriage more than we could have ever hoped or imagined is when we have been able to look beyond our own needs and to reach out together to help others.

A bonfire, built on a solid base and kept well fuelled, will keep burning in the rain, wind and snow and will be a source of warmth and hope for any who gather round it.

'It's just beautiful,' she whispered, gazing down at the ring on her finger. The emeralds on the eternity ring sparkled in the sunlight. Sarah and Jonathan were standing on the headland overlooking the harbour, watching their grandchildren throwing stones into the water below.

Sarah thought back to how they had stood on this headland thirty years ago, just after Jonathan had proposed. The landscape had looked quite different then. New developments had sprung up and the harbour was busier. The years had changed them both as well. 'For better, for worse' – those were the words that had kept them going through the tough times and the plain sailing. What would the next thirty years bring? Sarah looked up at Jonathan. He took her hand. 'I love you, Sarah,' he said...

Appendices

1 Are You Ready for Marriage?

It is not unusual at some time during your engagement to wonder, if only for a moment, whether you are making the right decision. However, if serious doubts persist, we recommend that you talk honestly to someone you know well and respect.

It takes great courage to postpone a wedding or even break off an engagement but, however hard, it is much easier to take action now than to live with a decision that you later regret.

In any event, you may find it helpful to answer the following questions individually.

The sharing test
Do I want to share the rest of my life with my fiancé(e)?

The strength test
Does our love give me energy and strength or does it drain me?

The respect test
Do I respect my fiancé(e)?

The habit test
Do I accept my fiancé(e) as they are now (bad habits and all)?

The quarrel test
Are we able to admit our mistakes, apologize and forgive each other?

The interest test
Do we have interests in common as a foundation for friendship?

The time test
Have we weathered all the seasons and a variety of situations together?

If you are unable to answer 'yes' to the questions above, we suggest you discuss your feelings with someone other than your fiancé(e).

FROM THE MARRIAGE PREPARATION COURSE MANUAL (ALPHA INTERNATIONAL), ADAPTED FROM *I MARRIED YOU* BY WALTER TROBISCH (IVP 1973)

2 Organizations to Inform About Changing Your Name

If you decide to change your name when you get married, don't forget to let people know! You will find below a list of organizations that you will need to inform about your name change. If you are moving house or opening a joint bank account, you will also need to inform these organizations your new address and (if appropriate) your bank details.

✱✎ ✔ Employer

✱✎ ✔ HMRC (HM Revenue and Customs) for tax and National Insurance records (obtain your reference and tax office address from your employer)

✱✎ ✔ Bank (mortgage and/or current accounts and saving accounts)

✱✎ ✔ Building society (mortgage and/or current accounts and saving accounts)

✱✎ ✔ Credit card companies

✱✎ ✔ Student Loans Company/other finance or loan companies

✱✎ ✔ Local authority (Council tax and register of electors)

✱✎ ✔ Department for Work and Pensions (if you are entitled to any benefits)

✱✎ ✔ Police (if you have any criminal actions against you or are on the Violent and Sex Offenders' Register)

✱✎ ✔ Land Registry (if you own land or property)

✱✎ ✔ Pension providers

✱✎ ✔ The Identity and Passport Service (apply for a passport in your new name)

✱✎ ✔ DVLA (apply for a new driving licence and vehicle registration certificate)

- ✔ Motoring organizations (breakdown organizations)
- ✔ Utility services (i.e. gas, electricity, water and sewerage providers)
- ✔ Telephone provider
- ✔ Internet provider
- ✔ Mobile phone provider
- ✔ Royal Mail
- ✔ Insurance companies (buildings, life, motor, endowments, contents etc.)
- ✔ Premium Bonds office
- ✔ Mail-order companies
- ✔ Doctor
- ✔ Dentist
- ✔ Vets
- ✔ TV licensing
- ✔ School/college/university
- ✔ Professional institutes and bodies
- ✔ Library, clubs, societies and associations
- ✔ Magazine subscriptions
- ✔ If either or both of you have a will, this should be renewed after you are married.

3 Wedding Invitations

The style and wording of the wedding invitation will be governed both by the style of the wedding and by your personal taste.

Formal invitation

A formal invitation is generally engraved in black or printed on folded white paper. The name of the guest is handwritten in the top left-hand corner.

The traditional wording for a formal wedding invitation is as follows:

Mr and Mrs James Brown
request the pleasure of your company
at the marriage of their daughter
Rachel

to

Mr Steven Williams
at Christ Church, Compton,
on Saturday 27th April
at 2.30 p.m.
and afterwards at
Leighton Hall

RSVP
12 HARLEY PLACE
HEYWORTH
NORTH SOMERSET
BS12 3YZ

Alternatively, the invitation can be set out as follows, leaving a space for the name of the guest in the body of the invitation:

Mr and Mrs Brian Stevens
request the pleasure of the company of

at the marriage of their daughter Ella
to
Mr Simon David Jenkins
at St Mary's Church, Westhampton,
on Saturday 6th December
at 12 noon
and afterwards at the Grange Hotel

63 Westhampton Road
Selbeigh
North Yorkshire
NY22 3PR

RSVP

The same wording can be used for a civil ceremony.

Individual family circumstances need to be reflected in the wording of the invitation. The basic guideline is that the host or hostess sends the invitation and their relationship to the bride should be made clear.

Traditional alternative wording to suit different family circumstances is set out below. However, there is no hard and fast rule, and the following suggestions are proposed as a guide only.

When the bride's mother is host:

Mrs Rosemary James requests the pleasure of your company at the marriage of her daughter...

(If the bride's mother has remarried, she would use her new husband's name, *Mrs Martin Yates [or Mrs Rosemary Yates] requests the pleasure...*)

When the bride's father is host:

Mr Thomas James requests the pleasure of your company at the marriage of his daughter...

When the bride's parents are divorced and neither has remarried:

Mr Thomas James and Mrs Rosemary James request the pleasure of your company at the marriage of their daughter...

When the bride's parents are divorced and the mother has remarried:

Mr Thomas James and Mrs Rosemary Yates request the pleasure of your company at the marriage of their daughter...

When the bride's mother and stepfather are hosts:

Mr and Mrs Matthew Yates request the pleasure of your company at the marriage of her daughter...

When the bride's father and stepmother are hosts:

Mr and Mrs Thomas James request the pleasure of your company at the marriage of his daughter...

When the bride and groom are hosts themselves:

Miss Charlotte James and Mr Robert Greene request the pleasure of your company at their marriage at...

When the hosts are unrelated to the bride:

Mr and Mrs Michael Williams request the pleasure of your company at the marriage of Fiona, daughter of the late Mr and Mrs Stephen Rees...

4 Invitation to a Service of Blessing

When a marriage takes place in a civil ceremony at a register office, it can be followed by a Service of Blessing.

An invitation to a Service of Blessing can read as follows:

Mr and Mrs Daniel Reed
request the pleasure of your company
at a Service of Blessing
following the marriage
of their daughter,
Laura
to
Mr Nicholas Grey

at _____

on _____

at _____

and afterwards at _____

RSVP
56 Pear Tree Lane
Bushbury
Wolverhampton
WV20 1UN

---

5 Invitation to an Evening Reception

If additional friends are invited to the ceremony and then to an evening reception, the wording of the usual wedding invitation can be as follows, but make clear that the invitation is for the evening party only. It can be helpful to have this invitation different in size from the main invitation so it can be easily distinguished.

Mr and Mrs James Brown
request the pleasure of your company
at the marriage of their daughter
Rachel
to
Mr Steven Williams
at Christ Church, Compton,
on Saturday 27th April at 2.30 p.m.
followed by an evening reception and barn dance
from 6.00 p.m. at Leighton Hall

RSVP
12 HARLEY PLACE
HEYWORTH
NORTH SOMERSET
BS12 3YZ

If the invitation is for the evening reception alone, it can take the form of an ordinary party invitation. Alternatively, the invitation can read:

Mr and Mrs James Brown
request the pleasure of your company
at a reception
following the marriage of their daughter
Rachel
to
Mr Steven Williams

at ....
on ....
at ....
RSVP
12 HARLEY PLACE
HEYWORTH
NORTH SOMERSET
BS12 3YZ

6 Order of Service for a Church Wedding

The forenames or initials of the bride and groom, the name of the church and the date of the wedding may all be printed on the front of the service sheet.

Printed on the inside will be the order of service and the words of hymns, readings and prayers or other appropriate information.

ORDER OF SERVICE
At the entrance of the bride
Trumpet Voluntary J.Clarke

HYMN
[words in full]

THE MARRIAGE

READING
1 Corinthians 13

ADDRESS
Revd Martin Stilwell

PRAYERS

HYMN
[words in full]

THE SIGNING OF THE REGISTER
During the signing of the Register
Solo

C. M. Widor: Toccata in F

7 Seasonal Guide to Flowers

All seasons

Daisy, freesia, gerbera, iris, lily, rose

Spring

Arum lily, auricula, bluebell, foxglove, freesia, gardenia, hyacinth, lilac, pansy, primrose, tulip

Summer

Delphinium, eucryphia, fuchsia, gardenia, geranium, honeysuckle, hydrangea, larkspur, lavender, lily, lisianthus, marigold, sunflower, sweetpea

Autumn

Alstroemeria, amaryllis, chrysanthemum, euphorbia, heather, hydrangea, hypericum berry, gerbera, ivy, orchid, snowberry

Winter

Amaryllis, anemone, Christmas rose, dark red rose, dendrobium, eucalyptus, fir, holly, hyacinth, ivy, jasmine, lily, orchid

8 Suggested Readings for a Church Wedding

Genesis 2:15–24

Psalms: 19, 34, 84, 85, 91, 121, 139:1–18

Ecclesiastes 4:9–12

Song of Solomon 8:6–7

Isaiah 40:25–31

Matthew 5:1–10

John 2:1–11

John 15:1–4, 9–17

1 Corinthians 13:1–8a

Ephesians 3:14–21

Ephesians 5:21–33

Philippians 2:1–11

Colossians 3:12–17

1 John 4:7–12, 21

9 Suggested Readings and Poems for a Civil Wedding

Poems, readings and music for civil ceremonies must not have any religious content.

The registrar can give you copies of collected poems, readings and music that are suitable. A few suggestions (first line only) are listed below:

A marriage... made of two fractional lives
Mark Twain

A walled garden Your marriage should have within it
Anon

If thou must love me, let it be for nought
Elizabeth Barrett Browning

It is not enough to love passionately
Anatole France

Let me not to the Marriage of true minds
William Shakespeare

Love is not breathlessness
Louis de Bernières (from *Captain Corelli's Mandolin*, see p.110)

Love takes time. It needs a history of giving and receiving
Barb Upham

The key to love is understanding
Anon

10 Suggested Music

Suggested hymns for church weddings

[first line only]

And can it be that I should gain

And did those feet in ancient time (*Jerusalem*)

Be thou my vision, O Lord of my heart

Come down, O Love divine

Dear Lord and Father of mankind

Glorious things of thee are spoken

Guide me, O thou great Redeemer

I cannot tell why He whom angels worship (tune of *Londonderry Air*)

Immortal, invisible, God only wise

I vow to you, my saviour/I vow to thee, my country

I will sing the wondrous story

Lead us, heavenly Father, lead us

Lord, for the years your love has kept and guided

Lord of all hopefulness, Lord of all joy (same tune as 'Be Thou my vision')

Love Divine, all loves excelling

Morning has broken

O Lord my God, when I in awesome wonder

O praise ye the Lord!

O strength and stay upholding all creation

Praise, my soul, the King of heaven

Praise the Lord! ye heavens, adore Him

Praise to the Lord, the Almighty, the King of creation

The King of love my Shepherd is

The Lord's my shepherd

Suggested classical music for weddings

* = probably not allowed at a civil ceremony

R = suitable during signing of the register

IN = suitable for the entrance of the bride

The following pieces are suitable for both church and civil weddings, unless otherwise indicated:

T. Albinoni: Adagio in G Minor* **R** or **IN**

J. S. Bach: Air on a 'G' String **IN**
Jesu, Joy of Man's Desiring* **IN**

L. van Beethoven: Moonlight Sonata **R** or **IN**
Symphony No. 9 ('*Choral*', last movement)

J. Charpentier: Prelude (from *Te Deum*) (the Eurovision Song Contest theme tune!)

J. Clarke: Trumpet Voluntary (*The Prince of Denmark's March*)

E. Elgar: Organ Sonata in G*
Imperial March (first movement)
Marches 1 & 4 (from *Pomp & Circumstance*)
Nimrod (from *Enigma Variations*) **R** or **IN**

G. F. Handel: Air & Hornpipe (from *Water Music*)
Overture, La Réjouissance and Minuet Finale (from *Music for the Royal Fireworks*)
Arrival of the Queen of Sheba (from *Solomon*) **IN**
Marches (from *The Occasional Oratorio and Scipio*)

F. Mendelssohn: Wedding March (from *A Midsummer Night's Dream*)* **IN**

E. Morricone: Gabriel's Oboe (from *The Mission*) **IN**

W. A. Mozart: Wedding March (from *The Marriage of Figaro*)

J. Pachelbel: Canon in D **IN**

H. Purcell: Rondeau (from *Abdelezzar*)

Trumpet Tune in D
Trumpet Tune in C (from *King Arthur*)

J. Stanley: Trumpet Voluntary in D

L. Vierne: Finale (from *Symphony I in D minor*)*

A. Vivaldi: Allegro [Spring] (from *The Four Seasons*)

R. Wagner: Bridal Chorus (from *Lohengrin*)*
Overture (from *The Mastersingers*) **IN**

W. Walton: Crown Imperial (Coronation March)
Orb and Sceptre (Coronation March)
Incidental Music (from *Richard III*)

C. M. Widor: Toccata in F (from *Symphony V for Organ*)*
Finale (from *Symphony VI for Organ*)*

Popular music

Any popular music can also be used to personalize your marriage
ceremony. Remember to check that suitable equipment to play music
is available.

Afterword

Rob Parsons,
founder and Executive Chairman
of Care for the Family

Introducing Care for the Family

I hope that you've enjoyed this book, and feel that you have gained some practical help and insight as you begin your married life together.

At Care for the Family we are committed to providing support that strengthens family life and helps those who are hurting because of family difficulty. Over the past twenty-one years hundreds of thousands of people have attended our seminars, and our staff of over a hundred supports single parents, those parenting children with additional needs, bereaved parents and those in a host of other situations.

When I helped found the charity in 1988, it was because I believed that it was important for families to be cared for. We work hard to produce world-class resources to help families and are keen to know whether what we provide makes a difference. Please let us know whether you found this book helpful by going to **www.careforthefamily.org.uk/ engagement** where you can complete a short survey and send us your views. We look forward to hearing from you!

If you are ever facing a difficult situation, or are looking for ways to make your family relationships even stronger, then give us a call on (029) 2081 0800. Much more information – including articles and advice – is available online at www.careforthefamily.org.uk.

And remember Care for the Family is *your* family charity. We are always there for you.

With very best wishes,

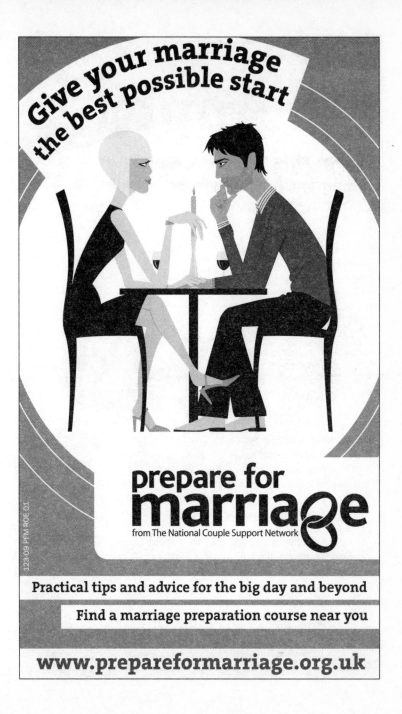

Give your marriage the best possible start

prepare for
marriage
from The National Couple Support Network

123-09 PFM ROE 01

Practical tips and advice for the big day and beyond

Find a marriage preparation course near you

www.prepareformarriage.org.uk

From this Step Forward

- marriage preparation for those forming a stepfamily

You can use this course as a couple, with or without the help of a facilitator. It will help you build a strong relationship on which to develop your stepfamily.

The course material is on one easy-to-use CD-Rom, so you can print off the material as many times as you like.

£19.99

From this Step Forward:

- Is a unique and flexible course
- Looks at practical, emotional and financial issues
- Explores issues with former partners and with the wider family
- Offers help in the couple relationship and in parenting relationships
- Can be used in groups or with just one couple at a time

"If we'd done the course when we started out, we would definitely have been more prepared for the challenges that lay ahead." (Isobel and Tony Parker)

124-09 FSF ROE 01

Order today at www.careforthefamily.org.uk/stepforward or phone (029) 2081 0800

The Astronomy Cafe

365 Questions and Answers from "Ask the Astronomer"

P9-DEJ-497

The Astronomy Cafe

365 Questions and Answers from "Ask the Astronomer"

Sten F. Odenwald

 W. H. Freeman and Company • New York

Interior Design: *Blake Logan*

Library of Congress Cataloging-in-Publication Data

Odenwald, Sten F.
    The astronomy cafe : 365 questions and answers from ask the
Astronomer / Sten F. Odenwald.
        p.   cm.
    Includes index.
    — ISBN 0-7167-3278-5
    1. Astronomy—Miscellanea.   I. Title.
QB52.O34   1998
520—dc21   98-2696
                                                                      CIP

© 1998 by Sten F. Odenwald. All rights reserved.

No part of this book may be reproduced by any mechanical, photographic, or electronic process, or in the form of a phonographic recording, nor may it be stored in a retrieval system, transmitted, or otherwise copied for public or private use, without written permission from the publisher.

Printed in the United States of America

Second Printing, 1998

Contents

Introduction

Have you ever wondered about the *big* picture? Have you ever taken a moment to think as deeply as you can about what is just above your head, just below the first impression, and not far from our inherent prejudices of how things ought to be? Some would call this a waste of time, an unproductive use of our limited energies and resources. Some of us find the time anyway. We seem compelled to do so and to relish those few moments like precious nuggets of gold stolen from the incessant tumult of our harried lives.

Like the children that we once were, you and I still find a moment to look at our world through glasses fashioned, not from cynicism, but from the sheer joy of being alive. And these glasses are framed not from a purposeful need to know, but from the sheer wonder of it all and the ever wistful question "Why?" Just the ability to ask a question is something that must be revered above all else. When questions probe the nature of our world and we see the telltale images of their answers, it is hard to feel that there isn't something divine in the simple act of asking a question itself.

How is it that we are so privileged to live at a time when the veil of ignorance has been so roughly peeled back from the world beyond our senses? We live in a physical world in which chaos is held at bay by laws and symmetries that, though alien, are understandable by organic creatures on the surface of a cold planet. We ask questions and by rational, logical detective work seem to win our way to answers.

It is a cliché used by many that we know hardly anything about the physical world and that "there are more mysteries in the world than can be dreamt of in our philosophies." Those people say that we seem to be constantly rewriting textbooks or, instead of finding answers, only creating new questions. This is simply superstition and fear speaking. We do indeed know many things about our universe—things of significance, things of lasting value. Of course there are always more questions to be asked, but we should not sit on the sidelines as naysayers and revel in how stupid we are. We should, instead, celebrate that in a few short centuries, we have pushed back ignorance so that the light of understanding now penetrates to the very foundations of our physical world, from the quark to the quasar.

How is it possible, in the face of this breathtaking accomplishment, to feel that we are still surrounded by the evil wolves of the unknown as we huddle around the glowing campfire of understanding? We call upon electrons to do our bidding. We walk on the moon and play golf there. We scramble on the face of Mars with our electronic proxies. These are not apologies to be had by a cowering humanity but claims to be staked against ignorance. As a measure of how much we have learned, you need only compare how long it takes to "build" an astronomer. In the nineteenth century, it used to take a year or two after high school. Now, as we embark on the twenty-first century, it takes nearly a decade—and that much time just to cover the ground already laid by answers to previous questions!

From the vantage point of my Web site the Astronomy Cafe (www2.ari.net/home/odenwald/cafe.html), I have had the great pleasure of replying to more than 3,000 questions submitted by casual visitors. This book is a synthesis of the most popular questions I have received and my answers. As you leaf through these pages, you will find many of the classical questions that an astronomer is asked by the general public. Some of the answers you may dimly recall from long-forgotten lectures by college professors. Other questions will seem surprising—a tribute to the constantly questioning mind. You will also encounter questions about astronomy that you might never have thought of asking, but someone very much like you did.

I have tried very hard to gear each answer to the level of the question, and for this reason this book reads unevenly. Some answers may even seem evasive, but they are written that way for a reason. We either have no concrete idea what the actual answer may be because of the lack of good data, or the answer that we can provide is, not by choice but by necessity, based on theoretical expectations and couched in very technical terms. Just because you can ask a question does not guarantee that you will always be able to understand the answer. In today's "I can do anything" age, such a comment could be considered the height of arrogance from a scientist, but then my stockbroker sometimes gives me answers to my financial questions that I cannot comprehend. That's life.

In most popular astronomy books, the topics unfold like some dialogue across the backyard fence, and you are attracted here and there to the pieces of the story that interest you. The advantage to be gained from reading this book is that it provides short direct answers to specific questions. Here you will find the most common and the most popular questions that other seekers have asked. You will not be forced to read the endless paragraphs of a conventional astronomy book in the hope of stumbling upon an answer. If your question is similar to one in this book, you are only a minute away from the best answer an astronomer (me) knows how to provide.

At the end of each answer is a bracketed list of numbers, such as [1959, 2080, 2053, 2021, 624]. These numbers are the file names for the on-line versions of answers at the Astronomy Cafe to the same or similar questions. Visit the Astronomy Cafe on-line to learn more about how to use these numbers to look up more information on your favorite questions at "Ask the Astronomer."

Now, stop leaning on the bookcase at the bookstore, buy this book, get some coffee, and get set for some answers that will knock your socks off!

Acknowledgments

I want to thank my wife, Susan Clermont, and my two daughters, Emily Rosa and Stacia Elise. For months, they have put up with my sneaking out of bed at 6:00 A.M. each day to work for a few hours answering questions and preparing this manuscript. As far as I know, they were asleep during those hours, but they tell me that my absence was noticed just the same. Someday my daughters may find their way to this book in our home or in some distant library, and perhaps look for their favorite answers among their father's writing, remembering dimly all those early morning hours he spent at the computer.

At W. H. Freeman and Company, Holly Hodder, my editor, was a constant source of encouragement and enthusiasm for this project. She recognized a gem in the rough, and it is through her convictions about this book that you now hold it in your hands. Diane Cimino Maass was the cheerful and hardworking project editor on this manuscript who made it all happen.

I would especially like to thank Dr. Carl Sagan for his profound influence. Although many have eulogized his passing far more eloquently than I possibly can, I would like it known that many of us looked upon him as a role model for science education for the general public. He was the first to professionally legitimize that activity and set a high-water mark for all of us to strive. The Internet has grown so rapidly, however, that we are all pretty much on our own without Dr. Sagan to show the way. This inspires us to use the Internet with respect and to foster in this new communication channel the same dedication, enthusiasm, and love of learning that he embodied.

I would never have undertaken a project like this were it not for the support of the more than 3,000 people who sent me their questions, and especially the 200,000-plus visitors to my Web sites, who chalked up some 3 million hits to its pages by December 1997. I would especially like to thank the following individuals who provided their farsighted and generous private financial support to help me maintain the Astronomy Cafe: Aline Akelis, Amarnath Annathur, Michael Barnes, Jason Barton, Michael Beam, Dan Benedict, Stephen Bishop, Burton Bloom, Stephen Bolger, Willis Boyce, Charles Buffler, Michael Burr, Peter Carini, Martin Coats, Norman Cormier, Richard Crawford, Elwood Downey, Jeffrey Doyle, Darrell Duane, George Ehlers, Dennis Fitzgerald, Michael Freeman, David Forty, Earl Gasner, Robert Gault, Don Goembel, Neil Goldstein, Charles Green, Milton Greek, Fred Heubner, Leonore Heiman, David Hoffer, Mary Hoffsis, Robert Hustwit, John Iatesta, Rebecca Iatesta, Ben Jackson, Douglas Jacoby, Andrew Jagusiak, W. Jastrzebski, Bruce Kennedy, Frank Klaess, Donald Koskinen, Elizabeth Kubala, Judith Konrad, David Lambert, Kent Land, R. Lang, Randolph Lechner, Dorn Lewin, Johnathan Loo, Shaula Massena, Daniel Medicis, Kirk Mueller, Robert Nemiroff, Phil Noss, Paul Oldenburg, Edward Packard, Wayne Page, Ben Patterson-Lin, Jerry Persall, John Peterson, Ramon Pinedo, Beth Purdy, Robert Rhodes, Peter Roode, Gonzalo Santos, William Schiffbauer, Michael Shank, Jeffrey Sherman, Louis Shornick, Steven Shumak, Fred Springer, John Stewart, H. Taylor, Ilya Taytslin, Abby Tromblee, Aaron Trudel, April Holladay Ttee, William Warner, Thomas Weil, Vern Weiss, William Wessman, Robert White, Ronald Williams, Todd Williams, Eric Wiseman, Bob Wright, Ronald Wyllys, Veryl Yarnes, and Jurek Zarzycki.

The Astronomy Cafe has also received two generous research grants from NASA, which were administered by the American Astronomical Society during 1996–1998 and for which I am grateful on behalf of public education.

To Emily and Stacia.
This, dear ones, is what Daddy has been working on
all those mornings while you were asleep!

Chapter 1

The Sun

ost of the questions I receive about the Sun at the Astronomy Cafe have to do with its basic properties of mass, age, temperature, brightness, and its future evolution. We are still learning more and more about the Sun every day. For example, its surface vibrates like a complex bell with a typical period of about 5 minutes, but without sensitive instruments you would never notice this at all. Physicists still cannot account for the dearth of neutrinos they are detecting, considering that the core of the Sun should be producing them in enormous quantities. Only in the last year have astronomers found a compelling explanation for what makes the outer layers of the Sun, its corona, more than 1 million degrees Kelvin hotter than its surface. In addition, sensitive Earth satellites have finally confirmed that the Sun's brightness is not constant. It increases and decreases with the sunspot cycle, and these changes have a measurable impact on Earth's climate and temperature. But the most popular questions have little to do with what astronomers would call the frontiers of research. Practical questions about why day and night are not of equal length at the equinox or what causes the green flash at sunset are by far the favorites.

1 Does our Sun have a technical name?

No, it doesn't. We are pretty much stuck with "sun" or "sol" or a number of other language-dependent names that have come up over the centuries. It's not really a big deal. Scientists don't go around creating new names for things unless there is an identifiable need. Renaming the Sun just to make it sound more technical is not a good enough reason. It is important in science to be as clear as you can about what you are talking about, and for the Sun there is no reason to fix something that isn't really broken. [1959, 2080, 2053, 2021, 624]

2 How old is the Sun?

The Sun is estimated to be 10–20 million years older than Earth, because that's about how long it takes to accumulate the material to form a solar system and planets, as we understand the physics of the process so far. By direct radioactive dating, we've determined that Earth is something like 4.7 billion years old, so the Sun is therefore just a tad older than that. There are uncertainties inherent in radioactive dating, so ages for the Sun from 4.6 to 4.8 billion years are probably reasonable. The oldest meteoritic material is about 4.9 billion years old and may predate the formation of the Sun itself. The cloud out of which the Sun and planets formed was probably already several hundred million years old before our solar system began to form. [1151]

3 Does the Sun have any moons?

Yes, they are called the planets. [2969, 2959]

4 Why are sunspots dark?

Sunspots are a magnetic phenomenon on the Sun. You can think of them as small pores on the surface of the Sun where lines of magnetic force enter and exit. The gas inside a sunspot can be about 1,500 kelvin cooler than the gas in the rest of the solar surface ($\approx$5,700 K) and, with the help of the pressure produced by the sunspot's magnetic field, remain in pressure balance with the rest of the gas in the Sun. If you were to rip a sunspot out from the solar surface, it would appear as a crimson red gas, glowing brighter than a full moon, with a temperature of just over 3,500 K. They only look black because at 3,500 K, they emit a lot less light than the nearby surface of the Sun at 5,700 K. In fact, they emit about $(3,500/5,700)^4$ or one-seventh as much light. [2854, 2508, 2447, 2271, 2056, 142]

5 Do the planets affect the sunspot cycle?

In a paper in the April 1965 issue of *Astronomical Journal,* astronomer Paul Jose described just such an effect. He noted that the Sun and planets orbit about a point called the barycenter of the solar system. This is a point in space located between 0.01 and 2.2 times the radius of the Sun from the Sun's center. What this means is that every 179 years, as seen from the Sun, Jupiter and Saturn return to the same spot in the sky. The sunspot record from 1610 to 1954 does indeed show evidence of this same period in the peaks and valleys of the 11-year sunspot cycle. By 1990, this paper was still being cited in the technical literature two to three times every year by researchers who study long-term changes in the Sun's sunspot cycles, luminosity, and other factors. The planetary effect cannot be due to the gravitational tides raised on the Sun by these planets, because the tidal forces of the planets at the solar surface is one-trillionth of the gravitational force at the Sun's surface. The actual mechanism that seems to be involved is still not understood. [1367, 923]

6 What are solar flares, and are they harmful to humans?

Solar flares occur when magnetic fields on the Sun's surface get tangled and reconnect, which causes the nearby gas in the Sun's atmosphere to be ejected at very high speeds and temperatures. (This is like when rubber bands are stretched to the point where they actually break.) Images obtained by the *Yohkoh* satellite (Plate 1) show the complex patterns of magnetic fields and heated gases in the Sun's corona. Yes, flares are a major problem for astronauts in space and can be lethal in terms of radiation doses, but for humans on Earth they are not a problem because the atmosphere is a very good shield. Indirectly, however, these flare events can be responsible for geomagnetic storms, which can cause power outages and difficulties with communications satellites. If you were on an operating table during one of these blackouts, the indirect effects of a solar storm could be lethal. [2939, 2930, 2929, 2898, 2418]

7 How does the solar wind work?

The surface of the Sun is an environment filled with ionized gas and magnetic fields. The magnetic fields are not randomly oriented in space but come in more or less two distinct types. Closed field lines emerge from the surface, loop up into the chromosphere or corona, and then connect back on the surface. These field lines are the ones that account for the beautiful patterns of heated gases you see in the *Yohkoh* X-ray image in Plate 1. Open field lines, however, stretch out into interplanetary space. Satellite observations directly show that the open field lines act like magnetic pipes down which the heated plasma from the solar corona and inner corona can escape if heated enough, usually by solar flares. These are seen as coronal holes in X-ray photographs of the Sun, and they come and go, depending on the activity level of the Sun. The dark patch at the top of the *Yohkoh* image of the Sun (Plate 1) shows what such a hole looks like. There is also a constant wind emitted by the Sun, due to the expansion of the solar corona. Much further out, beyond the orbit of Pluto, the solar wind rams up against the interstellar medium (see Figure 1) and produces a parabolic-shaped bow shock in the direction of the Sun's motion toward the star Vega. The *Voyager* and *Pioneer* spacecraft may soon detect this heliopause boundary, completing our understanding of the shape of the Sun's wind patterns. [2924, 2722, 1790, 1491, 1259]

8 Does the Sun give off smoke?

No, because the source of the Sun's energy is not from ordinary, sooty combustion but from thermonuclear fusion deep inside its core at temperatures of millions of degrees. The Sun, like many other stars, does produce a wind of particles, which travels through the solar system at about 450 kilometers per second. This wind consists of electrons and protons in an ionized gas called a plasma that is laced with a weak magnetic field. The density of this wind near Earth is about 5 to 100 particles per cubic centimeter. Some very old stars, such as Betelgeuse, the bright star in Orion, are in their red giant or supergiant phase and have outer layers that are at temperatures of only a few thousand degrees. Under these conditions, carbon and silicon atoms can combine to form dust grains and "soot," which are blown out into

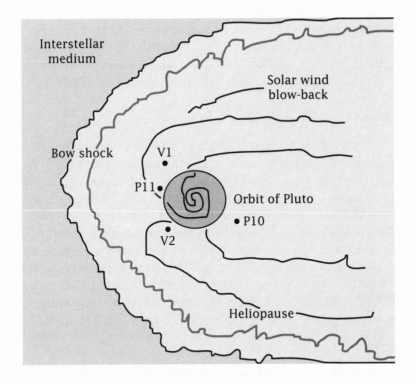

Figure 1 The shape of the solar wind as it impacts the interstellar medium to produce a comet-like bow shock. The motion of the Sun is to the left in the direction of the star Vega. Locations of the *Pioneer* (P10, P11) and *Voyager* (V1, V2) spacecraft are indicated.

space by radiation pressure. These stars really are producing smoke, but by a process of condensation not combustion. Some very old stars, such as IRC+10216, eject so much soot into space that they are enshrouded by a cloud that completely hides them from view. It is only with infrared detectors that we can see them shining brightly. [1836, 1835, 1171, 654]

9 If the solar wind can't rearrange the dust on the Moon, why does it blast dust from comets?

Because the escape velocity for matter on the surface of a comet is a thousand times lower than on the surface of the Moon. The escape velocity from comets is measured in centimeters per second. The gravitational field of the Moon provides *lots* of resistance for matter to waft away at a few centimeters per second, as it does in cometary tails, because the Moon's escape velocity is several kilometers per second. That's why the Moon isn't shedding a plume of dust behind it into space. [2882]

10 When is the Sun predicted to go nova?

The Sun will never go nova. A nova explosion requires that the star have a nearby companion star at about the distance of Earth from the Sun, and the companion star must be a white dwarf. The other star in this two-star, binary system has to be an evolved red giant that is shedding mass. When enough of this mass is gobbled up by the white dwarf, it detonates on the white dwarf's surface to produce a nova. The Sun has no companion star close enough to make this happen. In the future, millions of years from now, the bright star Sirius *may* become a nova, because it has a white dwarf orbiting it called Sirius B. Even so, Sirius B may be too far away from Sirius A to be an effective nova. [2542, 2490, 2130, 1153, 736, 391]

11 Will the Sun soon be passing through a dust cloud?

It sure looks that way! If you trust our knowledge of the solar vicinity, the next cloud passage could happen within 20,000 to 50,000 years. At the June 1996 meeting of the American Astronomical Society, astronomer Priscilla Frisch and her colleagues reviewed earlier proposals that the Sun may have already entered the edge of a nearby interstellar cloud (see Figure 2) called the Local Fluff a few thousand years ago. As described in a *New York Times Science Supplement* (June 18, 1997) article, the solar system is apparently moving along a path that is certain to take us closer to the nearby Scorpius-Centaurus expanding superbubble, which is a vast cavity in the interstellar medium that has been inflated by the action of hundreds of massive, luminous stars over the past few million years. The leading edge of the Scorpius-Centaurus superbubble, called Loop 1, seems to consist of an increasing number of cloudlets of varying size and density. The Sun, after apparently spending many hundreds of millennia in quieter regions of the interstellar medium, is apparently now moving nearer to the wall of this cavity.

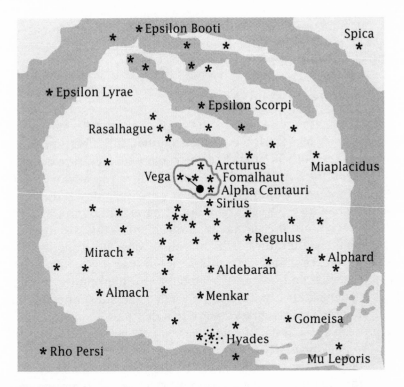

Figure 2 The neighborhood of the Sun out to 500 light years showing the brightest stars, the so-called Local Bubble void, and the locations of dust and gas (*shaded*). The Local Fluff cloud is shown near the Sun by a jagged closed line with the Sun near one edge. In reality, more than 1 million stars fill this field of view but most are fainter than the Sun. Only a handful of the brightest stars are shown.

When the solar system enters such a cloud, the first thing that will happen will be that the magnetic field and heliopause of the Sun (see Figure 1), which now extend perhaps 150 astronomical units (AUs) from the Sun, will be compressed back into the inner solar system. When this happens, Earth may be laid bare to an increased cosmic ray bombardment. To make matters worse, Earth's magnetic field is itself decreasing as we enter the next field-reversal era in a few thousand years. If Earth's field is "down" during the same time that the solar system has wandered into the new cloud, the cosmic ray flux near Earth could be many times higher than it is now. The atmosphere would shield us from this, but human space activities would run the risk of increased radiation exposure. Interplanetary travel in a few thousand years could be a real health hazard. [1372, 622]

12 Does water exist on the Sun?

As strange as it may seem, the answer is yes. Peter Bernath of the University of Waterloo in Canada studied the spectrum of a sunspot seen in 1991 that had the coolest temperature ever recorded on the Sun. According to an article in the January 1996 issue of *Discover,* he and his colleagues discovered that the spectrum had a very weak signature of water. Although I was not able to track down the formal announcement of this discovery in the technical literature, evidently water does not completely break down except at temperatures higher than 5,000 K, so steam can exist on the Sun. The amount of water implied by the measurement of the light from the Earth-sized sunspot would be enough to fill a lake 4 miles square to a depth of 300 yards. In the July 18, 1997, issue of *Science,* Oleg Polyansky and Jonathan Tennyson of University College, London, also found a sunspot with a temperature of about 3,000 K, and they found an exact match for the theoretical spectrum of water at this temperature in its infrared spectrum. The big question is how the water got there in the first place. One possibility is that some of it is left over from the interstellar cloud out of which the Sun and the planets formed 4.7 billion years ago. There could be a lot more water on the Sun just sitting around waiting to be detected. Water (steam) has also been detected in the atmospheres of the red supergiant stars Betelgeuse and Antares. This water was probably formed by direct condensation from the cool outer layers of these stars at temperatures of only a few thousand degrees. [381]

13 How do astronomers measure the temperature of the Sun without going there?

Suppose you heated a bar of iron to 3,000 K, and then, with a sensitive light meter, you measured how bright this bar was at wavelengths from the ultraviolet into the infrared. If you plotted the intensity on a graph, what you would find is that the intensity is not the same at all wavelengths but follows a very smooth pattern of increase and decrease. Physicists call this a blackbody curve. The brightness of the Sun plotted in this way also has the shape of a blackbody. The exact shape of this curve is uniquely related to the temperature of the surface emitting the light. Careful studies of this spectrum led to an estimated temperature near 5,750 K, give or take about 50 K. [2253, 2440, 1836, 1835, 1752, 1140]

14 Is the Sun shrinking?

Not that I know of. In fact, the Sun's radius is slowly increasing as it ages, and will double in size in the next five billion years or so, but this rate is, to my knowledge, immeasurable, because of the large number of other effects that have to be properly accounted for. [1281]

15 What would happen if the Sun vanished just after sunset?

If it just went away very cleanly with nothing left behind (a great science fiction plot, by the way), Earth would detect this loss 8.5 minutes later as the loss of the solar gravitational field (which travels at the speed of light). Earth would then behave as a free body unfettered by the solar gravitational field. Its speed would remain fixed at its tangential orbital velocity at the moment the Sun's field went away, and its trajectory would be a roughly straight line in the direction of the sky toward which it was moving at that instant. Only the Milky Way's gravitational field would now have much effect on Earth. What you would see is no daylight and a perpetual nighttime everywhere. The stars would still move in their 24-hour cycle, and the precession of the equinoxes would still occur. Over thousands of years, Earth astronomers would see familiar constellations being left behind and the bright stars shift in the sky. [1225, 358]

16 Have astronomers determined exactly how the Sun will change in the next 10 billion years?

In a research paper published in the November 20, 1993, *Astrophysical Journal,* astronomers I.-Juliana Sackmann, Arnold Boothrayd, and Kathleen Kraemer from the California Institute of Technology, University of Toronto, and Boston University, respectively, used the best stellar evolution models available to do just that. They "watched" as the Sun started out 4.6 billion years ago (byrs) with a luminosity of 70 percent of today's value and brighten to 2.2 times its current value by 6.5 byrs hence. A luminosity 10 percent more than the present value was reached in 1.1 byrs, and 1.4 times its present value some 3.5 byrs from now. This means that in 1.1 byrs Earth will experience a permanent moist greenhouse effect as the oceans begin to evaporate into the atmosphere, and by 3.5 byrs, a runaway greenhouse effect, similar to what Venus is enjoying, will be in place.

As the Sun evolves into a red giant, it grows to a luminosity of 2,300 times its present value and a size of 150 times its current extent, shedding about 27 percent of its mass and engulfing/incinerating the planet Mercury. It continues to evolve up the so-called Asymptotic Giant Branch and experiences at least four thermal pulses. After the first one, the Sun's size has swollen to 213 times its present size, but, at a mass of only 60 percent of its current mass, the orbits of the planets have crept outward from their present distances. Venus is now located about 1.22 times further from the Sun than where Earth is now. Earth has moved to about 1.7 times further out, so neither of these planets are engulfed by the Sun. The Sun has reached a peak luminosity of 5,300 times its current rate after the fourth thermal pulse. The timetable is as follows:

1. 11 byrs on the Main Sequence

2. 0.7 byrs cooling toward the Red Giant Branch

3. 0.6 byrs to ascend up the Red Giant Branch

4. 0.1 byrs on the Horizontal Branch

5. 0.02 byrs on the early Asymptotic Giant Branch

6. 0.0004 byrs on the thermally pulsing Asymptotic Giant Branch

7. 0.0001 byrs evolving to become a planetary nebula/white dwarf system.

The Sun has already spent 4.5 billion years on the Main Sequence, so it has another 6.5 billion years before it undergoes major structural changes. These are caused by the Sun reaching a critical point in its conversion of hydrogen into helium in its deep core. As far as life on Earth is concerned, beginning some 1 billion years from now, or probably somewhat earlier, the polar ice caps will permanently vanish and the oceans begin to evaporate, making Earth uninhabitable. I know we have more pressing problems today, like paying the rent and balancing the federal budget, but we better have some plans for getting us off this planet. A billion years is not a very long time. [391]

Chapter 2

The Solar System

We have all learned about the solar system since grade school, but the questions being asked today favor only a few issues among all the possibilities. By far the most popular one is about the planetary conjunction that will take place on May 5, 2000. Hundreds of people have expressed concern that this alignment will destroy Earth, and it doesn't seem to make any difference what I say about tidal forces and gravity being too weak to do anything or that these things have happened before with no ill effect. There also have been many questions about the existence of Planet X, a purported tenth planet. Some even wonder why we still call it Planet X and do not give it a real name, perhaps unaware that astronomers are not in the habit of naming something until it is discovered. Other imponderable questions include, "Why is Pluto the ninth planet?" and "Will other planets ever collide with Earth?" For a time, one of the favorite questions was whether a planet could ever explode.

In astronomical research, the questions that are the most actively researched have to do with the details of how the solar system and planets formed from a primordial gas cloud. Many of the details of this process have been worked out, and detailed studies of the composition of ancient meteorites and the surfaces of planets have accelerated this research enormously. Also, astronomers have begun to detect disks of gas orbiting distant young stars and can now explore the question of solar system and planet formation by looking at infant planetary systems. We have also entered an age when individual planets can be detected around nearby stars. During the *next few decades, we will learn just how unique our solar system is and whether conditions for the origin of life are common or rare.*

17 Is there a way to remember the ordering of the planets in the solar system?

There are a number of phrases you can use in which the first letter of each word is the first letter in the name of the planet. Here are a few of my favorites:

Mary's Violet Eyes Made John Sit Up Nights Pondering.

Matilda Visits Every Monday, Just Stays Until Noon Period.

Mr. Valiant Eats Many Jelly Sandwiches Under Nate's Piano.

Mother Vera Thoughtfully Made Jelly Sandwiches Under No Protest.

Most Very Eager Mercenaries Just Shoot Until Nothing Persists.

And here are some that I have concocted:

Many Vast Emotions May Jell Silently Under Nine Planets.

More Velocity, Ensign, May Just Save Us Needless Pain.

Mr. Vega Enjoys Many Jewel-like Stars Under Nightly Promenades.

Many Vague Emotions Might Just Solidify Under Nightly Prodding.

My Very Enraged Mother Just Stealthily Unplugged Ned's Pool.

[2907]

18 Will the conjunction on May 5, 2000, destroy Earth?

First of all, a conjunction happens when two or more bodies in the solar system (planet, Sun, asteroid, comet) appear close together in the sky. Some conjunctions can be so close that one of the bodies actually seems to pass behind the other, producing what astronomers call an occultation. Grand conjunctions happen when several planets over the course of days or weeks appear to gather together into one part of the sky either before sunrise or after sunset. Some are not very spectacular, especially if they are spread out over more than 90 degrees of the sky, but occasionally you can get very tight conjunctions spanning only a few tens of degrees. This will happen on May 5, 2000, just as it has at least two or three times in the twentieth century.

The grand conjunction near May 5, 2000, will involve all the bright planets together in the same part of the sky, but the conjunctions actually span almost a full month on either side of this date, and the Sun will be in the way, so that visually it will be a rather poor sight. As with all planetary conjunctions, the gravitational effect on Earth will be nil. There have been many of these grand conjunctions in the past, including one during December 1997, and the historical record shows that absolutely nothing happened. Physically, there is no reason to expect any effects, gravitational or electromagnetic. The only effects will be those caused by mass hysteria—a far more powerful force than gravity—which can cause riots, buildings to explode, crime waves, and the like.

People are looking for something spectacular to mark the new millennium, which actually starts on January 1, 2001, but doomsday watchkeepers will find nothing in the planets on May 5 except their own imaginations. The only crisis that will befall us will be the so-called year 2000 software problem, which could bring down thousands of computers worldwide. Planetary conjunctions are a lot more common than the nonastronomer imagines. Even so, as portents of doom, conjunctions were absent from the skies during some of the most major calamities of the twentieth century. Table 1 is the definitive list of all the interesting solar system events for the year 2000. [2518, 2500, 2497, 2496, 2494, 2490, 2307, 2120, 1499, 1318, 943, 888, 803, 678, 100]

19 What was the most spectacular planetary conjunction in the past or will be in the future?

John Meeus described 15 planetary groupings that have occurred or will occur between the years 1007 and 2100 within 30 degrees of longitude from the Sun. The most recent was on February 5, 1962, when the Sun was in total eclipse, and you could see Mercury, Venus, Mars, Jupiter, and Saturn all within 13 degrees of

Table 1 **The year 2000 is anticipated to be an exciting year.**
Here are some of the astronomical phenomena and events you
should be looking forward to, including the great conjunction
on May 5. Many people believe it will destroy Earth, but there is
absolutely no scientific evidence that it will affect Earth in any way.

Conjunctions

Planets	Date	Sep.	Planets	Date	Sep.
Mercury-Venus	3/15	2.5	Venus-Mars	6/21	0.3
Mercury-Venus	4/28	0.3	Venus-Jupiter	5/17	0.1
Mercury-Venus	7/2	5.0	Venus-Saturn	5/18	1.2
Mercury-Mars	5/19	1.0	Venus-Uranus	3/4	0.1
Mercury-Mars	7/7	5.3	Venus-Neptune	2/22	0.5
Mercury-Mars	8/10	0.1			
Mercury-Jupiter	5/8	0.8	Mars-Jupiter	4/6	1.1
Mercury-Saturn	5/10	2.3	Mars-Saturn	4/16	2.4
Mercury-Uranus	1/28	1.3			
Mercury-Neptune	1/20	2.4	Jupiter-Saturn	5/31	1.2

the eclipsed Sun. An even tighter grouping occurred on September
15, 1186, when the Sun was partially eclipsed and the planets
were within 12 degrees of the Sun. The next grand conjunction will
occur on May 5, 2000, with the planets within 16 degrees of the
Sun, but there will be no eclipse, so you will have to see it in two
installments—just before sunrise and just after sunset. The most
interesting visual presentation will occur on September 8, 2040,
when the planets Mercury through Saturn will be at longitudes
from 20.4 to 29.8 degrees to the east of the Sun. Just after sunset,
these planets will appear like a swarm of objects within a region
9.5 degrees or so in diameter. The Moon will be 15.7 degrees from
the Sun in the same region, and in a first crescent phase. See the
article in the August 1997 *Sky and Telescope* for descriptions of
other spectacular conjunctions we have missed. [2307, 2120,
1298, 888, 134]

Table 1 (*Continued*)

· ·

Calendar Events

	Date	Time
Spring arrives	3/20	7:36:19 UT
Summer arrives	6/21	1:48:46 UT
Fall arrives	9/22	17:28:40 UT
Winter arrives	12/21	13:38:30 UT
Easter Sunday	4/23	
Jewish Calendar Year 5761	9/30	
Moslem Year 1421	4/6	
Solar Rotation Number 1958	1/1	

Lunar Events

	Dates of occurrence
Moon occults Uranus	1/9, 2/5, 3/2, 3/31
Moon occults Neptune	2/4, 3/2, 3/30, 4/26
Moon occults Venus	3/4
Moon occults Mercury	7/29
Partial solar eclipses	2/5, 7/1, 7/31, 12/25
Lunar eclipses	1/21, 7/16

Sep. = the separation between the planets taking part in the conjunction measured in degrees. For a comparison, the full Moon is about 0.5 degrees in diameter. UT = universal time.

20 Will there be global flooding caused by upcoming planetary conjunctions?

No. There have already been many planetary conjunctions involving the largest planets in the solar system, and none of these had any measurable effect upon Earth. [2900, 2314, 2304, 2302]

21 Can the gravitational pulls of the planets in conjunction affect humans or Earth?

No. The only physical force is that of gravity, and the so-called tidal effects of planets are completely overwhelmed by the direct gravitational influence of the Sun and Moon on Earth's crust. As you can see in Table 2, even under the best of circumstances, the total gravitational force of all the planets in their closest orbital locations to Earth equals only 10.65 newtons, a standard unit of force measurement, and this is less than 2 percent of what the Moon contributes each month. The tide-producing gravitational force is even smaller, because it varies as the inverse third power of the distance. The combined gravitational effects of the planets are entirely dominated by the influence of Jupiter. There might be a measurable enhancement to Earth's water tides, but this effect would be at the millimeter level and not actually detectable. [2900, 2304, 803]

22 Where is the tenth planet located?

No tenth planet (Planet X) has yet been discovered. So-called mini-planets and large asteroids like Ceres do not count. Part of the difficulty in searching for Planet X is in deciding what defines a planet. If Pluto is a planet (even this has been disputed), how about something two or three times smaller, making it just a little bigger than the asteroid Ceres? Astronomers can pretty much rule out an object as big as Jupiter orbiting a little further out than Pluto, because its gravitational influence on Pluto's orbit would be pretty obvious. But a planet as large as Earth at twice Pluto's distance would be almost undetectable. Thus, the answer is that we simply don't know if a bona fide tenth planet exists beyond the orbit of Pluto if its mass is too small and it is far enough away. There seems to be plenty of smaller objects outside the orbit of Neptune, however (see Figure 3), and more are being found every year. Astronomers Jun Chen and David Jewett recently found a trans-Neptunian object, 1997TL66, about 300 miles across (one-fourth the size of Pluto) orbiting more than twice as far out as Pluto, so who knows; in 10 years a really big object

Table 2 Interesting planetary facts. A collection of frequently requested quantities, including how fast the planets and the Moon move in their orbits, the time it takes light from the Sun to arrive (light travel), and how much sunlight (solar power) reaches a planet compared to Earth. Both the distance from the Sun and the amount of sunlight are presented with the value at Earth assigned 1.0 unit.

Planet	Distance (AU)	Solar Power	Gravitational Force	Tidal Force	Light Travel (minutes)	Moons	Orbit Speed (km/sec)
Mercury	0.38	7.1	0.03	165	3.2	0	47.9
Venus	0.72	1.9	1.80	25,200	6.0	0	35.0
Earth	1.00	1.00	—	—	8.3	1	29.8
Moon	0.002	1.00	377	630,000,000	0.02	0	1.0
Mars	1.50	0.44	0.07	526	13	2	24.1
Jupiter	5.20	0.037	3.20	2,990	43	15	13.1
Saturn	9.50	0.011	0.22	100	79	17	9.6
Uranus	19.10	0.0027	0.008	2.0	159	15	6.8
Neptune	30.00	0.0011	0.003	0.5	246	8	5.4
Pluto	39.40	0.00064	0.00001	0.001	330	1	4.7

Note: Gravitational force is the force in dynes on a 100-kg human. The tidal force is the force exerted by the planet upon the whole Earth in multiples of 1 million dyne/cm.

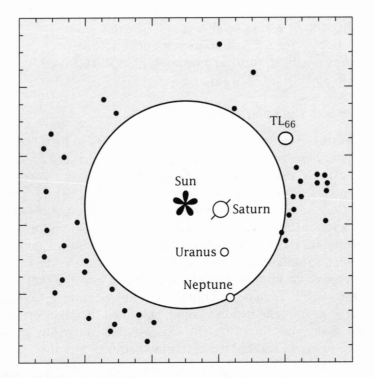

Figure 3 Location of trans-Neptunian bodies recently discovered outside the orbit of Neptune (*shaded region*), including a particularly large body (*not shown*) nearly as large as the giant asteroid Ceres and located between the orbits of Mars and Jupiter.

may be detected further out. [1771, 908, 770, 574, 392, 311, 304, 125]

23 How many hypothetical planets have been searched for but not found?

There have been various objects proposed as a new planet in the solar system over the past few thousand years. Ancient Greeks believed in the Counter Earth, and it was thought that the morning star Lucifer and the evening star Persephone, which we now know as Venus, were two different planets. There have also been reports of a planet inside the orbit of Mercury called Vulcan, to account for perturbations in Mercury's orbit before the advent of Einstein's theory of general relativity. Today, the search continues beyond the orbit of Pluto but with little success. For a great list

and collection of essays on this subject, have a look
at the Students for the Exploration of Space archive
(www.seds.org/billa/tnp/hypo.html). [1771, 1204, 908, 770, 574,
392, 350, 304, 261, 176, 125]

24 How was the solar system formed?

As far as observations of other young stars seem to be telling us,
it seems to have begun with a collapsing cloud that contracted
into a flattened disk. As the Sun began to form out of the center
of one such spinning disk, the material in the disk began to grow
in size from small micron-sized dust grains to asteroid-sized
bodies a kilometer across and then to large bodies hundreds of
kilometers across. These bodies then collided to form 1,000-
kilometer protoplanets, whose strong gravity fields made them
very effective vacuum cleaners in their orbits, causing them to
grow explosively in mass in only a few hundred thousand years.
Evidently, to start the process going, you need to make certain
that the disk is not too turbulent, because this causes the small
particles to hit each other too fast and shatter before they can
grow big enough.

Astronomers have detected dusty, orbiting disks around
hundreds of young stars. We have yet to see planets form, but we
know that several nearby stars have orbiting planets, so it's just a
matter of time and technology before we will be able to study the
whole process in detail. [2983, 1893, 1873, 1332, 1275, 962]

25 Where do planetary rings come from?

They may have been formed at the same time as the planets
themselves and are just left over junk that never could get
together to become moons because of the strong planetary
tidal gravitational forces. One of the moons of Saturn observed
by the *Voyager 2* spacecraft more than a decade ago seems to
have disappeared. All that remains, according to Hubble Space
Telescope observations, are two curiously shaped new moonlets.
The speculation is that the moon spied by *Voyager 2* got hit by
some object and shattered into two or more fragments that are
now on different orbits around Saturn. If stuff like this can happen
in 10 years, think of what kind of mayhem can happen in a billion
years to create planetary rings. [535, 58]

26 Where do the planetary moons come from?

Apparently, they can either be captured into orbit or formed out of the accreting gas that went into the planet itself. In the case of the larger moons of Jupiter and Saturn, they were probably formed from material accreted by the planet into a disk. The smaller outer moons and, for example, the two moons of Mars were captured asteroids. Our own Moon may be material ejected from Earth and mixed with the material from a large body that collided with Earth when it was first formed. This material later accumulated into the Moon. Thus, moons can have a variety of origins. [332, 329, 328]

27 Why do the planets orbit the Sun in the same plane?

We think that this is a reflection of the way in which the cloud that collapsed to form our Sun was rotating. Computer models of such collapsing, rotating clouds show that they rapidly form into a flattened disk. The planets formed out of this disk will orbit the new star in the same plane as the original disk of gas out of which they accreted. [1893]

28 What happens at the second focus of elliptical planetary orbits?

Elementary geometry tells us that an ellipse has two centers, which are called foci. The orbits of planets are elliptical, with one focus occupied by the Sun, and it is at this point in space that the gravitational field of the Sun emanates. But what happens at the second focus of the planetary orbit? Nothing at all. This is a good example of where a mathematical view of the physical world sometimes provides additional information that nature simply doesn't use for anything interesting. [2675]

29 Can a planet ever explode?

No. There is no known physical phenomenon that would allow a planet by itself to suddenly explode through the action of some internal mechanism. Some low-grade science fiction stories may use this to generate a story line, but the truth of the matter is that no chemical or nuclear process can produce enough energy to disassemble Earth against its own gravitational binding energy. [2940, 180]

30 Which planet is hotter, Venus or Mercury?

The surface temperature of Mercury is regulated by its closeness to the Sun and is about 430 Celsius (806 degrees Fahrenheit) at local noon. Because of the greenhouse effect on Venus, the surface temperature is regulated by the trapped infrared energy, which cannot escape back into space to balance what Venus receives from the Sun, as is the case for Mercury. This means that the surface temperature of Venus is far hotter than on Mercury, in the neighborhood of 472 Celsius (882 degrees Fahrenheit), even though it is twice as far from the Sun and receives one-fourth as much sunlight as Mercury. [2788, 2484]

31 How much energy do the planets get from the Sun compared to Earth?

If we use 1 unit as the norm for Earth, then the insolation for the other planets follows the inverse-square law, as you can see in Table 2. On Pluto you would receive nearly 1,600 times less warmth than you do on Earth. [2977]

32 Does the solar system have a barycenter?

A barycenter is a point in space where two bodies, such as Earth and the Moon, will appear to orbit, and it is also the point in space where the mass of a binary system will appear to be concentrated if you were to view the system from a great distance away. The solar system is a collection of thousands of bodies orbiting the Sun, and it does indeed have its own barycenter. The barycenter is located just outside the surface of the Sun, but its position in space changes in a complex loop-de-loop pattern, depending on the locations of the planets, mostly determined by where Jupiter is located, because Jupiter has the most mass of all the planets. [2927, 1482, 1195, 923]

33 How fast does light travel from the Sun to each of the planets?

It takes 1.5 seconds for light to get to the Moon from Earth; 499.0 seconds for light to travel from the Sun to Earth; and 5.5 hours to get from the Sun to Pluto. Table 2 lists the light travel times from the Sun to each planet. [89]

34 Is there life on other planets in our solar system?

Not so far as we know. With the exception of Mars and the satellite of Jupiter called Europa, no other places in the solar system are even close to having the right temperatures and prospects for liquid water. The satellite Titan and the atmosphere of Jupiter, however, may have a complex soup of organic molecules, including some amino acids and simple proteins in a prebiotic state. But no one seriously expects to see living bacteria anywhere else but on Earth or, at best, under the surface of Mars. [1482, 1195, 572]

35 How is the mass of a planet determined?

The most direct way is by measuring the orbit distance and period of an orbiting satellite. By Newtonian mechanics, the period and distance are very simply related to the mass of the primary body. Some planets, such as Mercury and Venus, do not have satellites, so you may have to send one there yourself, as NASA has done, and measure how the planet perturbs the trajectory of a passing artificial satellite. The idea is the same. You can also get a fair approximation by knowing the size of the planet and assuming a typical density for its composition. [1564]

36 If the atmosphere of a planet contains methane, does that mean it smells bad?

Well, it all depends on how you carry out the experiment. If you landed on the planet's surface and stuck your nose out of the spacesuit, it would be frozen so quickly that your sense of smell would fail before your brain had a chance to register anything. So, I would say that the planets Saturn, Uranus, and Neptune do not have a bad smell, because there is no way for a human to ever conduct the experiment. Of course, methane gas on Earth does not have a foul odor. It is odorless unless it is mixed with other trace gases. Usually, wherever methane is formed organically on Earth, there are plenty of trace gases to choose from, especially a variety of noxious compounds of sulfur. [2549, 2177, 1172, 533, 419]

37 Was there ever a planet between the orbits of Mars and Jupiter?

The consensus is that material in this part of the solar system would not have had the chance to assemble itself into much of a planet because of the tidal influence of Jupiter. Even if you added up all of the material in the asteroid belt, you would not get more mass than we find in Saturn's little moon Rhea (about 2.3×10^{24} grams), which is a moon only 1,200 kilometers in diameter. We are not talking about a genuine planet like Mars or even one of the large satellites of Jupiter, such as Callisto or Ganymede. Once upon a time, there were lots of bodies a few hundred to a few thousand kilometers across, but they eventually were captured as moons or crashed into the growing bulks of the existing planets, leaving behind large craters. Perhaps in what is now the asteroid belt, two or more of these bodies collided.

We know that asteroids come in stony and iron-nickel varieties. Also, microscopic studies of their crystalline structure show that many of the asteroids come from about five or six distinct families; perhaps these families represent the original bodies that collided billions of years ago to form the rubble we now see. In addition, the crystals in the meteorites from the asteroid belt are big enough so that the rock must have cooled slowly, as though it were part of larger bodies once upon a time. There is plenty of evidence that the asteroids were once a smaller number of bodies that collided. But again, these bodies were much smaller than what we now call planets, and they probably were no bigger than a few hundred kilometers across. [261]

Chapter 3

The Planets

E ndless questions about Mars, Europa, and Pluto seem to be the
rule of the day on the topic of the planets. The general public has
picked up much of the excitement in the professional community
about whether conditions for life exist elsewhere in the solar system.
Still, there are plenty of questions about basic planetary properties,
such as whether Jupiter has a ring, why Mercury and Venus don't
have moons, or why it is that Uranus is tilted. There are also many
questions about the hypothetical Planet X, and I am astonished
that some people accept its existence as a given and wonder why
astronomers have not given it a better name. There has also been
the question about how astronomers pronounce "Uranus" during
professional talks.

38 Has evidence for fossil life been found on Mars?

At a press conference on August 6, 1996, a team of scientists
at the Johnson Space Center led by David S. McKay, a veteran
of the study of lunar rocks from the Apollo program, described
their evidence that microscopic fossils resembling ancient Earth
bacteria were found in a meteorite recovered from Antarctica in
1984. Daniel Goldin, the head of NASA, stated that "NASA has
made a startling discovery," calling it "exciting, compelling, but
not as yet conclusive."

The surface of a small part of the ALH84001 meteorite was photographed using a scanning electron microscope, which showed that it appeared to be covered by a fine surface with many elongated bodies, either exposed or partially embedded in the carbonate-rich material. The longest of these are 200 nanometers long, and the smallest are about 100 times smaller than the smallest known Earth microfossils recovered from 3.8-billion-year-old Australian rocks. In appearance, they resemble images of Earth nanobacteria on calcium carbonate. The team admitted up front that they had no confirming evidence of cell walls or a chemistry for the microfossils that is uniquely biological in origin. The team acknowledged that each of their threads of evidence was not conclusive, but that taken together they added up to a plausible and even convincing story that they have detected microfossils in Martian rock. Further details can be found in the August 7, 1996, issue of the *Washington Post*. [1876, 1874, 1844, 1520, 1447, 1429, 1428, 1427]

39 Is it possible for life to exist on Mars?

Yes, it is. We are finding bacteria living under almost impossible physical conditions here on Earth—buried in solid rock for millions of years, eating rock, swimming in acid, and enjoying high temperatures near the boiling point of water. In comparison, the subsurface conditions on Mars must be quite comfortable to new species of bacteria, but we have no proof. The prospects for finding fossil bacteria dating from several billion years ago, when Mars was very Earth-like, are very good and that's why there are many plans afoot to visit Mars and search for fossils. The exploits of the *Pathfinder/Sojourner* mission on the surface of Mars in July 1997 (Plate 2a) have revealed the surface to be geologically complex, but chemically similar to Earth, and who knows what future prospectors will uncover once they dig below the surface. Many of us remain optimistic that something interesting will eventually turn up. [2991, 2150, 2029, 2014, 1875, 1739, 1738, 1710]

40 Is there really a face on Mars?

Sure, and many other shapes that we place a lot less emphasis on. There are facelike features on many planets and moons. But there are so few of them that they can easily be explained as shadows and erosion features without getting "weirded out" on other, more sensational explanations. My favorite astronomical image is shown in Plate 3, which comes from the Hubble Space Telescope. It is a processed image of the planetary nebula MyCn18, which looks disconcertingly like an alien eyeball staring out from the center of the nebula from this dying star. [2052]

41 Can Venus be seen in the daytime?

Yes, if you know exactly where to look and use a telescope. Seeing a daytime Venus is best accomplished within a few hours after sunrise; by noon, it is impossible to see Venus except with a small telescope pointed in exactly the right direction on a steady mounting. [2756, 2698, 898, 567, 526]

42 Why does Venus rotate backward from the other planets?

The best explanations still favor some dramatic event that occurred while Venus was being formed. It is known from the cratering evidence we see on a variety of planetary surfaces that soon after the planets were formed, there were still some mighty large miniplanets orbiting the Sun. One of these may have collided with Earth, dredging up material that later solidified into our Moon. The satellites of the outer planets are probably representatives of this ancient population of bodies. Venus may have experienced an encounter with one of these large bodies in which the material didn't form a separate moon, but was absorbed into the body of Venus. The result is that the spin direction and speed for Venus was seriously altered from their initial orientation. [50]

43 What are the two theories accounting for the surface of Venus?

There is the thin crust theory and the thick crust theory. If Venus has a thin crust, its internal heat escaped into space long ago, and the crust is now frozen in time with no tectonic activity. This doesn't explain why the crater distribution is so random or why there are seemingly no old craters. If Venus has a thick crust, it is ultimately unstable because the internal heat of the planet cannot easily escape into space. In this scenario, every 750 million years, the surface turns itself inside out in a catastrophic episode. Then, after Venus has lost its load of trapped heat, the crust begins to slowly thicken again, until at long last the internal heat convection process again drives the crust to break up and turn inside out. All the while, the radioactive decay of elements in the core continues to generate heat inside the planet. This periodic turnover may take a million years or less, followed by nearly a billion years of nothing happening, except that meteors will continue to fall and produce craters. What we now see are the craters generated in the crust since the last turnover.

Personally, I think it is an intriguing theory, and a simple seismic measurement will tell us whether Venus is in this regime or not. If its crust is thin, say 20–30 kilometers, then this periodic turnover cannot happen, and we will have to look elsewhere for explaining the weird cratering record. If it is thicker than, say, 50–100 kilometers, then episodic turnover may be favored.

44 Could a comet impact on Jupiter trigger thermonuclear fusion in its atmosphere?

Deuterium fusion can occur at temperatures just under 1 million K. But the maximum impact velocity of an asteroid with Jupiter is equal to Jupiter's escape velocity (60 km/sec) plus the comet's velocity, which is usually about 20 km/sec, for a total of 80 km/sec. This works out to a maximum temperature of only about 220,000 K. But the problem is that deuterium is such a minor constituent of the atmosphere, 1 part per 100,000 atoms of hydrogen, that you would not get much of an effect, and certainly not the fusioning of the atmosphere, because the other atoms would act as dampers to the fusion reaction. [2937, 584, 583]

45 Is the center of Jupiter really an Earth-sized diamond?

We don't really know. It is certainly very hot, probably 56,000 K, and very dense, and it seems to me that any stable compound such as crystalline carbon in diamond form could not exist at these temperatures and pressures. In fact, I see no reason why the core would not be some type of exotic, superdense, plasmalike state with ionized atoms of helium, carbon, nitrogen, and oxygen all mixed together. [2786, 2707, 2270, 2048, 533]

46 Could Europa support life?

Europa is the smallest of the Galilean satellites of Jupiter and has a diameter of 3,050 kilometers. From models of its interior based on its size, mass, and likely composition, astronomers have predicted that its interior is about 10 percent water and 90 percent silicate material. The core silicate region could be at a temperature of 2,800 K, heated by a combination of radioactive element decay and the gravitational stresses produced by Jupiter's proximity. There is an ice crust about 10–50 kilometers thick floating on top of a sea of liquid water, which is 200 kilometers or so thick. The water layer has a temperature ranging from 350 K nearest the core to 270 K just below the ice crust. It is exciting to think that three prerequisites for life—water, energy, and organic compounds—may be present inside Europa. Whether organic life could emerge from this slurry is not known. NASA plans to launch probes in the twenty-first century to penetrate the icy crust and find out. [1481, 833, 274]

47 How thick are Saturn's rings?

Voyager 2 flew by the rings and showed them to be thousands of individual ringlets. Some rings were only a few kilometers wide. The thickness of the ring plane is deduced to be fewer than 100 meters, making the rings the thinnest objects in the solar system. [2176, 129]

48 Have there been any recent discoveries about Neptune?

Take a look at Jonathan Lunine's article in the September 1996 issue of *Sky and Telescope* for an up-to-date review of what we now know about Neptune. Despite the *Voyager 2* flyby in 1989, Neptune still remains a planet shrouded in considerable mystery. Of all the planets, it emits far more energy (2.6 times!) than it receives from the Sun possibly because of the energy trapped during its formation. The atmosphere consists of methane, ammonia, and hydrogen sulfide and flows in zones parallel to the equator. Occasionally, and for reasons not understood, portions of the atmosphere erupt in storms with an enormous dark spot that comes and goes as local haze conditions vary. Neptune's satellite Triton is now regarded as an interloper captured by

Neptune perhaps as few as 500 million years ago, but not before it disrupted Neptune's original satellite system, causing several to eventually collide to form the ring arcs. Because of its great distance from the Sun, it may be a very long time before we fully understand this planet significantly better than we do now. [2945, 2663]

49 Were the satellites of Uranus created before or after the planet got tilted?

If the tilt arose by a violent collision, it is hard to imagine such an event not seriously affecting the orbital plane of the satellites. This argues very strongly for the collision happening before the formation of the satellites. The satellites currently orbit in a plane that is in the equatorial plane of Uranus and tilted with the axis of the planet in the same way. [2061, 1943]

50 Has Pluto been demoted to the status of a nonplanet?

Pluto is a small planet, but despite debates over the past decade whether it is a planet or a large asteroid, it remains classified by Dr. Brian Marsden and the International Astronomical Union as the smallest planet in the solar system. Most of us are comfortable in defining any object larger than Pluto as a planet and any smaller than Pluto as an asteroid or planetesimal. Whether it is an escaped moon or a big comet nucleus is irrelevant. For more on these debates, have a look at the August 1994 issue of *Sky and Telescope*. [2004, 51]

51 What objects besides Pluto have been found outside Neptune's orbit?

Currently, 28 large bodies at distances between 35 and 46 astronomical units have been discovered, most since 1992 by astronomers Jane Luu at Harvard University and David Jewett at the Massachusetts Institute of Technology. Figure 3 summarizes their locations beyond the orbit of Neptune. One of these objects, QB1, is nicknamed "Smiley" and is located 44 AUs or 6.5 billion kilometers away. It is 280 kilometers across, about one-eighth the size of Pluto. In 1997, Luu and Jewett announced the discovery of an even larger body, 1996TL66, with a size of 470 kilometers, which made many people excited about a "new planet," but it is too small to be called a planet, which some astronomers feel only marginally applies to Pluto itself. Pluto and its moon, Charon, and the cometary body Chiron (Kowal's Object), just outside the orbit of Saturn, are trans-Neptunian objects believed to be members of the inner edge of the Kuiper Belt—a vast system of billions of icy bodies, many destined to become comets. A class of objects called the Centaurs have orbits that cross the orbits of the giant planets and are believed to be the missing link between the Kuiper Belt population and short-period comets.

For more information, see the Centaurs web site (cfa-www.harvard.edu/cfa/ps/lists/Centaurs.html) and the Trans-Neptunian Objects site (cfa-www.harvard.edu/cfa/ps/lists/TNOs.html) for more details. Also, look at the February 1996 issue of *Astronomy* for more information. [392, 311, 304]

52 Why don't Mercury and Venus have moons?

Because they are too close to the Sun. Any moon with too great a distance from these planets would be in an unstable orbit and be captured by the Sun. If they were too close to these planets, they would be destroyed by tidal gravitational forces. The zones where moons around these planets could be stable over billions of years is probably so narrow that no body was ever captured into orbit or was formed there when the planets were first being accreted. [332, 328]

53 If you dropped a dead body on Mars, would it start life there?

While it is true that there are anaerobic bacteria living inside the human body, it is inconceivable that these bacteria, which have evolved in symbiosis with the water-rich tissues in terrestrial fauna and flora, would find the desiccated, low-pressure, low-temperature, and high-ultraviolet-radiation environment of Mars very favorable. There are, however, terrestrial bacteria that have adapted to many different niches deep inside Earth, or in some of the most hostile environments you can imagine, that might find some places on Mars rather homey. [2029]

54 Are the moons of Mars really moons or are they asteroids?

They are both. The moons of Mars are captured asteroids that have taken up permanent orbit around Mars, probably since the past billion years or so. Photographs of their surfaces show that they look almost identical to objects such as Ida (Plate 4), Gaspara, and Matilda, which are known asteroids that spacecraft have flown by since 1992. [327]

55 What are some of the details about Pluto?

It is about 3.6 billion miles from the Sun (about 40 times the Earth-Sun distance) and orbits the Sun every 249 years. It is 2,300 kilometers in diameter and has a density of about 2 gm/cc, which means it is an icy body with little rocky material in it.

Pluto has a single satellite, Charon, which orbits the planet every 6.4 days. It faces the planet the same way our Moon faces Earth, always showing the same face to Pluto. Charon seems to be rich in water ice, but no methane or ammonia is present. Its diameter is only 1,186 miles, and its mass is insufficient to hold an atmosphere. Pluto does have a tenuous atmosphere of methane, but the planet is too small to retain it, and it must be continuously leaking away as it is generated from the surface's methane ices, which are sublimating into gas without passing through a liquid state at these low pressures.

The Hubble Space Telescope recently photographed the surface of Pluto, but because Pluto is so small and far away, the photographs only show large splotches of light and dark areas. Visit the Space Telescope Science Institute web site (www.stsci.edu/) and follow the links to their collection of recent photographs in their image archive. [1775, 1596, 1123, 771, 364, 304, 51]

Chapter 4

The Earth

E arth, our home world, is still a somewhat mysterious planet to some people. I am amazed by the number of questions received at the Astronomy Cafe that have to do with what would happen if Earth stopped spinning, if the Moon suddenly vanished, or even why this planet spins at all. Many people ask questions about why the longest night of the year doesn't happen exactly on the winter solstice and why it is that we do not feel Earth spinning at 1,000-plus miles per hour. After answering more than 180 questions about our planet, there was not a single question that had not already been answered. My favorite question is, "How long will Earth remain habitable?," because the answer is very different than the one we are often obliged to provide after discussing the future evolution of the Sun. The answer is much closer to a few hundred million years than it is to the 6 billion years until the Sun becomes a red giant and engulfs Mercury and Venus.

56 Is Earth really shrinking?

We don't know for sure. The planet Mercury shrank as its core cooled. We expect that Earth could also shrink a bit in the next, say, 10 billion years as its core cools. If we use Mercury as a model, which shrank perhaps 10 kilometers in 5 billion years, we *might* expect Earth to shrink by 0.002 millimeters in one year—an undetectable rate. [2982]

57 Is Earth's pole shifting?

Yes, and it wobbles on many different time scales, all the way from millions of years as the continents move around down to day-to-day microshifts due to changes in the location of air masses and the effects of earthquakes. This is not a theory and is quite easily measurable with modern timekeeping technology. As shown in Figure 4, even the annual motion of the pole can be substantial if you are standing near the North Pole. Each spot shows where the rotation axis of the earth emerged from its surface.

The Chandler wobble has a period of about 14 months and an amplitude of ±0.7 seconds of arc. The north and south poles execute roughly a circular path about the nominal polar directions. If you were standing at the mean geometric north pole, the Chandler wobble would carry the actual pole on a circle about 25 meters in radius and at a speed of about 1 foot per day around

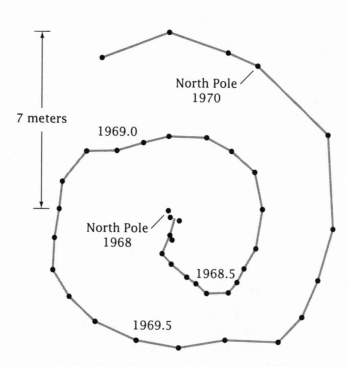

Figure 4 If you were to stand exactly at the North Pole, this plot shows by how many meters the pole has shifted between 1968 and 1970 during one episode of polar wander.

this circular path. No two Chandler wobbles are exactly the same, and the "orbits" change in radius from cycle to cycle.

Superimposed on the Chandler wobble are higher-frequency daily disturbances at the 0.001 second of arc level that are due to the motion of air masses, weather systems, and other daily influences. For more on this, have a look at the National Earth Orientation Service Web site (maia.usno.navy.mil/), particularly the discussion on leap seconds and why we need one every year. [2819, 2679, 2200, 2086, 1965, 1758, 1727, 1726, 1725, 1720, 728, 523, 396, 278]

58 Is Earth's magnetic field changing?

Indeed it is. It currently has a strength at Earth's surface of 0.6 gauss, which are the units we use to measure magnetic field strength. But long-term observations, summarized in Figure 5, show that it is decreasing at a rate of about 0.07 percent per year. If the current decline continues, in 1,500 years it could have a strength of practically zero. Because the magnetic field and the atmosphere help to shield the biosphere from cosmic rays and charged particles from the Sun, there *may* be a minor health hazard to astronauts posed by Earth losing its magnetic field.

The geologic record also shows that, in addition to its strength changing, Earth's north-south polarity flips every 250,000 years

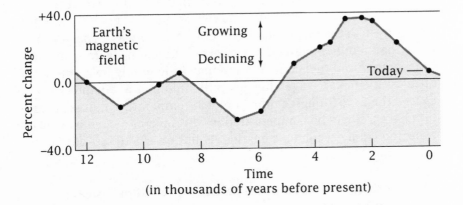

Figure 5 The changing strength of Earth's magnetic field between 10,000 B.C. and 2000 A.D.. We are in a period of decline that has lasted since 500 B.C..

or so. There are no identifiable effects from previous flips in the fossil record. We know that many species of bacteria, birds, and fish can sense the direction of the magnetic field and use it for migration and to find food in murky waters. These animals may perish when the field changes and they can no longer rely on it to orient themselves to find food or migrate. No one really knows if the condition of zero field will last 5 years, 10 years, or 500 years. Stay tuned. [1686, 1213, 816, 279]

59 Will there be a restructuring of Earth's magnetic field in the near future that will result in Earth's end?

No. There will not be any major change in Earth's magnetic field for many thousands of years. Even if Earth's magnetic field vanished, it would have no effect on the physical integrity of the planet, because the energy carried by the entire magnetic field of Earth is insignificant compared to either Earth's rotational energy or its kinetic energy as it orbits the Sun. [2941, 2411, 2232, 1077, 816, 279]

60 Are we currently in an ice age that has lasted millions of years?

We are living through a long period when ice ages come and go, but, given the average length of such ice ages in the past, we may be coming to the end of an inter–ice age period called the Holocene epoch, which has lasted about 15,000 years (see Figure 6). This period includes the rise of human agriculture and long growing seasons, which have let us multiply as a species to more than 5 billion members. However, human-made greenhouse heating by fossil fuel consumption may indefinitely delay the onset of the next ice age, due any millennium now! Whatever causes the 2- to 3-degree dips in global temperature that send us into ice ages may be compensated by the several-degree increases expected from greenhouse heating. Pollution is at last good for something! [2872]

61 Why does the Moon produce two water tides on Earth and not just one?

Because it is not the gravitational force that is doing it; it's the change in the gravitational force across the body of Earth. On the

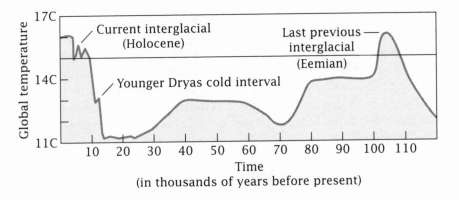

Figure 6 Average global temperature changes during the past glacial and interglacial periods back 110,000 years from the present. The current average temperature is near 16 degrees Celsius and is the highest it has been since the Eemian interglacial period 110,000 years ago. The current warm interglacial period (Holocene) has lasted 15,000 years and may be about to end.

side nearest the moon, this tidal gravitational force is directed toward the Moon. Particles on Earth's surface would be tugged toward the Moon, because the force of the Moon is slightly stronger at Earth's surface than at its center, which is an additional 6,300 kilometers from the Moon.

On the side of Earth opposite the Moon, the Moon is tugging on the center of Earth slightly more than it is on the far side, so once again the resultant force on a particle on the far side of Earth is directed away from Earth's center. Another way of thinking about this is that the gravitational force of the Moon causes Earth to accelerate slightly toward the Moon, which causes the water to be pulled toward the Moon faster than the solid rock. On the other side, the solid Earth leaves behind some of the water that is not as strongly drawn toward the Moon as Earth. This produces the bulge on the side of Earth away from the Moon. [380]

62 Why are there no ocean tides at the equator?

Tides are a very complex phenomenon. For any particular location, their height and changes in time depend to varying degrees on the location of the Sun and the Moon and on the details of the shape of the beach and coastline, coastline depth, and prevailing ocean currents. The tidal bulge of the Moon follows along the path on Earth's surface that intersects with the orbital plane of the Moon. This plane is tilted 23.5 degrees with respect to the equatorial plane of Earth. The result is that near the equator the difference between high tide and low tide is actually rather small, compared to other latitudes that are closer to the ground track of the tidal bulge. [2792]

63 Do auroras give off heat?

Many people have seen the northern lights, also called the Aurora Borealis, and it is hard to avoid the impression that the night sky is not aflame. But from direct measurements by rocket payloads, we know that auroras do not represent combustion nor do they give off heat. They glow by the same mechanism as the gases in a typical fluorescent bulb and this is not an incandescent process that produces heat. Having said that, there is some heat energy that is produced when high-speed electrons strike the atmosphere. For Earth, this thermal heating effect is pretty minor and does not lead to a visible glow. On Jupiter, however, the incoming currents of particles are so energetic that the atmosphere inside the jovian auroral regions is heated to thousands of degrees in the upper atmosphere. [2913, 1880, 1858, 1856]

64 What causes auroras to have different colors?

The electric currents that enter the atmosphere several hundred kilometers above the ground are invisible, until they slam into atoms of the atmosphere. The chief constituents of the atmosphere are nitrogen (78 percent) and oxygen (21 percent). Different colors occur because these atmospheric constituents are stimulated by energetic particles from the Sun and Earth's radiation belts, and they do so in slightly different ways. The green color comes from oxygen atoms being stimulated to emit light as the electrons collide with the atoms and cause the electrons in the oxygen atoms to take quantum jumps. The atoms emit light at a single frequency, which we see as a green light. Between 400 and 1,000 kilometers above the ground, auroras first become visible, but by about 100 kilometers, the atmosphere is too dense for the atoms to give off enough light between collisions among themselves. At lower altitudes, nitrogen emits a faint blue color and a pinkish color. Because the nitrogen atoms emit light faster than the oxygen atoms, the lower blue-pink parts of many auroras seem to move faster than the upper, slower parts controlled by the more sluggish emission of the oxygen atoms. [1899, 1851]

65 What would happen if you traveled through an aurora?

First, the air where auroras are formed is a pretty good vacuum. You might notice a faint glow all around you but not within about 10 meters, because the excited gas is pretty thin. Auroral curtains are less than 1 kilometer thick. We see auroras dramatically because of their contrast with the dark sky. This contrast may not be as spectacular when you are right inside it, and because the region is being bombarded by energetic electrons, I would also suspect that you would build up quite an electric charge. [1854, 1853, 799]

66 Can you hear an aurora?

Native people living in the arctic regions of Alaska, Canada, Scandinavia, and Siberia sometimes claim they hear rustling or crackling sounds. Auroras never get closer to Earth than 100 kilometers or so, and no known physical mechanism can transmit sound waves to the ground from such "near space" altitudes. For a long time it was thought the brain was fabricating these sounds. From the sight of auroral fires in the sky it simply filled in the sounds it was expecting to hear. Recently, physicists have discovered that pulses of electromagnetic energy from the rapidly changing auroral electric fields can produce a discharge near the ground, and that pointed objects such as pine needles can transduce this energy into local sounds such as cracks and hisses. Experiments have shown this actually happens, even in lightning storms, when a crackle is sometimes heard at the same time as the flash, but long before the thunder arrives. [1856, 1852]

67 How long will Earth remain habitable?

Calculations always seem to show that at the present time, 4.5 billion years after its birth, the Sun will change its luminosity by about a factor of 2 in the next 5 billion years. In the next billion years, the amount of solar radiation reaching Earth will increase by 8 percent. This doesn't sound like much, but climate modeling studies indicate that a 0.1 percent increase in solar radiation causes a mean global temperature increase of 0.2 degrees Celsius. From this, we can estimate that our 8 percent increase in solar radiation will cause a 5 degree increase in the mean solar temperature over the next 300 million years. This means we are now talking about an average global winter temperature of 25 degrees Celsius and very few places where we can expect to see snow and ice. The mean summer temperatures would be closer to 30 degrees Celsius.

A recent review of long-term climate variations among the inner planets by Michael Rampino and Ken Caldeira suggests that the long-term outlook may be very bleak, if you take into account the carbon dioxide gas in the atmosphere. In their 1994 *Annual Reviews of Astronomy and Astrophysics* article, they discuss how the amount of carbon dioxide in the atmosphere is sensitive to temperature. When you add this into the equation, the slight increase in the Sun's output could translate into a global mean temperature exceeding 80 degrees Celsius in the next 1.5 billion years. Thanks to the greenhouse effect, the evaporation of Earth's oceans would be well under way 1 billion years from now, and only thermophilic (heat loving) bacteria would find this environment comfortable. We can assume that millions of years before this happens Earth will have already become uninhabitable. Life more complex than a bacterium has only been around for 600 million years, so it looks like we are about halfway through the "golden years." To me, this is rather uncomfortably short, because it suggests that in perhaps as short a period as a few hundred million years, living on Earth would be unbearable. [79]

68 How do you think Earth will finally come to an end?

For life on this planet, it seems certain that once the Sun continues to evolve into a slightly brighter star, the surface temperature of Earth will increase by 20 to 50 degrees Celsius. More water will be evaporated from the oceans, thereby increasing the greenhouse heating of Earth. This will turn into a runaway process, probably in another 500–700 million years and will convert Earth into a twin of Venus. It will be impossible for life of any kind, except perhaps thermophilic bacteria, to survive. The final coup de grâce will be delivered some 5 billion years later, when the Sun becomes a red giant star and its surface swells to envelop the orbits of Mercury and Venus. Earth may well lose its atmosphere at this time.

More immediately, there are many asteroids that periodically cross Earth's orbit, and new ones are discovered every month. Many of these will probably impact Earth with the same force and consequences as the one that struck Earth 65 million years ago and caused the mass extinction of most of the dinosaurs. Still, there are many, many known asteroids in the 100-meter to 500-meter class that could deliver a major blow to Earth's biosphere, possibly in the next 10,000 to 100,000 years. Millions of people might die from direct consequences of the impact, such as coastal tidal waves. [1886, 1260, 189]

69 Is Earth about to crash into the asteroid belt?

Not a chance. The orbits of Earth and the asteroid belt are much too stable for anything like that to happen. [2721]

70 Did the asteroid that hit Earth 65 million years ago affect Earth's orbit?

A body about the size of the asteroid Ida (Plate 4) hitting a 12,000-kilometer planet isn't going to do much. The mass of Earth is 10^{27} grams and a 10-kilometer asteroid roughly similar to Ida is about 10^{19} grams, so the energy of Earth in its orbit will only be affected by the ratio of the two masses, or 1 part in 10 million. As a guess, this is not going to be enough to change Earth's orbit by more than a few centimeters. [1713]

71 How much energy would it take to explode Earth?

An amount equal to about the total gravitational potential energy of Earth, or about 2.5×10^{39} ergs. This is equal to something like 10 billion billion Hiroshima bombs, give or take a few. A more astronomical way to think about this is that you would need as much energy delivered to the core of Earth as the Sun produces in 10 days, and this would dissipate the mass of Earth to infinity. Do not attempt this experiment yourself. [2940]

72 If the Sun stopped shining, when would Earth cool to absolute zero?

Absolute zero is 0 degrees Kelvin, and Earth cannot drop to absolute zero, because the universe would keep it above 2.7 K. Without the Sun, the only energy reaching the surface of Earth would be the heat from its own interior. All you have to do is go down a kilometer or two, where deep diamond miners work, and you are already up to a temperature of 140 degrees Fahrenheit or more. If the Sun went away, Earth would readjust itself to a heat flow where the outer surface is no longer warmed by the Sun. My guess is that this internal heat flow is not enough to keep the surface of Earth above the freezing point of water and that, after perhaps a month or so, the latent solar heat stored in the oceans and crust would be exhausted. The temperature would stabilize probably somewhere below 200 K and be maintained thereafter by the heat flux from Earth's interior for a few billion years. Perhaps the oceans would not freeze solid, but a thin, deep, liquid layer might survive for millions of years or more, providing some warmth for bacteria but not much else. [2895, 2158, 1793, 1628, 629, 617]

73 How is the distance to the Sun determined from Earth?

The most accurate way is to first use celestial mechanics to determine the orbit of an asteroid, such as Eros. At a given date, calculate its distance in astronomical units (the Earth-Sun distance). Then, you bounce a radar pulse off the asteroid to get its distance in kilometers. You can then deduce the value of the Earth-Sun distance in kilometers. There is no other way to do this accurately, because, from celestial mechanics and observations, all we get are the relative distances to the Sun and planets. To get an absolute distance, you need to find an independent way to determine one of the required interplanetary distances. Planets are so far away that parallax techniques from the surface of Earth do not work very well. Detecting reflected radar pulses is the most direct way, because you get the distance at a given instant, exactly, from the time delay and the speed of light. Radar pulses have been transmitted and received even from Saturn, nearly 1 billion miles away. (The current value for the astronomical unit is 149.598 million kilometers.) [638, 63]

74 When Earth's magnetic field reverses, does its rotation also switch?

No, it doesn't, because, although the magnetic reversals can be easily identified in rock, there is no evidence whatever that the rotation of Earth falls to zero then spins back up. This is impossible from simple physics, without turning Earth's surface molten, because of the enormous heat dissipation that would result. The amount of energy stored in the rotation of Earth is enormous, and it would have to be dissipated and restored somehow in order to change its spin. This rotational energy would be enough to melt the crust. [2763, 1077, 772, 279, 278]

75 How much mass does Earth gain from the solar wind?

Not much. The density of the solar wind is only a few dozen atoms per cubic centimeter traveling at about 450 kilometers/sec. This represents a flow of atoms across an Earth-sized area of about 5×10^{26} atoms/sec. For hydrogen atoms, this is about 1 kilogram/sec or 70,000 kilograms per day. The problem is that these particles are usually charged and would be deflected by Earth's magnetic field, and very little of this gets into the atmosphere, perhaps only a few kilograms per day. [2924, 2723, 2722, 1790, 1171]

76 Why is Earth tectonically active and not Mars or Venus?

Mars is evidently too small, and because it doesn't have a strong magnetic field, its core must be solid and not fluid. Perhaps it simply cooled off too quickly to have a crust thin enough to form plates. As for Venus, it also doesn't seem to have a liquid core, because it has no magnetic field. Some astronomers think that its crust is so thick that it cannot break into plates that move, but every 750 million years or so, heat builds up from decaying radioisotopes inside the planet, causing a catastrophic melting of the core and the churning of the crust like oatmeal in a pot. No feature is seen anywhere on the surface of Venus that is older than 750 million years, unlike Earth. We will not know what is going on inside these planets until we can plant seismographic stations on their surfaces, like we did on the Moon. [2560]

77 What is a Schumann resonance?

Believe it or not, Earth behaves like an enormous electric circuit.
The atmosphere is actually a weak conductor, and if there were
no sources of charge, its existing electric charge would diffuse
away in about 10 minutes. There is a cavity defined by the surface
of Earth and the inner edge of the ionosphere, 55 kilometers
up. At any moment, the total charge residing in this cavity is
500,000 coulombs. There is a vertical current flow between the
ground and the ionosphere between 1 to 3×10^{-12} amperes per
square meter. The resistance of the atmosphere is 200 ohms. The
voltage potential is 200,000 volts. There are about 1,000 lightning
storms at any given moment worldwide. Each produces 0.5 to
1 ampere, and these collectively account for the measured current
flow in Earth's electromagnetic cavity.

The Schumann resonances were predicted to exist in 1952 and
were first detected in 1954. They are resonant electromagnetic
waves that exist in this cavity. Like waves on a spring, they are
not present all the time but have to be excited to be observed.
They are not caused by anything internal to Earth, its crust,
or its core. They seem to be related to electrical activity in the
atmosphere, particularly during times of intense lightning activity.
They occur at several frequencies between 6 and 50 cycles per
second, specifically, 7.8, 14, 20, 26, 33, 39, and 45 hertz, with
a daily variation of about ± 0.5 hertz. As long as the properties
of Earth's electromagnetic cavity remain about the same, these
frequencies remain the same. Presumably, there is some change
due to the solar sunspot cycle as Earth's ionosphere changes in
response to the 11-year cycle of solar activity. Schumann
resonances are most easily seen between 20:00 and 22:00
universal time (UT).

Given that Earth's atmosphere carries a charge, a current, and a
voltage, it is not surprising to find such electromagnetic waves.
Much of the research in the past 20 years has been conducted
by the Department of the Navy, which investigates extremely
low frequency (ELF) communication with submarines. For more
information, see Hans Volland, ed., *Handbook of Atmospheric
Electrodynamics* (CRC Press, 1995). Chapter 11 is on Schumann
resonances and was written by Davis Campbell of the Geophysical
Institute, University of Alaska. There is also a history of this
research and an extensive bibliography. [768]

78 How do astronomers know that Earth had a different rotation period long ago?

Geologists discovered sedimentary tidal deposits near ancient coastlines dating from about 750 million years ago, and the layering sequence of the sediments could be traced in the rock. By counting the layers during a particular dating sequence, they deduced that Earth was rotating about once every 18 hours. There is an article about this by astronomers from the University of Arizona in the July 5, 1996, issue of *Science.* By studying the laminations in tidal sediment deposits from Utah, Indiana, Alabama, and Australia, they found that some 900 million years ago the day was only 18 hours long, and there were 481 days to the year. [1733, 1726, 1725, 1720, 1688]

79 Can you slow Earth's rotation artificially?

Not so that it made any difference. Humans have made a measurable change in the rotation period of Earth by several microseconds just by damming up all the fresh water into vast reservoirs containing trillions of tons of water. This has happened mostly in the equatorial temperate zone, where most humans live, and, dynamically, this is just where you would want to move mass to have the greatest effect upon a planet's rotation. There may be a weak interaction between this activity and the weather over the long term, and perhaps even in the strength of Earth's magnetic field, which may be very sensitive to the rotation rate of Earth. [772]

Chapter 5

The Moon

To me, the most boring category for questions is the Moon. Sure, it is a pretty sight in the sky, but I often have to pull my hair out to come up with a few dozen interesting questions about it, but this hasn't been a problem for visitors to the Astronomy Cafe. I have logged more than 260 questions on the topic of the Moon, ranging from "When is the next blue moon?" to "Can you buy land on the Moon?" One question for which I had no answer, at least initially, was what is the name for the second new moon of a month. The answer was eventually provided by a visitor to the web site who filled me in on this great mystery. Eclipses, phases, and lunar tide effects are also fascinating for many people, but most of my answers to those questions have been just gentle reminders of what people should have been taught in grade school. Still, I learned a thing or two about proxigean spring tides, at what depth moonquakes occur, and what the current ideas are for explaining the moon illusion. The most unusual question? Well, it probably had to be whether astronomers have a technical name for the Moon. I now receive very few new questions about the Moon, so I imagine that the questions that have been answered at the Astronomy Cafe are probably a complete sample of what nonastronomers are capable of coming up with, for which I am thankful.

80 How can you tell the difference between an ordinary full moon and a blue moon?

If a full moon is the second one in the same month, it is called a blue moon. Because there is not a whole number of lunar cycles in every year (29.53 days for a lunar synodic month times 12 does not equal 365 days), every three years or so there are two full moons in one month. It's as simple as that. Table 3 is a list of monthly full moon names, and Table 4 is a list of dates for blue moons until the year 2028, including 1999 and 2018, which will have two blue moons, in January and March. The term "blue moon" has nothing to do with color, although a blue moon observed from Great Britain in 1954 did look distinctly blue. Patrick Moore, a British author of many popular astronomy books, has described several other sightings of genuine blue moons—in 1944 in the United States, in 1949 in Queensland, Australia, and in England on

Table 3 Names of the full moons during each month.

Month	American Folk Name	Ojibwa Indian Name
January	Wolf Moon	Great Spirit Moon
February	Snow Moon	Sucker Spawning Moon
March	Sap Moon	Moon of the Crust of the Snow
April	Pink Moon	Sap Running Moon
May	Flower Moon	Budding Moon
June	Strawberry Moon	Strawberry Moon
July	Buck Moon	Middle of the Summer Moon
August	Sturgeon Moon	Rice-making Moon
September	Harvest Moon	Leaves Turning Moon
October	Hunters Moon	Falling Leaves Moon
November	Beaver Moon	Ice Flowing Moon
December	Cold Moon	Little Spirit Moon

Table 4 The dates for the second full moon of the month (blue moon) until the year 2031. Note that 1999 and 2018 will have two blue moons. Time of day is given in universal time at Greenwich, England. For Eastern Standard Time subtract 5 hours and for Pacific Standard Time subtract 8 hours.

Year	Month	Day	Time
1999	January	31	16:07
1999	March	31	22:49
2001	November	30	20:50
2004	July	31	18:06
2007	June	30	13:49
2009	December	31	19:13
2012	August	31	13:59
2015	July	31	10:44
2018	January	31	13:27
2018	March	31	12:37
2020	October	31	14:50
2023	August	31	1:36
2026	May	31	8:46
2028	December	31	16:49

September 26, 1950. According to Moore, who witnessed the 1950 event: "The moon was in a slightly misty sky and had a kind of lovely blue color comparable to the electric glow discharge. I never saw something similar before." Apparently, this phenomenon has been reported by many people all over the world. It is believed to be caused by dust in the atmosphere at very high altitudes, and the 1950 event seen in England may have been produced by an unusually heavy season of forest fires in

Canada. The fires may have added dust to the atmosphere, causing the Moon to appear blue. [2992, 2745, 1302, 1268, 1064, 426, 390, 152, 3]

81 Why does the harvest moon look bigger than other full moons?

The explanation for this moon illusion is still not known. It is not an atmospheric phenomenon, and the Moon really does seem to be larger on the horizon than when it is high up in the sky, particularly in September during the harvest moon. The Moon obviously does not change its apparent size, because if you hold a penny at arm's length, it will cover the Moon on the horizon and high over head. There must be an eye-brain basis for this effect, just as there are many other optical illusions that also fool the eye.

The Moon Illusion, edited by Maurice Hershenson (Erlbaum Associates, 1989) is a book dedicated to this phenomenon and covers the pros and cons of the most common explanations for this illusion, some going back to Aristotle's time. The most popular explanation is that it has to do with the eye seeing familiar-sized objects, such as trees and buildings, at the horizon with which to compare lunar size and not having similar reference objects high up in the sky. Other explanations involve atmospheric refraction, which is greater at the horizon than it is high in the sky. Even the human brain and the way it processes visual information has been implicated. The bottom line is that the Moon illusion is so deeply linked to the general problem of human space perception that the experts do not as yet understand all of the physiological factors that contribute to the illusion. [2259, 847, 122]

82 What is the youngest moon after the new moon ever seen?

The youngest first crescent moon after the new moon is about 18 hours old and very hard to see, because it is so close to the Sun that you have to look for it just as soon as the western edge of the Sun sets below the horizon. Many amateur astronomers have international competitions to see who can see the youngest moon. The December 1996 issue of *Sky and Telescope* reports that the record for observing the youngest crescent is held by Steven

O'Meara of Massachusetts, who observed a 15.5-hour moon on May 24, 1990, under virtually perfect conditions. [729]

83 Is the full moon seen the same everywhere on the same date?

No. Astronomers define when a full moon occurs by its phase as seen at the standard meridian on Earth, which passes through Greenwich, England. This defines Greenwich mean time (GMT), which is also called universal time (UT). All predictions and forecasts are based on planetary positions and celestial events on this time standard. If a full moon is reported to occur at 3:00 UT by the calculations, a lucky bloke living in England will see it at 3:00 A.M., but someone in New York will have seen it the previous day at 10:00 P.M. because of the five-hour time zone difference. [2100, 1465]

84 Does the full moon have any effect on humans or animals?

None, except that, unlike animals, humans can talk themselves into making such correlations happen as self-fulfilling prophecies. Both of my daughters were born on the full moon, but the hospital nurseries were practically empty that day, and no nurse made any comment about the full moon. Had the nursery been full, they would have made comments and remembered them, thereby passing on the faulty observation to others. This one-sided recall is a well-known phenomenon in psychology. [2244, 1934]

85 Can you get a moon burn in the tropics from the full moon?

No. You need ultraviolet, B-type light to get a skin burn, and none of this is reflected from the surface of the Moon from the Sun. Besides, the Moon is 10,000 times less bright than the noonday Sun and is already worth a sunblock protection factor (SPF) of 10,000! [2846]

86 Is it an accident that the Moon is just big enough to cover the Sun in a total eclipse?

It seems to be. If we look at the other moons in the solar system, there is a whole range of apparent angular sizes for satellites or moons as seen from the surfaces of the planets. Earth just got lucky. My big complaint is that we were gypped by only getting one moon. [229]

87 Does the Moon have an atmosphere?

Yes, it does, believe it or not. In 1993, Boston University astronomers Brian Flynn and Michael Mendillo detected the emission of sodium gas around the Moon by using a special instrument that covers the Moon and then detects the faint light produced by sodium atoms. As reported in the July 9, 1993, issue of *Science,* they detected the sodium cloud exosphere all the way to the lunar surface. Overall, the atmosphere has a density of 50 atoms/cc and is a million times less dense than Earth's atmosphere. [961, 652]

88 How long could the Moon hold on to an atmosphere as dense as that of Earth?

A ballpark estimate could be fewer than 10 million years, but this would be a handsome overestimate, because the leakage rate will accelerate as the density of the atmosphere diminishes. My best wild guess would be something like a few hundred thousand years. [2845]

89 Is it true that the Moon is moving away from Earth?

Yes, and this has been confirmed by more than a decade of lunar ranging experiments using the laser retroreflectors left on the Moon by *Apollo* astronauts. It has also been verified by looking at fossil deposits. In both cases, the rate works out to be about 3.8 centimeters per year, and the fossil sediment layering records show that this motion has been constant for more than 900 million years at this same rate. [1711]

90 What do we now know about the patches of ice on the Moon?

The *Clementine I* satellite conducted a radar experiment that measured the reflectivity of the Moon's surface directly below the orbiting spacecraft. A few of the orbits passed over a couple of craters on the Moon's south polar region. It has been known for some years that portions of the crater floors have been in total darkness for thousands or even billions of years. On December 3, 1996, astronomer Paul Spudis of the Lunar and Planetary Laboratory in Arizona announced that *Clementine* discovered that these same shadowed areas coincide with radar reflections that are normally found associated with rock that contains ice on Earth. As described in the February 1997 issue of *Sky and Telescope*, however, the discovery on the Moon only involved a single pass worth of data, so confirmation is desperately needed before we get too excited. Recent follow-up radar studies of these regions at the Arecibo Observatory in Puerto Rico by astronomer Donald Campbell of Cornell University (see *Astronomy*, September 1997 issue) do not confirm the existence of the *Clementine* anomalous radar reflectivity patches, so the original detection may just have been radio noise. These things do happen.

By the way, astronomers Martin Slade of the Jet Propulsion Laboratory in California and Bryan Butler and Duane Muhlman of the California Institute of Technology reported in the October 23, 1992, issue of *Science* how they used the 70-meter Goldstone dish to transmit and receive radar pulses from Mercury. Their mapping of the reflectivity of the planet showed that the polar regions gave a very strong return signal very similar to the ices found on the polar caps of Mars and the surfaces of the satellites of the outer planets. Although ice on the Moon may be less of a sure thing, there is little dispute from the large amount of data from the Mercury mapping program that some subsurface ice exists there. The radio pulses can probe many meters below the surface of the planet and that's the most likely place to find ice on Mercury. [2781, 2471, 2341, 2206]

91 Have any new craters been seen in the 100 years of lunar photographs taken from Earth?

The problem is that any impact big enough to leave a crater that is visible from Earth and more than a hundred meters across would have been a spectacular impact, and no one would have missed it. Impacts of just about any size kick up so much rock and dust that even an impact that leaves behind a crater too small to be easily seen in a survey photograph would produce a collateral plume of rock and dust and a flash of light from incandescent material, which I suspect would be detectable. [1816]

92 Have gold, silver, or diamonds been found on the Moon?

According to the *Lunar Sourcebook* (Cambridge University Press, 1991) no silver or diamonds have been discovered in the moon rocks collected by *Apollo* astronauts, but gold has been found at a level of about a few nanograms per gram of lunar rock. Give or take a few grams, this is about equal to a single grain of rice (0.5 grams) added to 500 tons of beach sand (500 million grams). It is believed this gold is deposited by meteorites, because the isotopic abundance of this gold compared to iridium is the same as what is found in many terrestrial meteorites. [2987, 2398, 1020]

93 What is a proxigean spring tide?

The Moon follows an elliptical path around Earth that has a perigee distance of 356,400 kilometers, which is about 92.7 percent of its average orbital distance from Earth. Because tidal forces vary as the third power of distance, this little 8-percent change translates into a 25-percent increase in the tide-producing ability of the Moon upon Earth. If the lunar perigee occurs when the Moon is between the Sun and Earth, it produces unusually high spring high tides, called the proxigean spring tides, and these happen about once every 18 months or so.

The very interesting book *Tidal Dynamics,* by Fergus J. Wood (Reidel Publishing Company, 1986), discusses these tides and their environmental consequences at great length. There are many recorded instances of unusually high storm conditions or coastal flooding during the proxigean times. On January 9, 1974, the *Los Angeles Times* reported, "Giant Waves Pound Southland Coast." During the past 400 years, there have been 39 instances of extreme proxigean spring tides, where the tide-producing severity was near the theoretical maximum. [1423, 809]

94 Exactly how did Earth and the Moon get locked into synchrony?

Apparently, when the Moon was very young, it was also much closer to Earth. This means that because the effect of Earth's gravitational tide upon the Moon varies as the third power of the distance, the young, molten Moon was tidally deformed. It may have been spinning quite rapidly then and was not locked into its orbital period at all. But as the Moon drifted away from Earth and the Moon solidified, it apparently froze in a memory of this highly deformed initial state, and *Apollo* radar altimetry showed this in the early 1970s. The reason the Moon is now synchronously locked is probably because it inherited a nonspherical shape from its close tidal phase, and this fossilized tidal bulge has been used by Earth as handles to slowly lock the Moon into its synchronous state during the past few billion years. In the future, as the Moon continues to move further away from Earth, the orbital period of the Moon will increase to more than 50 days, and its rotation period will also decrease to the same period. [2848, 2448, 2417, 1353, 277, 247]

95 Is there a name for the second new moon in a month?

When I first received this question at the Astronomy Cafe, I said that I didn't know of any such names, but then several readers contacted me and said that the second new moon is sometimes called the Finder's Moon, the Secret Moon, or the Spinner Moon. You learn something new every day. [1295]

96 Will Earth always appear in the same location in the sky as seen from the Moon?

The first time I answered this question I got it wrong because I tried to answer it by juggling the geometry in my head! The correct answer is that Earth remains fixed in the lunar sky during the entire lunar month; however, the background constellations do change. Take two balls to represent the Earth and Moon and connect them with a stick so that the same hemisphere of the Moon-ball always faces the Earth-ball. You will easily see that Earth must remain fixed above the lunar horizon as the Moon orbits Earth. From the Moon, Earth goes through a complete set of phases so that when it is new moon, Earth is fully illuminated. The "full earth" bathes the darkened Moon in a ghostly blue earthshine, so from the lunar surface it is never actually fully dark with such a bright, fixed light in the sky. The full earth is about 10 times brighter than the full moon. [1905, 1678]

Chapter 6

Meteors and Comets

E veryone seems captivated both by Comet Hale-Bopp and the prospects of Earth being hit by a large asteroid in the near future. Several made-for-TV movies have raised many questions about the consequences of such impacts and have consistently underestimated their horrific consequences. Hale-Bopp, which appeared in 1997, even produced accusations that astronomers were covering up information on alien spacecraft accompanying the comet by not allowing large observatories to photograph the comet. The Astronomy Cafe has received many questions about great comets of the past and when they were discovered. I have provided information about how much mass Earth acquires from meteoritic material every day and why fireballs are so spectacular and even answered questions about how we would detect and destroy a comet or meteor about to hit Earth. I think I've scared many people by announcing that we are investing only a few million dollars to identify and track objects that could cause enormous damage to our civilization, and that, at best, we would probably only get a few months' notice of the impending catastrophe, because these bodies are so hard to see at great distances. Many people became quite indignant about this, and I have told them to write their congresspersons! I still think that nothing will be done about this kind of threat until one of these objects takes out a city or causes other widespread destruction. Then there will be congressional hearings, some finger-pointing, and hopefully a more serious attitude about this subject. Right now, your safety is in the hands of about five astronomers and graduate students in Arizona. Sleep well!

97 Was Earth almost hit by an asteroid on March 23, 1989?

Yes. There was a near miss that went unnoticed because the Moon was so bright that the asteroid was lost in the glare. The object was discovered by astronomers eight days later and cataloged as 1989 FC. According to an article in the June 1989 issue of *Sky and Telescope,* it was 300 meters in diameter and passed within 690,000 kilometers of Earth. This is less than twice the distance to the Moon from Earth and only 20 times the distance from Earth to our orbiting communications satellites. Had it hit, we would have had a crater bigger than the Barringer Meteor Crater in Arizona. Many cattle and sheep would have died. [2879]

98 Is there an asteroid that will hit Earth in the near future?

Astronomers Donald Yeomans and Paul Chodas of the Jet Propulsion Laboratory in California computed the orbits of all known asteroids until the year 2200, using specially designed, high-precision orbital dynamics software. They write in the book *Hazards due to Comets and Asteroids,* edited by Tom Gehrels (University of Arizona Press, 1994), that about 100 asteroids and comets will indeed come within 40 million kilometers of Earth. This is about the distance between Earth and Venus at the latter's closest approach, but Table 5 includes asteroids and comets that have passed or will pass by Earth within 9 million kilometers and quite a few within a few times the Earth-Moon distance. This is much too close for comfort as planetary encounters go.

You will note from Table 5 that the asteroid 1863 Antinous gets within 565,000 kilometers of Earth, which is only a bit more than the distance from Earth to the Moon! Now, before you get all excited, the asteroid 1991 VG passed within 565,000 kilometers of Earth on December 4, 1991, and no one got terribly worked up about it. Also, the calculations can easily be in error by amounts up to 50,000 kilometers, depending on the exact details of the actual gravitational perturbations the asteroid experiences with many other bodies in the solar system. Still, this list bears careful study. It just covers those asteroids that we have already discovered. There are thousands more out there, dozens are discovered every year, and one of them could have the name "Earth" engraved on it. For a look at what a typical asteroid looks like, see the spectacular image of Ida and its moonlet Dactyl taken by the *Galileo* spacecraft

Table 5 **Asteroids that have come very close to Earth in the past or are predicted to do so by the year 2194.** So far, we have been lucky, but each year astronomers discover a new asteroid that comes very close, because only then are they easily seen. As the asteroid surveys continue, many more close calls are expected to be discovered in the next 10 years.

Predicted Close Calls

Asteroid	Distance (kilometers)	Date
1863 Antinous	565,000	April 1999
4179 Toutatis	689,000	December 2012
4179 Toutatis	748,000	November 2008
2340 Hathor	838,000	October 2086
2340 Hathor	970,000	October 2069
1991 JX	980,000	June 1999
2101 Adonis	1,060,000	February 2177
1986 PA	1,064,000	April 2001
4660 Nereus	1,180,000	February 2060
1980 WF	1,155,000	January 2001
1992 FE	1,218,000	March 2000
3362 Khufu	1,288,000	January 2001
4179 Toutatis	1,530,000	September 2004
4581 Asclepius	1,800,000	March 2051
2100 Ra-Shalom	2,114,000	September 2000
1990 OA	2,200,000	July 2070
4660 Nereus	2,200,000	February 2071
3361 Orpheus	2,450,000	April 2194
4183 Cuno	3,390,000	June 1998
1990 OS	8,750,000	November 2003

Table 5 (Continued)

....

Observed Recent Close Calls

Asteroid	Distance	Date	Size (meters)
1994 XM1	102,900	12/9/94	9
1993 KA2	147,000	5/20/93	6
1991 BA	160,000	1/18/91	7
1994 ES1	162,000	3/15/94	7
1995 FF	426,000	5/27/95	18
1996 JA1	440,000	5/19/96	220
1991 VG	565,000	12/4/91	50
4581 Asclepius	676,000	3/22/89	280
1994 WR12	705,000	11/24/94	140
1937 Hermes	720,000	10/30/37	900

Note: For comparison, the Earth-Moon distance is 350,000 kilometers or 224,000 miles.

in Plate 4. Many of the smaller satellites in the solar system, such as the moons of Mars and Jupiter, look like this. [2779, 2590, 1648, 884, 844, 704, 80]

99 What would the Cretaceous impactor have looked like from the ground?

About 65 million years ago, an asteroid several kilometers across and called the Cretaceous impactor hit Earth near the Yucatan Peninsula of Mexico and Central America. The impact apparently altered Earth's climate long enough to kill off all of the large dinosaurs and helped set the stage for the emergence and eventual dominance of mammals, such as ourselves.

The object would have entered the atmosphere more than 100 kilometers up and in 5 seconds or so impacted the ground. An asteroid 2 kilometers across, from a viewing distance of 100 kilometers from the impact site, would have a size about twice the diameter of the full moon, but the surrounding fireball would have been much larger. An instant before it impacted, the fireball would probably have filled half the sky at this distance. Sound travels at about 300 meters/sec, and the supersonic shock wave from the impact would have taken about 5.5 minutes to reach you. From 100 kilometers the streaking of the fireball through the sky would have been silent. The shock wave would have looked like a solid wall of high-temperature gas and rock mixed together into an incinerating 2,000–5,000 kelvin wall of flames. The brightness of this fireball would have been amazing. At contact with the atmosphere 100 kilometers up, its solid body alone, heated to more than 2,000 degrees, would have been larger than the Sun, which means that from the ground you would have been bathed by light from a new, moving mini-sun many times the apparent brightness of the Sun itself. Just before impact, the 5,000-degree fireball would have covered most of the sky with a brilliance many times greater than the Sun itself. Even the word "blinding" fails to describe what you would have seen. These are my best back-of-the-envelope estimates. Actual research suggests that the Cretaceous impactor, given the angle of its trajectory on impact, sent out a searing wall of flames that may have engulfed many parts of North America thousands of kilometers from the impact site. [2771]

100 What would happen if a large object hit Earth?

By the end of 1992, astronomers had discovered 163 asteroids with orbits that crossed Earth's orbit. These Apollo-Amor class of asteroids are prime candidates for eventual impacts with Earth in the distant future. The largest of these is 1627 Ivar, which is 8 kilometers across and contains 1 trillion tons of mass. Smaller asteroids are much more numerous as a rule of thumb. According to the best estimates, objects 3 meters across impact Earth every year and deliver about 2 kilotons of TNT of energy. Objects 100 meters across collide with Earth every few hundred years and deliver the equivalent of about 2 megatons of TNT. A 1 kilometer–sized object impacts Earth every 10 million years or so and delivers about 100,000 megatons of TNT.

Table 6 shows how the consequences of impacts depend on the size of the asteroid. For ocean impacts of objects about 300 meters across, the tidal waves (tsunamis) produce more damage

Table 6 **Estimates of the expected damage to Earth from the impact of asteroids of various sizes.** Note that impacts on land usually cause considerable local damage but limited global effects, while ocean impacts produce effects on most of the globe via tsunamis.

Asteroid Size	Yield (megatons)	Crater (kilometers)	Effect
75 m	100	1.5	Land impact destroys major metropolitan area, e.g., Washington, D.C., or Paris.
350 m	5,000	6.0	Land impact destroys an area the size of a small state; ocean impact produces tsunamis.
700 m	15,000	12.0	Land impact destroys an area the size of Virginia or Taiwan; ocean impact produces major tsunamis.
1.7 km	200,000	30.0	Land impact affects climate, ozone; tsunamis from ocean impact destroy coastal communities.
3.0 km	1 million	60.0	Large nation destroyed, widespread fires from ejecta, and major climate change.
7.0 km	50 million	125	Mass extinction, global conflagration, and long-term climate change.

than an equivalent impact on land. Fortunately, humans occupy so little of the surface of Earth that, although these impacts happen about once every century or so, in the past no one was around to see them.

Ocean impacts of bodies in the 700-meter range would produce major tidal waves that would reach the shores of many continents. For asteroids in the 1- to 2-kilometer range, these waves would be 300 feet high and travel 20 or more kilometers inland, putting at risk about 100 million people, or 2 percent of the world population. Such an object would be discovered several days in advance by direct detection by NORAD, so the question is whether enough people could make it to safety. Traffic jams out of urban centers near coastlines could easily last a week or so. [2784, 2728, 2613, 975]

101 How should a near-Earth asteroid be deflected?

Many scientists believe that launching nuclear-tipped rockets to deflect or fragment the intruder would be a good strategy. A laser, on the other hand, could deliver heat to the surface of a cometary body and evaporate it to produce a jet of gases emanating from the point of contact at high speed. Over time, this might provide enough thrust to affect the comet's orbit. It would not work as well with the more common solid, rocky bodies, because the power delivered to those surfaces would be insufficient to vaporize solid rock.

There is a lot of work to be done on both these issues. We do not have rockets out there waiting to be launched on three-weeks notice, and we do not have any firm ideas about whether a given explosion will deflect or fragment a near-Earth object. Aside from a few study groups, there is no concerted effort by any nation to develop a fleet of rockets on standby alert that would be ready to go if such an object was discovered next month. We humans are master procrastinators. The likelihood that you will be in some way affected by such an impact either physically or economically during your lifetime is about the same as dying in an airplane accident, when averaged over all of the 6 billion people on our planet over a 70-year period. Humans only respond to an imminent crisis, so I am afraid we will have to experience the deaths of millions of people in a future impact before we take this possibility seriously. Do you feel lucky? [2537, 1453, 977, 974, 895, 848]

102 Has anyone ever been hit by a meteor?

Yep! And there have been plenty of near misses too! On October 9, 1992, a meteorite slammed into a parked 1980 Chevy Malibu then owned by Michelle Knapp in Peekskill, New York. Plate 5 shows the damage sustained by the car. As described in the February 1993 issue of *Sky and Telescope,* it was a 27-pound meteorite, probably related to a spectacular meteor that was seen in the sky of neighboring states shortly before impact. Many people saw the meteorite, and its tentative trajectory followed a shallow entry near the border of Virginia and West Virginia and traveled north-northeast. The car, with its damaged rear end, was purchased by a rock collector and is now an attraction at national rockhound and meteorite conventions. There have been other falls in which meteorites have crashed through houses, and even a grazing strike with a human, which, fortunately, was not fatal. According to *Sky and Telescope* (January 1954), Mrs. Hewlett Hodges of Sylocuga, Alabama, was struck in the hip on November 30, 1953, by a meteorite that crashed through her living room ceiling. [501]

103 How many meteors enter Earth's atmosphere every day?

Lots! Astronomers at the University of Adelaide in Australia have been using radar to monitor incoming meteors. When meteorites slam into the atmosphere, they produce trails of ionized gas. As reported in the *Nature* (March 28, 1996), the AMOR radar installation in New Zealand was used for a year to detect 350,000 faint echos from very small meteorites, with sizes between 0.01 to 0.1 millimeters or about the size of large dust grains. This works out to nearly 1,000 every day, just from this one site alone. The estimates are that on any given day Earth intercepts about 19,000 meteorites weighing more than 3.5 ounces, of which fewer than 10 every year are ever recovered. Earth acquires about 100 tons per day of dust-sized micrometeoroids. [896]

104 In Akron, Ohio, in the 1960s, the entire sky was lit up by a fast-moving object bigger than the Moon with molten colors on the surface but no tail. What was it?

An eyewitness writes: "In the summer of the mid-1960s in Akron, Ohio, around 9:00 P.M. the entire sky lit up like high noon seconds before anything was visible. Then a fireball appeared several times larger than the Moon. It had every color and a boiling surface moving slow enough to see molten colors moving on the surface. No tail. It made a hissing sound. When it disappeared, the sky stayed bright for a second or two. The rumbling sound went away slowly. The entire event lasted about 5 seconds." This "Ohio fireball" was briefly described in the December 1967 issue of *Sky and Telescope*. It happened on September 10, 1967, at 8:50 P.M. and was observed from northern Ohio. It moved from east to west and broke up into two smaller bodies near Oberlin. The eyewitness was probably right underneath the ground track of the fireball. Very few humans are privileged to be in the right place at the right time to see nature at its most awesome.

Although most meteors are produced by particles of dust no bigger than beach sand entering the atmosphere at high speeds, occasionally some of the larger chunks of rock that wander interplanetary space hit the atmosphere. These chunks can be anything from basketball-sized to the size of small cars. These rare collisions are what we see as fireballs. If you are lucky, you will see perhaps one or two of these in your lifetime. [2836]

105 What is a comet?

A comet is a ball of water and carbon dioxide ices mixed with dust grains and perhaps small rocks and even complex organic molecules. Before the solar system was formed, the cloud out of which it formed had countless trillions of these bodies mixed in with a cloud of various gases of carbon monoxide, hydrogen, formaldehyde, ammonia, and so on. By a process we still do not understand, this gas clumped up into cometary bodies that probably measured from 1 centimeter to tens of kilometers in size. Today, all that remains around the solar system of this original cloud are the numerous cometary bodies that occasionally get kicked into orbits that bring them into the inner solar system. Because the reservoir of these cometary bodies, called the Oort Cloud, is so vast, we will continue to see comets for billions of years, even after most of the asteroidal bodies have vanished. [2731, 2299, 1719, 918]

106 How big do comets get?

The actual icy core of a comet, called its nucleus, can be anywhere from a kilometer across to 50 kilometers across for the rare supercomets, like Hale-Bopp. By the time they enter the inner solar system and their ices begin to turn to gas, they billow like clouds into objects with cores thousands of kilometers across and tails that can stretch tens of millions of kilometers as the ices in the nuclei are heated and give off gas and dust clouds and streamers. The nuclear regions can produce halo clouds of particles and gas called comas, which are larger than the diameter of the Sun! [2965, 2298, 2121]

107 Why do some comets have two tails?

Comets produce gas and dust in large quantities as they approach the Sun and the inner solar system. The gas can be ionized by the harsh ultraviolet light from the Sun, so that comet tails contain a complicated mixture of dust, ionized gas, and neutral gas. The reason a comet develops two tails is because the ionized and neutral gases go one way in space, because they are affected by the magnetic fields and gases in the solar wind, but the dust is less sensitive to the solar wind and continues to go its own way. Generally, the dust tails follow along the orbit of the comet, and the gas tail follows in the direction of the outgoing solar wind at that location. Sometimes the ionized gas undergoes complex and rapidly changing motions as it interacts with kinks in the solar magnetic field. This produces cusps and kinks in the tail that travel from the head of the comet down the gas tail in a matter of hours or days. [2805, 1882]

108 Why aren't comets captured by planets when they come close?

They move too fast and are too far away from most planets to be captured by them. Believe it or not, by the time you see a spectacular comet in the sky, it can be literally tens of millions of kilometers from Earth. Jupiter has managed to capture a handful of cometlike bodies as its outer satellites, but, generally, the capture of a single body by a planet is very difficult, because just the right amount of angular momentum and kinetic energy have to be shed for the body to be inserted into a stable orbit. With the impact of Comet Shoemaker-Levy on Jupiter, the comet's orbit actually intersected Jupiter itself, producing one of the most spectacular interplanetary events ever seen. [2883, 2738]

109 How do astronomers compute the orbit of a comet?

First you have to make at least three observations of the location of the comet in the sky, during which time the comet has to move an appreciable distance along its orbit. Then, these sky coordinates are translated into ecliptic heliocentric coordinates, and an ellipse is "fit" through the three data points to get the six parameters that define an orbit in space. As more observations become available, a better fit can be achieved. The dimension and orientation of the ellipse give its inclination, size, eccentricity, and period, among other defining orbit elements. [2936, 594]

110 How fast is Comet Hale-Bopp moving through space?

Usually objects falling "from infinity" have speeds near the local escape velocity. For the inner solar system, this is very approximately 30 km/sec or 69,000 miles per hour. [2868, 2729, 2726, 2594, 2093, 1619, 1090]

111 Is it a conspiracy that no major observatories have photographed Hale-Bopp since October 1996?

Everyone loves a good conspiracy theory, but you won't find evidence for one here. How do you hide a celestial phenomenon from the whole world? The problem is that comets are so big that large telescopes are useless for studying them. In the February 1997 issue of *Astronomy,* there is a photograph taken with the world's largest electronic camera, on the Canada-France-Hawaii Telescope on Mauna Kea. It is a 3.5-meter telescope and nearly as big as the Hubble Space Telescope. In the December 12, 1996, science section of the *New York Times,* it was reported that astronomer Harold Weaver of the Applied Research Corporation in Landover, Maryland, took a photo of the nucleus of Hale-Bopp with the Hubble Telescope. [2851, 313]

112 What would the surface of Hale-Bopp look like up close?

From spacecraft studies of Halley's comet, the surface would be pitted with craters and fault lines. Heaps of rocks and dust would probably be piled up everywhere, because the ice that originally bound them into a conglomerate has evaporated. There would be many active (and some inactive) vents spewing jets of water vapor and gases into the coma of the comet. There would also be a haze of vapor and frozen ices that would surround the nucleus and grow thicker as the comet gets nearer the Sun. Think of a dirty iceberg covered with dust and gravel and exposed icy patches. [2773]

113 What is your opinion about the recent discovery of thousands of minicomets pummeling the Earth every minute?

More than a decade ago, Louis A. Frank, a noted space physicist at the University of Iowa, proposed that the dark spots seen in ultraviolet photographs of Earth from space were caused by compact, water-rich bodies pummeling Earth's atmosphere more than 1,000 kilometers above the surface at a rate of several per minute. If this water ever reached the surface, it would fill the world's oceans to their present level in fewer than 1 billion years. His revolutionary conclusion was met with considerable resistance, despite the fact that he was a leading world figure in space research at the time. No one faulted him for his care in analyzing the data, only in the provocative conclusion he embraced to explain the numerous "holes" he was seeing in Earth's ultraviolet satellite images.

In 1997, after analyzing data from a new ultraviolet imager he had developed and which flew on NASA's *POLAR* satellite, not only did Frank see in the data the same holes viewed a decade earlier, but the holes were now large enough not to be single-pixel blemishes or data dropouts. Moreover, with images taken in a specific band sensitive to the emission of light by water, he offered to the scientific community not just holes but, as Plate 6 seems to show, the long streak of a minicomet just before impact. As an astronomer, I have a problem with this image, because *all* digital images show not only the object you are seeing, but also background noise from all the other pixels. As Plate 6 shows, these noisy pixels somehow have been scrubbed from Frank's image, which means that we are not seeing a true image of what *POLAR* saw but an altered image designed to enhance the minicomet trail. Without the rest of the pixels, we cannot tell just what this minicomet really is photographically.

Presumably, all this activity appears to occur more than 1,000 kilometers above Earth, well above the orbits of the space shuttle, but now there are far more observatories in space and none has ever seen such a frenetic level of activity. No one understands where these minicomets, which are the size of a house, might come from. No one understands how they can remain so unobservable, although Frank says that if you observe the sky for about 100 hours, you, will see one or two of these impact flashes with a fleeting brilliance equal to Venus.

Airborne infrared observatories, such as the NASA Kuiper Airborne Observatory, work at very high stratospheric altitudes, precisely because these altitudes are so dry and free of water in any form. If the water comet scenario is correct, no one can understand where all the water goes before it gets to the stratosphere. According to Frank, most of this water never makes it below the tropopause. Some scientists legitimately ask why these 20-ton comets have not changed the surface of the Moon in any detectable way. Why haven't the seismometers on the Moon recorded these impacts? Frank says they are of such a low density that their impacts go unnoticed and their water is immediately ejected into space because of the low lunar escape velocity.

There are many questions raised by these observations and no good answers, assuming that the data have been interpreted correctly. And in the astronomy business, you have to be very, very careful how you interpret data. The jury is still out on exactly what it all means. The recent data obtained on these minicomets are very provocative, and there are now five papers by Frank working their way through the professional refereeing process at several scientific journals. For more information about where this controversy stands, see articles in *Sky and Telescope* (August 1997), *Scientific American* (August 1997), and *New Scientist* (July 12, 1997). You might also want to visit Frank's web site to get his personal point of view (smallcomets.physics.uiowa.edu/), and at which he, rightly or wrongly, portrays himself as an underdog that has been unjustly subjected to much ridicule, hardship, and loss of scientific respect since he put forth his idea. [11021, 10782]

114 How fast do the nuclei of comets rotate?

Observations of Halley's comet by the *Vega* and *Giotto* spacecraft, as well as ground-based studies in the 1980s, showed two nuclear rotation periods of this potato-shaped comet nucleus. A 2.2–2.4-day period, and a 7.4-day period. Not enough is really known about other comets to unambiguously determine a rotation period, but their periods are most likely the same to within a factor of 10. [2299]

115 How much notice would we get from a asteroid like the one that hit Earth 65 million years ago?

This asteroid was several miles across, and, hopefully, in the next 10 years we will have identified most of the objects that have orbits that cross that of Earth. In principle, one could then make forecasts such as the one described in the answer to question 98, that would be reasonably accurate for a few years at a time, given all the gravitational perturbations that can occur between such bodies and the other objects in the solar system. If we did not know of the existence of the asteroid prior to impact, we might only have a week's notice or less, depending on its trajectory. The problem is that during the days and weeks just before impact, such an object would be moving almost directly toward Earth and not have much of a motion across the sky. This makes identifying asteroids on the basis of rapid motion in the sky very difficult. All we might see would be its increase in brightness from a starlike object. If it happened to be in or near the plane of the Milky Way, it would easily be confused with background stars in such a nightly search. Traveling at 30 kilometers/sec, by the time it got to the orbital distance of the Moon, deep-space radars might detect the object, which would only be about 34 hours from impact. [2590, 2537, 2154, 975, 974, 896, 501, 80]

116 Can an asteroid have an atmosphere?

An asteroid such as Ceres, which is 380 kilometers in radius, has a mass of about 10^{24} grams. Its escape velocity is something like 600 meters per second. The rule of thumb is that in order to remain captured, an atmosphere must not have a mean thermal speed more than one-sixth the escape velocity from the body. Thus, the atoms in the Ceres atmosphere cannot be moving faster than about 100 meters per second. The speed of an atom of gas depends on its mass and the temperature to which the gas is heated. For Ceres, its surface temperature is about 200 K, and for very heavy xenon atoms weighing about 2×10^{-22} grams, their typical speeds are about 200 meters per second. This is within a factor of 2 of the critical velocity given the asteroid's mass. This means that Ceres might have had an atmosphere made up mostly of xenon gas early in its history, but most of this has probably been lost by now, blasted into space by all the meteoritic impacts on its surface over the millennia. Still, we won't know until we get there. [1457]

The stars are one of the more popular categories at the Astronomy Cafe—more than 350 questions covering everything from individual stars to whether you can see stars in the daytime from the bottom of a well. The nature of the Star of Bethlehem has been a seasonal favorite near Christmas, and there have been many requests for information about specific stars, such as Polaris, Alpha Centauri, and Eta Carina. There are many opportunities in my answers to review what astronomers now know about how stars evolve and to reassure everyone that the Sun will never become a supernova. These things don't just happen out of the blue but depend on the mass of the star, and the Sun simply doesn't have enough to make its future evolution quite this spectacular. I particularly enjoy discussing Betelgeuse, which is an ancient supergiant star near the Sun and one that astronomers are confident will become a supernova in the next million years or so. It will be a spectacular sight, and for many months out of the year we will have two suns in the sky with no nighttime, as either the Sun or Betelgeuse will be above the horizon. Other questions that are particularly interesting to me and popular with the public are "Why are there no green stars?" and "Is there a constellation called the Poop?"

117 What do stars look like up close?

Probably very much like the Sun but with colors that depend on their surface temperature. Some have sunspots that come in cycles or are perhaps permanent or absent, depending on the convectiveness of their outer layers. Some stars may even have spots that cover sizable fractions of their surface area. The surfaces of the cooler stars will boil and convect like hot cereal on a stove top. Very hot stars will have calm and featureless surfaces, because they are fully radiative in their outer layers and have no convection cells. In close binary systems, the stars will be very distorted and have lots of surface magnetic activity in sunspots and flares. [2967]

118 How often do stars explode in space and become shooting stars?

Stars do not become shooting stars, which are what some cultures call meteors. These are just sand-sized pieces of rock and cometary ice chunks that enter Earth's atmosphere. [2963]

119 Can I get a star named after my wife on our anniversary?

When I was a student at the University of California, Berkeley, in the 1970s, I bought an acre of land on Mercury for $25, but that was for some noble, charitable cause. The International Astronomical Union is the only sanctioned body that has the authority to name celestial bodies. Any names that you or a commercial enterprise care to attach to a celestial body would not be legally recognized, nor would they be used by the astronomical community in technical journals and other scientific literature. Naming conventions are strictly adhered to for both solar system and deep-space objects. What is the point of naming something if the name is not recognized by any agency? [27]

120 How hot do stars get?

The Sun is about 5,770 K. Newly formed white dwarfs and neutron stars can have temperatures above 200,000 K for a few years before cooling rapidly to below 50,000 K. For normal stars that still have internal energy supplied by thermonuclear reactions, temperatures as high as 50,000 K or so have been seen in what astronomers call Wolf-Rayet stars. Only about 100 of these are known to exist in the entire Milky Way. Stellar core temperatures, on the other hand, can get even hotter. The core temperature of the Sun is near 14 million K. In the center of a star about to go supernova, temperatures as high as several billion kelvins can occur. [2966, 185]

121 How long does it take for stars to form?

Computer models suggest that the initial phase of the collapse of a gas cloud takes a few million years. Most of the collapse into a prestellar object occurs during this period of time. After about 10 million years, the object has stabilized as a young star. [2984, 1121, 612, 183]

122 How old do stars get?

The life of a star depends only on the amount of mass of the star. The smaller its mass, the longer it lives. As shown in Table 7, stars that are 10 times the mass of the Sun will last about 20 million years, and stars with about the Sun's mass last about 14 billion years. Stars about one-tenth the mass of the Sun last 500 billion years or longer. These are rough estimates, but they can be made very precise by astronomers who study the physics of how stars evolve and change with time. As for the average lifetime of a star, it turns out that the average star in the Milky Way is about half the mass of the Sun and will live about 50 billion years. [2961, 1997, 655, 614, 611, 608, 607, 585]

123 If stars come in colors, why do they all appear white to the eye?

This is a complicated subject, but the sensation of color comes in part from the difference between retinal cone and rod cells in the human eye. The cones are not very light sensitive, and below a fixed threshold, they stop responding. The rods, however, are very sensitive photoreceptors, even at low light levels, but they only sense black and white, or, more correctly, they are monochromatic. When you look at the brightest stars with the naked eye, or when you use a telescope to concentrate the light that falls on your retina, the light can be above the threshold at which the cones register color, but for the thousands of other stars in the skies fainter than these brightest stars, only the

Table 7 **The basic properties of stars, including their approximate colors, surface temperatures, mass as compared to the Sun's mass, and their lifetimes.** The most massive stars in the Milky Way have not been around as long as humans.

Type	Color	Temperature (kelvins)	Mass (Sun = 1)	Approximate Life (years)
O	Blue	50,000	40	1 million
B	Blue-white	20,000	10	20 million
A	White	10,000	5	400 million
F	Yellow-white	8,000	2	2 billion
G	Yellow	5,000	1	14 billion
K	Orange	4,000	0.5	50 billion
M	Red	3,000	0.2	140 billion

monochromatic rods see anything and do not pass on color information to the visual cortex of the brain. There is also the problem that the retinal cells do not respond in the same way to the incoming light at each wavelength. The product of this response with the way that the light from each star is naturally distributed in wavelength apparently also leads to the sensation of blue or white for stars much hotter than the Sun, as indicated in Table 7. [1534, 1035, 619, 266, 72]

124 Why aren't there any green stars?

The color of a star is a combination of two phenomena. The first is the star's temperature, which determines the wavelength (frequency) where the peak of its electromagnetic radiation will emerge in the spectrum. A cool object, like an iron rod heated to 3,000 K, will emit most of its light at wavelengths near 9,000 angstroms in wavelength. A very hot object, at a temperature of 30,000 K, will emit its light near a wavelength of 900 angstroms. The amount of energy emitted at other wavelengths is precisely determined by the body's temperature and by Planck's radiation law. But color is another matter.

Color is a perception we humans have because of the kinds of pigments used in our retina. Our eyes do not sense light evenly across the visible spectrum but have a greater sensitivity for green light and somewhat less for red and blue light. If I were to figure out how hot a star would have to be for its peak of its emission to be in the green area of the human color spectrum near 4,000 angstroms, I would estimate that the temperature of the star would have to be about 10,000 K. There are many such stars in the sky. The two brightest of these A-type stars are Vega in the constellation Lyra, and Sirius in Canis Majoris. But if you were to look at them in the sky, they would appear white, not green! This is not the same sequence of colors you see in a rainbow (red, orange, yellow, green, blue), because the distribution of energy in the light source is different, and in the case of the rainbow, optical refraction in a raindrop is added.

So, there are no genuinely green stars because stars with the expected temperature emit their light in a way that our eye combines into the perception of whiteness. For more information on star colors, have a look at the article by Philip Steffey in the September 1992 issue of *Sky and Telescope,* which gives a thorough discussion of stellar colors and how we perceive them. [72]

125 Was Sirius ever a red star?

Sirius is the brightest star in the sky for northern observers during the winter months. Looking through ancient reports of its color, however, it was occasionally identified as a red star. A decade or so ago, there was a lot of interest in this issue, and astronomers were perplexed that the white dwarf accompanying Sirius could have gone from a red giant to a white dwarf phase in only a few thousand years, leaving no trace of any circumstellar gas behind. Usually, this evolutionary transition leads to a planetary nebula and expanding gas that lasts tens of thousands of years. The red Sirius mystery seems to have been resolved in a study of the literature of the Greek-Roman period in which the alleged red moniker used to describe Sirius had nothing to do with its actual color, but with some other usage of the term "red," which had other meanings at the time. I'm sorry to be so vague, but the bottom line is that the red Sirius mystery is no longer a mystery to astronomers, thanks to some sleuthing by historians familiar with the literature of the time. [2283]

126 Why isn't Ophiuchus a zodiacal constellation?

Beats me! Ophiuchus is a constellation that star charts show is located in the zodiac between the constellations Sagittarius and Scorpius. If you look at any star chart, you will see that the narrow path that the planets and the Sun move along, called the ecliptic, passes through the 12 classical zodiacal constellations, plus it comes within 0.5 degree of the northern corner of Orion, 0.25 degree from the northwest corner of Cetus, 1 degree from the northeast corner of Sextans, and it passes through the entire southern quadrant of Ophiuchus. With a little more precession of Earth's spin axis, no doubt the ecliptic will also include pieces of Orion, Cetus, and Sextans. The problem is that constellation boundaries have been redrawn several times in the past five centuries. Astronomers don't care, and astrologers only use the classical, ancient definitions of where the zodiacal constellations are located. Ophiuchus would be no doubt an unlucky thirteenth house, so it is simply ignored. [1640]

127 Can you hear stars?

Yes, you can, but it requires a radio telescope and a way of converting the electromagnetic signals into audio signals. The sound is typically very monotonous and noisy, the audio analog of what you see on your TV screen when no station is broadcasting. Pulsars, however, can be heard to pulse dozens of times a second. The sound from other stars doesn't change during the few minutes you usually listen, and it sounds like ocean waves hitting a beach or some strange wind. The most interesting and eerie sounds are those of Earth and Jupiter. You hear whistles and peculiar choruses of sound that slide up and down in pitch like some alien electronic singing. [2969]

128 What is a red giant star?

A red giant star is a star like our Sun that is in the last stages of its life. Hydrogen fusion reactions have become less efficient in the star's core, and with the gravitational collapse of the hydrogen-poor core, the fusion reactions occur in the hydrogen-rich shell surrounding the core. This increases the luminosity of the star enormously (up to 1,000 times the Sun) and the star expands. The outer layers then cool to only 3,000 K or so and you get a red star, but its size is now equal to the orbit of Mercury, Venus, or even Earth. After a few more million years, the star evolves into a white dwarf–planetary nebula system and then it dies. The closest red giant is Beta Andromedae, also called Mirach. It is about 75 light years from the Sun and has a luminosity about 75 times that of the Sun. [2958, 2942, 2336, 2224, 587]

129 Are there more grains of sand on the beach than stars in the universe?

Not by a long shot. And if the universe is infinite, then the answer is a flat no. In our visible universe alone, there are 100 billion galaxies, each with a few billion stars on average, which gives you 1 billion times 100 billion or 100 billion billion (10^{20}) stars. A grain of sand is perhaps 1 millimeter in diameter and weighs 0.003 grams, so this gives you 3×10^{17} grams for the anticipated beach sand, if one grain of sand equals one star. The mass of Earth is 6×10^{27} grams, but most of this is in the interior, not on continental shelves or ocean bottoms. The critical amount of beach sand would have to weigh a half billionth of the mass of Earth, which is unreasonably high. So, there are far fewer grains of sand on the beach than stars in the universe and probably around a million stars for every grain of sand. [2865]

130 Does the Nemesis star really exist?

In the early 1980s, astronomers Marc Davis and Richard Muller of the University of California, Berkeley, proposed that the apparent 25–30-million-year ebb and flow in the cratering record of Earth might be caused by a small, dim, dwarf companion to the sun called Nemesis. It would be in a highly elliptical orbit with a size of 90,000 AUs and a period of 26 million years. A similar periodicity was claimed for the pattern of ancient biological extinctions in the fossil record by David Raup and John Sepkoski of the University of Chicago in 1986. The basic idea is that this star would perturb the Oort Cloud and send millions of comets raining down on the inner solar system. Astronomers no longer take this idea seriously in light of the uncertainties in the extinction and cratering history data. The star would be so loosely held by the Sun's gravity that its interaction with other stars would likely eject it from any orbit with respect to the Sun. See *Cosmic Catastrophes* by Clark Chapman and David Morrison, (Plenum Press, 1989) for more on Nemesis. [744]

131 What is the furthest star we know about?

One of the stars furthest from Earth that I know about is V12, or Variable 12, in the galaxy NGC 4203. This galaxy is located 10.4 million light years away. The star is about 10 million times brighter than our Sun. The Hubble Space Telescope is such a powerful telescope, that it can also see less luminous stars in the Messier 100 galaxy (see www.stsci.edu/pubinfo/PR/94/49.html for variables in this galaxy), located in the Virgo cluster of galaxies, which, according to astronomer Wendy Freedman at the Carnegie Observatories in Pasadena, California, is now determined to be at a distance of 56 million ± 6 million light years. Supernovae are individual stars, and many of these have been detected in galaxies more than 1 billion light years away as they flare to brilliance and temporarily outshine their entire host galaxy. [609, 615]

132 What is the most massive star we know about?

The most massive star known in the Milky Way galaxy is Eta Carina, and it has an estimated mass of about 120 times that of the Sun. In the nearby Large Magellanic Cloud, the star HDE 269801 weighs in at 190 times the mass of the Sun. These stars are so hard for nature to make that there are only a handful of them in a galaxy as big as the Milky Way, which contains more than 200 billion stars. Eta Carina is located 8,200 light years from the Sun. We do not think that stars can get heavier than about 200 times the Sun's mass, because the pressure caused by the light they emit into space becomes so enormous that it causes these stars to evaporate, losing large quantities of their mass back into space in a few thousand years. The lifetimes of such massive Wolf-Rayet stars are literally only a few tens of thousands of years. [2278, 2196, 609, 184, 183]

133 Has anyone determined what the Star of Bethlehem might have been?

There have been many ideas bandied about over the years. Astronomers have considered supernovae and planetary conjunctions as the most likely prospects, but neither is convincing to everyone. A supernova has definitely been excluded because they are lengthy affairs that take a week to reach maximum brilliance and months to vanish. Also, all the supernova remnants younger than 5,000 years are known to us, because they are powerful X-ray and radio sources. None dates from 2,000 years ago.

In the December 1986 issue of *Sky and Telescope,* Roger Sinnott, an associate editor at the magazine, discussed the various astronomical phenomena that might explain the Star of Bethlehem. An April 1987 letter to this magazine by James DeYoung and James Hilton at the U.S. Naval Observatory had further comments to make about an unusual planetary conjunction between Venus and Jupiter that occurred on June 17, 2 B.C. This conjunction would have been very spectacular, because Venus and Jupiter came within 25.5 arc seconds of each other, and because at that time Jupiter had a size of 32 arc seconds, and Venus 25.6, they would have appeared to be a single bright "star" in the sky in the constellation Leo, a constellation identified with the Jews by the Ancients.

Other pertinent articles in *Sky and Telescope* include: "Thoughts on the Star of Bethlehem" (December 1968), "Computing the Star of Bethlehem" (December 1986), "The Star of Bethlehem" (April 1987), and "The Coins of Antioch" (January 1992). [341,93]

134 Is there a rogue star that will eventually end life on the Earth?

Astronomers Joan Garcia-Sanchez and Robert Preston at the Jet Propulsion Laboratory have used the recent *Hipparchos* satellite data to identify stars that will pass close to the Sun during the next million years. One of these is a star called Gleise 710, now about 63 light years away in the constellation Ophiuchus and described in the August 1997 issue of *Sky and Telescope.* This "bad boy" seems to be on track to approach within 1 light year of the Sun about 1 million years from now, which is a distance estimated to be well inside the Oort Cloud. That could unleash a hail of comets into the inner solar system and make life very uncomfortable for us for thousands of years. It will also make for some spectacular night skies, as this red dwarf star glows brightly at a visual magnitude of +0.6, making it one of the brightest stars in the entire sky. [764]

135 How far is Proxima Centauri from Alpha Centauri?

Alpha Centauri A, B, and Proxima Centauri are members of a three-star system about 4.3 light years from the Sun in the southern constellation Centaurus. Alpha Centauri A and Proxima Centauri have a separation of 12,560 AUs, or just over 1 trillion miles. The common expectation has long been that planets cannot exist around stars in a multiple-star system. Recent computer calculations of planetary orbital dynamics suggest that if the planets formed within a few times the Earth-Sun distance from any of the three stars in this system, they can survive for billions of years before being ejected. No one has ever detected any hint of planets bigger than Earth around these three well-placed stars, although the Hubble Space Telescope has recently been used to search for them. [1849, 1548, 1546, 1411, 693, 375]

136 Can you see stars from the bottom of a well?

From the bottom of a 50-foot well that is 6 feet in diameter, the sky would subtend the same angle to the eye as a 1.5-inch diameter tube of 1 foot length held up to the eye. If you do this experiment in the daytime, you will see that no stars come out by sighting through such a tube. This experiment was actually performed in England by, I believe, amateur astronomer and science author Patrick Moore, who used a smokestack and a group of students. He selected a time when the bright star Vega should have been in view through the opening, but the results for sighting this bright star at the bottom of the smokestack were negative. [241]

137 Can astronomers predict when a star will become a nova or a supernova?

Not really, at least not so that it matters. Novae are produced in binary (two-star) systems in which one of the two stars is a white dwarf or a neutron star and the other is a normal star, usually a red giant that has a distended outer atmosphere. Some of this material can be captured by the dense neutron star companion via a process called Roche-lobe overflow. Depending on a variety of factors, the dense companion will flare up as a nova periodically or simply blow itself to pieces as a Type I supernova. The dynamics of the nova process are sufficiently complex that we do not yet have a good way to predict when outbursts will occur from a cold start unless the process is periodic, which seems to be the case for some reoccurring novae.

We have good theoretical reasons to believe that supernova precursor stars will be red supergiants, if their heavy element content is like that of the Sun, or perhaps blue supergiants, if they have somewhat lower heavy element abundances than the Sun, as was apparently the case for Supernova 1987A in the Large Magellanic Cloud. For more about this, read Al Mann's *Shadow of a Star* (W.H. Freeman, 1997). A few thousand years before it becomes a supernova, the star may have a composition that suggests a great deal of chemical enrichment of its surface by convection from its nuclear core. There may be a sudden increase in the velocity of its stellar wind and the thickness of its circumstellar dust envelope. As we learn more about the theory behind the explosion, we can better anticipate just what kinds of things to look for observationally. [2334, 1041, 966, 965, 141]

138 What exactly happens to a star about to go supernova?

This is still a subject of intense study using sophisticated computer models, but what seems to happen is as follows. Once a significant amount of iron ash has accumulated in the core, the core begins to collapse and heat up, but by this time the temperature is more than 1 billion degrees kelvin. At these temperatures, neutrinos are produced in such huge quantities that they transport energy out of the interior of the star into space. At the same time, the gamma ray photons produced by fusion reactions in the core carry so much energy that each time they slam into an iron nucleus, the nucleus shatters into 13 helium nuclei and the gamma ray photon is lost from the core. This means that the core loses internal support from light pressure as the gamma rays are absorbed by the iron nuclei. Meanwhile, the iron nuclei are prevented from fusing into heavier nuclei because of an insurmountable energy barrier. The net result is that the core continues to collapse, produces more neutrinos, and loses still more internal pressure. This process runs away with itself until the density of the core, in a matter of hours, becomes so large that the neutrinos can no longer escape. In virtually an instant, the neutrinos dump most of their energy into the outer layers of the collapsing core and trigger an explosion. A shock wave travels from the outer core, out through the star's extended atmosphere (it is a red supergiant star by this time), and when this breaks through we see the huge pulse of light that signals the supernova explosion. Because for every reaction there is an equal and opposite one, the expanding shock wave also spawns an inward-traveling shock wave that implodes the core of the star either into a neutron star cinder or a black hole. The details depend on the mass of the core when the supernova detonates. [2954, 2008, 186]

139 Are any stars about to go supernova?

My favorite candidates are Eta Carina and Betelgeuse, but we are talking anywhere from thousands to hundreds of thousands of years, or maybe tomorrow morning! Between 1958 and 1975 the Palomar Supernova Search program photographed 3,000 galaxies in clusters every moonless night and found 281 supernovae. A search of the International Astronomical Union daily discovery reports showed that on February 7, 1997, Supernova 1997Z in the galaxy NGC 3261 had been discovered, making it the twenty-sixth supernova that year alone. Now, just in case you really want to feel nervous, among the brightest stars in the sky there are many that are massive stars destined to become supernovae and end up as black holes. These stars are Polaris, Rigel, Alnilam, Alnitak, Betelgeuse, Antares, and Deneb. Most of the stars in the constellation Orion are only 1,500 light years away and are massive O- and B-type stars that are prime candidates for supernovae. Betelgeuse will go first, probably within another million years or less. After 100 million years or so, all the other stars that make up the constellation will blow up one by one. Our solar system will be rocked by the expanding shells from these stars for millions of years once the fireworks begin. [2978, 2861, 2574]

140 How close can we be to a supernova without being damaged?

The star Betelgeuse is a good supernova candidate, about 1,500 light years distant. I think this is uncomfortably close, but for some real excitement, let's put the limit at about 10–50 light years, even though there are no supernova candidates this close. Once a star explodes, after thousands of years, it will produce a vast bubble of ionized and X-ray-emitting gas that can measure hundreds of light years across. Anything inside would be bathed for hundreds of thousands of years by enhanced fluxes of cosmic rays and X-rays. I can imagine that kind of environment inside the solar system being like a bad period of solar activity but lasting thousands of years. This would make interplanetary travel hazardous without the proper and expensive shielding. There would be decades, even centuries, when the many filaments and other irregularities in the supernova ejecta pass through the solar system and make interplanetary travel possibly lethal. [2742, 2360, 1803, 1380, 347]

141 Do you have any information on the North Star?

Also called Alpha Ursa Minoris and Polaris, this magnitude +1.99 star is classified as a F8 Ib star, which means it is a very luminous supergiant with an orange-yellow color and a surface temperature near 4,000 K. It is currently about 54 arc minutes from the true north celestial pole, and by the year 2102, it will be less than the Moon's diameter from the pole, or 27.5 minutes of arc. Polaris is a double star with a companion star about 18 arc seconds distant that orbits Polaris every few thousand years, at a separation of about 2,000 times the Earth-Sun distance. Polaris moves through space at a speed of about 20 kilometers/sec and is at a distance of about 360 light years. It has a luminosity of about 1,600 times that of the Sun. It is also a variable star, but the amplitude of its brightness change is only 0.1 magnitudes with a period of about 3.9 days, and this variability has decreased below 0.05 magnitudes in the past decade, causing some astronomers to think that it is evolving into a stable star. There is also an unseen companion star to Polaris that has a period of 30 years, but it would have to be a faint dwarf star to have escaped detection against the bright glare of Polaris itself. [1945, 1847]

142 Are stellar distances known for certain or are they just theoretical?

They can be determined with a variety of distance indicators, based on a series of empirically derived measurement principles that themselves are based on direct measurements of stellar parallax or on knowledge of the Cepheid period-luminosity relationship. This is empirical knowledge based on direct observation and only very weakly on some theory. Of course, everything we do is based on some theory about what to expect including the rising of the Sun each morning. The distance information we have is the most fundamental and heavily verified element of astronomical knowledge that we work with and on which everything else in astronomy hinges to set the scale of the rest of the universe. The most basic distance measure, used for thousands of years by surveyors on Earth, is the parallax. The *Hipparchos* satellite remeasured the parallaxes of more than 120,000 reference stars and a million others. The distances to galaxies were changed by *Hipparchos* when the previous distances to them were found to be about 10 percent too small, based on the new parallax measurements of certain crucial stars called Cepheid variables. It is satisfying that this ultraprecise study resulted in only a 10 percent change in the distances to all objects further away than about 300 light years. [2552, 2540, 2278, 2123, 1981, 1639, 1565, 615, 375]

143 What would happen to a planet orbiting a star that has gone supernova?

If the star lost more than half its mass, the planet's speed would exceed the escape velocity from whatever remains of the star, and the planet would be ejected from the solar system. The enormous flow of particles ejected from the star, assuming 10 solar masses, a shell thickness of 1 million kilometers, and a radius equal to Earth's orbit, would be about 10^{19} atoms/cc traveling at 10,000 km/sec. When it strikes an Earth-like atmosphere and the particle energy is converted to heat, it would be like injecting a gas into our atmosphere with a temperature of 5 billion degrees. A planet like Earth would probably not be vaporized, but its atmosphere would be boiled off into space to join the expanding supernova remnant. If the planet were far away, like the orbit of Neptune at 2 billion miles, the flow of particles would be reduced by about 460 times, and the expansion of the gas would probably reduce its energy so that distant planets might be able to hold on to some of their atmospheres. Most of the ejected matter would clear out of the solar system within a few weeks or months, but there is lots of other matter being accelerated by the trapped magnetic fields to make for a constant flux of lethal radiation within the newly formed cavity plowed out by the passing shock wave. The planetary surfaces would be bombarded by a hellish cosmic-ray flux for thousands of years, and it is hard to believe life could survive. [2861, 2742, 2574, 1803, 1380, 585]

144 How many stars are there like the Sun?

A lot! If you just ask how many stars there are in our local vicinity of the Milky Way that have the same color (spectral class G) and luminosity (main sequence class V), my copy of C.W. Allen's *Astrophysical Quantities* (Athlone Press, 1973) says that there are 0.0063 of these stars per cubic parsec. This doesn't sound like a lot, but if you were to consider Earth sitting at the center of a sphere extending just 324 light years in radius, the volume equals 4,188,000 cubic parsecs, and 4,188,000 times 0.0063 equals 26,384 stars similar to the Sun.

In terms of an exact match, the Sun is classified by its temperature (5,770 K) and luminosity as a G2 V star. But any planet located at a distance of 93 million miles from such a star would see the same yellow star with the same amount of heating at its surface. The nearest G2 V star to the Sun is Alpha Centauri, at a distance of 4.3 light years.

From here we can ask whether these solar wanna-bes also have 11-year sunspot cycles and all the other detailed features of our Sun, but the important point is that there are a lot of Sun-like stars that Earth would be equally proud to orbit. [75]

Chapter 8

Other Planetary Systems

The subject of other planetary systems would have been a very short and tedious topic to offer were it not for the fact that within six months of the Astronomy Cafe going public, astronomers from San Francisco State University and other, international institutions reported a steady stream of detections of Jupiter-sized planets orbiting stars within 100 light years of the Sun. This produced endless rounds of questions about what these planets are like, whether there could be life on them, and what the chances are for life in the rest of the universe. I was, however, quite amazed that hardly anyone asked how it was that astronomers were detecting these planets now, given that the search has been going on for decades. It seems that the general public is far more interested in what we know, than how we come to know it, while astronomers, if given a chance, are very happy to discuss how they carry out their observations and arrive at their conclusions.

For a time, a new star with an orbiting planet was announced nearly every month, but I was a bit surprised to see the public's enthusiasm for this topic wane steadily, so that by the time the Astronomy Cafe had amassed 3,001 questions, only 61 had to do with this category. It bothered me to no end that the public was so bored by this subject, and all I can think of is that after 30 years of Star Trek and Star Wars, the public simply assumed that planets around other stars was a given that needed no experimental confirmation. This is kind of like the search for Planet X, where the outcome of its eventual discovery seems to be a foregone conclusion and that astronomers should just get on with giving Planet X a proper name.

145 How do astronomers detect planets around other stars?

As a planet orbits a star, the star's position in the sky will shift by a small fraction of an arc second or so over the orbital period of the planet. Unfortunately, many of the stars for which some effect was seen, such as Barnard's Star, could never be confirmed. Then, about five years ago, astronomers detected a change in the frequency of pulses from a pulsar and were able to use the Doppler effect to determine the pulsar's change in velocity. This led to the discovery of two planets orbiting the pulsar. As they moved, they caused the velocity of the pulsar through space to change slightly, and this speed change caused a measurable Doppler shift in the pulsar's frequency. In 1996 Geoff Marcy and Paul Butler of San Francisco State University used spectroscopic data from a new instrument at the Lick Observatory in California to search for a similar Doppler shift in the light from more than 100 bright nearby stars. They discovered periodic speed changes of about a few tens of meters per second in several candidates, including 51 Pegasi, shown in Figure 7, and when they used supercomputers to model the possibilities, they found evidence for several massive planets.

In addition to these reasonably direct methods, it may also be possible to detect the existence of planets by studying the gas surrounding a star. For example, the star Beta Pictoris was discovered to have a flat disk of material orbiting it and extending more than 200 times the distance of Pluto from the Sun. But Hubble Space Telescope studies of the core of this disk show that it has been evacuated of material. This is exactly what you would expect to find if planets were busily ejecting or accreting material out from this region, which in the case of Beta Pictoris is about the diameter of our own solar system. Also, astronomers have begun to suspect that the reason why some planetary nebulas, such as MyCn18 (Plate 3), look so unusual is that the expanding star has absorbed the mass from orbiting planets, and the angular momentum from these planets stirred up the gases of the expanding stellar atmosphere. This would explain why planetary nebulas are not always perfectly round like the shape of the star. There are also numerous, small globules found in nebulas, such as the Helix Nebula (Plate 7) and the Great Nebula in Orion, which have sizes only a few times larger than our

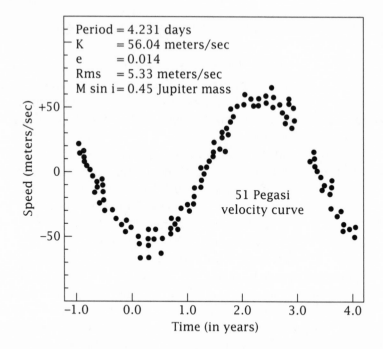

Period = 4.231 days
K = 56.04 meters/sec
e = 0.014
Rms = 5.33 meters/sec
M sin i = 0.45 Jupiter mass

51 Pegasi
velocity curve

Figure 7 The speed of the star 51 Pegasi relative to the Sun during a 4.3-year period, based on many measurements (*dots*). The total speed change of the star is about 50 meters per second toward (negative) and away (positive) from the sun.

solar system, so we know that clumps of gas of about this size are common in nature. [2908, 2441, 1909, 1898, 1645, 1243, 1143]

146 Could the Hubble Telescope see planets around other stars?

Under certain circumstances and with the right instruments, yes, it could. A planet cannot be seen just by measuring the "wiggle" of the star it orbits. This takes very high precision astrometry or spectroscopy over many years to detect. Planets could be detected, as they have already been by astronomers Geoff Marcy and Paul Butler, by monitoring the frequencies of many spectral lines from the star to a precision of 10 meters per second. Ground-based telescopes, like the Keck and Gemini telescopes in Hawaii, among others, will be the champions of this method, using their enormous light-gathering apertures in excess of 10 meters.

Planets could be detected by their reflected light by the Hubble Space Telescope (HST) because the optics and seeing conditions in space are superior to anything on the ground. The Space Telescope Imaging Spectrometer (STIS) was installed in the 1997 servicing mission and has a special occulting mechanism that will allow searches for Jupiter-sized planets around nearby stars. A Jupiter-sized planet orbiting a star 3 light years away at the distance of Jupiter from the Sun, will be seen about 5 arc seconds from the star. Only HST's perfect optics, the STIS occulting mechanism, and no distortion will allow astronomers to search for faint objects within a few arc seconds from a nearby star. [2483, 779, 765]

147 Is there compelling evidence that there is a planet orbiting 51 Pegasi?

This is a barely visible star in the constellation Pegasus, which in recent decades has been studied for signs of orbiting planets as part of several intensive searches of hundreds of nearby Sun-like stars. I think the evidence of some periodic change in the velocity of 51 Pegasi, shown in Figure 7, is very compelling. For decades, various groups of astronomers have detected peculiar perturbations in the motions of stars. I am happy with the recent spate of confirmations of the earlier studies and the new detections by such groups as San Francisco State University's Geoff Marcy and Paul Butler and David Latham's Harvard-Smithsonian collaboration, among others. We have clearly entered a new productive style of doing the research, with a growing acceptance of the techniques being used and their results. This is truly a watershed moment in history. We now know of more planets outside our solar system than inside it! [2990, 1870, 1553, 1496, 1205, 569, 456, 455]

148 What is the latest count on the number of extrasolar planets?

Table 8 is a list of stars for which some evidence for an unseen, planet-sized companion has been identified as of December 1997. [2858, 2740, 1505, 1075, 123, 108]

Table 8 **Planets detected around nearby stars as of December 1997.** The first group of 14 stars includes a total of 19 planets for which the astronomical evidence is exceptionally strong. Also shown is a list of stars suspected to have planets but for which additional confirming observations are required.

Stars with Confirmed Planets

Star and Planet Designation		Type	Distance	Orbit Size	Mass of Planet
51 Pegasi	b	G4 V	42	0.05	1.35
55 Cancri	Ab	G8 V	44	0.11	0.8
Tau Bootes	Ab	F7 V	49	0.046	3.9
Upsilon Andromedae	b	F8 V	54	0.054	0.6
Rho Coronae Borealis	b	G0 V	55	0.25	1.13
47 Ursa Majoris	a b	G0 V	46	2.1	2.5
55 Cancri	Ac	G8 V	44	4.0	5.0
Lalande 21185	b, c	M2 V	8.2	10.0	2.5
HD 114762	b	F9 V	91	0.39	10
70 Virginis	b	G5 V	78	0.43	6.4
16 Cygni	Bb	G2 V	78	1.7	1.6
B1257+12	A, B, C, D	pulsar	2,600	0.19, 0.36, 0.47	0.015, 3.4, 2.8
B0329+54	b, c	pulsar		2.2, 0.03	7.0, 2.3
B1620−20	c	pulsar		38	10

Table 8 (*Continued*)

· ·

Stars Suspected of Having Planets

Star and Planet Designation		Type	Distance	Orbit Size	Mass of Planet
M Draconis	c	M4 V	47	Not known	Not known
Gleise 229	B?	M1 V	19	44	20–50
van Biesbroek 10		dM8			5
BD+68 946		M3V	16		8
BD+43 4305		dM4	16		9
Stein 2051A		M4V	18		18
CC 1228		dM3	38		22
Barnard's Star		M5V	6	3.7, 3.9	0.7, 0.5

Type = type of star. Distance = star's distance from us in light years. Orbit size = distance of the planet from the star in terms of the Earth-Sun distance of 1 AU. Mass of planet is given in multiples of the mass of Jupiter, except for the pulsar planets, which are given in multiples of the mass of the Earth. Visit the Exoplanets web site (www.physci.psu.edu/~mamajek/exo.html) for the most recent updates on the search for extrasolar planets.

149 How many other solar systems do astronomers think there are?

Lots. I think that a plausible estimate is that one in five stars has a planetary system of some kind. The recent discoveries in 1996–1997 of planets orbiting some nearby stars is just the tip of the iceberg, because the instruments that were used could only detect very large planets like Jupiter in very pathological orbits. There must be an even larger number of stars that have smaller planets, and it is hoped that in the next decade new generations of instruments will be good enough to detect them. [1179, 1075, 982]

150 Which is the nearest planetary system to the Sun?

At the American Astronomical Society meeting on June 10–14, 1996, astronomers George Gatewood and his colleagues at the

University of Pittsburgh's Allegheny Observatory presented astrometric data on the nearby star Lalande 21185 that seemed to show a wobble due to the orbit of an unseen, Jupiter-sized planet orbiting every 30–35 years. Lalande 21185 is an M2.1 V main sequence red dwarf star with a luminosity about 200 times less than the Sun and a mass of about 0.3 times the Sun. It is the fourth closest star to the Sun after the Alpha Centauri/Proxima Centauri system, Barnard's Star, and Wolf 359. Its distance is 8.3 light years, about half a light year closer than Sirius. [2390, 1961, 1205]

151 Who is studying Barnard's Star these days?

Dr. Sprague Van de Kamp at Yerkes Observatory in Illinois was the premier observer of Barnard's Star in the 1960s. He originally made the claim that an unseen planetary companion had been detected in astrometric data of this star, contained in more than 20,000 photographic plates covering decades of observations. However, in 1973 George Gatewood at the Allegheny Observatory in Pennsylvania performed a new statistical analysis of the original data and concluded that there was, in fact, no significant evidence for such a perturbation produced by a body similar to the one that Van de Kamp had proposed. Hubble Space Telescope observations of Barnard's Star in 1995 have now demonstrated that no objects more massive than Jupiter are in orbit around Barnard's Star with periods less than 600 days. The implied orbital distance is about 2 AUs. Still, as for many stars, one can never say conclusively that no planets are in orbit, only that objects with more than a specific amount of mass cannot be closer than a particular distance, beyond which their perturbations fall below the statistical noise level of the measurement process itself. Note, however, at the distance of Barnard's Star, our own Sun would execute a roughly 12-year wiggle due mostly to Jupiter, but the amplitude of this wiggle would only be about 0.005 arc seconds. This is at the very limit of many astrometric techniques. Sadly, Van de Kamp did not live long enough to see the dawning of a new age in detecting new planetary systems, not by measuring star positions, but by measuring their spectroscopic velocity changes. [2837, 2673, 1569]

152 How many planets do you think there are with intelligent life?

This is impossible to estimate, because we know that the evolutionary road from bacteria to humans on Earth was plagued by random and very, very fortunate events. These events, such as the Cretaceous impactor 65 million years ago by opening up millions of new evolutionary niches literally overnight, helped to make advanced mammalian intelligence possible. There may be billions of planets out there with bacteria as the highest life forms and only a handful having life more intelligent than dinosaurs. [2751, 2383, 2165, 2072, 2039, 1680, 1385, 1320, 1179, 625]

153 What are the scales of the newly discovered solar systems compared to ours?

Very approximately, the detected Jupiter-sized planets around 51 Pegasi and 70 Virginis would be located inside the orbit of Venus. The planet around 47 UMa is located out by the asteroid belt in our solar system, and Lalande 21185's planet is at the distance of Jupiter. Table 8 gives more details, and using the distances given in astronomical units, you can draw a scale model of these systems yourself. [1206]

Chapter 9

Black Holes, White Holes, and Worm Holes

he topic of black holes, white holes, and worm holes has been
extremely popular, and although it has received fewer than 125
questions, it has generated more hits than many other topic areas
of the same size at the Astronomy Cafe. I receive many requests
from young students looking for ideas for science-fair projects on
black holes. The amount of enthusiasm for this topic is so great that
there seems to be a great many armchair physicists out there. This
actually bothers me quite a bit, because, inevitably, they begin their
letters to me with a statement like, "I do not know much mathematics
and physics, but I have a theory about black holes I want you to look
at." Then, they make assertions about black holes that are quite
wrong and launch into some proof that physicists do not understand
something obvious about gravity or black holes. I credit this lack of
humility to our current fascination with empowering individuals to
believe they can do anything.

People are mostly fascinated by what is inside a black hole
and whether black holes can be used for space travel. My favorite
question of all has to do with how gravity can escape a black hole but
not light. I actually had to do quite a bit of reading in the technical
literature to come up with an answer I felt confident about. Frankly, I
had never really bothered with this question myself, and the answer
turned into more than just a quick plunge into the library. Some
people have asked for a firm commitment from me that black holes
are now recognized as a fact of nature rather than just a theoretical
possibility. Thanks to the spectacular results from the Hubble Space
Telescope, it has been easy to provide this reassurance, as far as

our current observations are able to tell us. I have also been able to explain some of the peculiar relativistic effects that distant observers would see as a black hole forms and its prior stellar state winks out. It is hard to imagine anything stranger than the split reality seen by someone falling into a black hole in a matter of minutes and a distant observer concluding the whole passage took millions of years for the same journey. I've also happily reassured the public that the nearest known black holes are several thousand light years away, despite how common they seem to be in science fiction stories.

154 What is a black hole?

A black hole is a region of space into which matter has collapsed and out of which light may not escape. There are two main types—the Schwarzschild black hole that does not rotate and the Kerr black hole that does. Unlike the prediction by the eighteenth-century French mathematician Pierre Simon de Laplace, who used ordinary Newtonian physics, a black hole has a very sharp boundary in space known as the event horizon.

Event horizons are regions around gravitational singularities where infinite red shifts and infinite time dilation can occur. In Table 9 you can see what some of the gravitational time dilation effects look like as you get closer and closer to the mathematical limit of the event horizon of a very massive black hole. If you fall into a black hole, you will see nothing dramatic happen at the horizon, and, assuming you can survive the gravitational tidal stresses trying to pull you apart, you can enter the black hole after only a few seconds of your spaceship's time. To a distant observer, however, a much longer span of time than just a few seconds would appear to pass. But to actually get the highest time dilation factors, you would have to be less than a meter away from the event horizon, and by then both you and the distant observer would agree that you are at the horizon for any practical purpose of defining your condition.

There is a precise mathematical prediction of the radius of this horizon, which for objects that do not rotate depends only on the mass of the object that has collapsed through its event horizon. For every unit of mass equal to that of the Sun, the radius grows by 2.7 kilometers. The most massive black holes known are a

Table 9 **How slow your spaceship's time would pass if people far away from the black hole were to watch each of your days on the ship pass as you entered the black hole's event horizon.** All estimates are for a supermassive black hole 1 billion times the mass of the Sun and whose radius, R, equals 2.7 billion kilometers.

Ship's distance from the horizon	The distant observer sees this much time elapse
R + 1,000,000,000 kilometers	2 days
R + 1,000 kilometers	5 years
R + 1 meter	4,260 years
R + 1 centimeter	43,600 years
R + 1 micron	4.5 million years

billion times the mass of the Sun and are as big as our entire solar system. [2632, 2338, 1995, 1972, 442]

155 Is the edge to a black hole a smooth one, or is it a sharp boundary in space?

In Newtonian physics, escape velocity smoothly decreases the further from a body you get. For black holes described by general relativity, this is not the case at all. As seen from the vantage point of an outside observer, the event horizon is extremely sharp. For Schwarzschild black holes, it is a mathematically perfect, spherical surface where light is infinitely red shifted. To observers falling into the black hole, other than lethal tidal effects, they experience nothing peculiar, except that once they cross this mathematical surface by even 1 millimeter, they can never turn back to escape the black hole. Actually, to distant observers, the region near a black hole can be very messy indeed, as shown in Figure 8. If the black hole is being fed by infalling gas, it can emit X-rays and gamma rays and have a very complex magnetic field capable of producing flares. These emissions from the infalling matter have been detected for many different types of objects, including X-ray binary stars and even quasars, which is why astronomers think

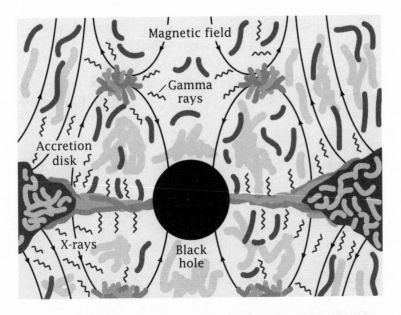

Figure 8 The hypothetical appearance of the gas and magnetic fields just outside a black hole based on interpretations of the data to date. Magnetic field reconnections accelerate the gas to nearly the speed of light in jets perpendicular to the accreting disk of gas. Temperatures in the inner edge of the disk are more than 10,000 K, so the gas shines by X-ray light much as solar flares do. Accelerated plasma glows in gamma-ray light, which flares and changes rapidly in intensity over minutes, hours, or months, depending on the size of the black hole and the precise way that magnetic fields accelerate matter.

they all involve black holes, although of vastly different sizes. [2425, 670]

156 How big and hot can black holes get?

According to theoretical expectations, the biggest black holes are actually the coldest, because their so-called Hawking temperature is measured in billionths of a degree above absolute zero (zero degrees Kelvin). The hottest black holes are microscopic in size and have fewer than 1 trillion grams of mass. Their temperatures increase from a few thousand degrees to trillions of degrees Kelvin as they evaporate into still-lower-mass objects. As for size, the biggest known black holes contain several billion times the

Sun's mass and are about 3 billion kilometers in radius. These supermassive black holes lurk in the cores of quasars and other "active" galaxies. We know of no black holes with more than 10 billion times the mass of the Sun. The universe is probably not old enough to grow such unspeakable monsters, but in the distant future, there may indeed be many such hypermassive black holes to reckon with. [2973, 570, 331]

157 Is the temperature inside a black hole absolute zero?

Theoretically, the outside portion that we see from far away can have a definable temperature because it emits Hawking radiation, but this temperature, though small, is not absolute zero (zero degrees Kelvin). Inside, because space itself is collapsing, nothing is in equilibrium long enough for temperature to be a meaningful way of describing anything. [2495, 988]

158 How do black holes form?

They form from massive stars that become supernovae. Their core regions implode, and no known force can withstand the force of gravity once the imploding mass gets close to its eventual size as a black hole—a size determined by the so-called Schwarzschild radius of the mass. Large supermassive black holes probably form by simply eating vast quantities of stars and gas every year for billions of years.

Black holes that form in our universe from the collapse of very massive stars actually form objects that do not become true black holes until an infinite amount of time passes for those of us outside watching. This is because the mathematical black hole condition only describes the so-called asymptotic end state of such objects after they have settled down. Because of the gravitational time dilation effect, we will see this process take thousands and even millions of years, although someone riding on the surface of a collapsing body will judge this to take less than a second. To someone watching from far away, the star's surface will actually wink out very quickly as it gets close to the horizon limit and cause the object to become black, but the actual surface is still just hovering micrometers outside the horizon as seen by us. The last few centimeters of travel takes a very long time to finish, as seen by us watching outside. This is why black holes are sometimes called frozen stars. Unless they were formed at the big bang itself, there simply has not been enough time, as judged by us well outside the horizon, to see the original mass fall completely inside the black hole's event horizon. [2042, 1969, 1808, 1682, 1355, 1185, 643]

159 If from far away nothing gets inside a black hole, how do they accrete and grow?

Matter does not have to fall through the event horizon to make a black hole for outside observers. All it has to do is get close enough to the horizon, by literally a few millimeters, so that it experiences a large relativistic dilation factor. The emitted light will be highly red shifted from gamma-ray energies to radio wavelengths during this last few millimeters of travel. As seen by a distant observer, the matter will cease to emit detectable light or energy, and within a few seconds, the last possible photon will have been emitted by the object's surface into our universe. If the object is accreting matter, the matter falls toward the horizon and then seems to slow down and stop before winking out. Only to an infalling observer will the matter actually be seen to pass across the horizon and fall into the black hole singularity, but this is never observable to the distant observer in a finite amount of time. [2450, 2319, 1238, 732]

160 If I fell into a black hole, would the universe collapse before I passed across the event horizon?

Mathematically, this might indeed happen, as strange as that sounds. Based on the external clock attached to the distant reference frame of the universe, your motion toward the event horizon reaches highly relativistic speeds once you get within a few millimeters of the radius of the black hole's event horizon. As seen by the distant observer, your clock slows down enormously. By your clock, it will not take you long to reach the horizon, perhaps only a few seconds, and you may not feel any tidal effects at all if the hole is big enough. The outside universe will appear to advance billions of years into its own future, and if it is a closed universe, there are not many billions of these years to spare.

As shown in Table 9, by the time you are within a micron of the event horizon, the external universe clock will be ticking at a rate of nearly 5 million years for every one of your days. As you get even closer, the time dilation factor increases sharply, and, in principle, you would not be able to outlast the rest of the universe collapsing in a mad rush behind you. [2592, 2386, 1912, 1881]

161 If you could survive a trip into a black hole, what would you see?

Frankly, no one knows. I have never seen any calculations that attempt to predict what the victim would actually see inside the event horizon. Instead, the black hole solutions that come from general relativity theory usually identify different regions inside the event horizon only in terms of their geometric properties. There must be enormous optical distortions that would make the scene look like something out of a carnival fun house, and the radiation, depending on its source, would have various amounts of red shift or blue shift. Beyond that, I cannot even begin to speculate. [2750, 2717, 2452, 2343, 496, 475]

162 If a black hole entered our solar system, would it head for Earth?

No, but, depending on its mass, it would sure make life very uncomfortable for us. A Jupiter-sized black hole would be only a meter across and detectable only by the substantial perturbations it would make as it crossed the orbits of the planets. For a solar-mass black hole only 5 kilometers across, not only would planetary orbits be perturbed, but some planets might even be ejected from the solar system entirely, and this from an object only the size of a large city. [2586]

163 How do astronomers study black holes when they can't see them?

We "see" them by their gravitational effects on nearby stars, which they are often eating or causing to move at very high velocities just before the stars enter the black hole. The core of a galaxy that "weighs" 1 billion times the mass of the Sun but has only a few million visible stars in it in a small volume of space is a prime candidate for having a black hole. Also, a binary star system where the total mass is, say, 20 times that of the Sun but the only visible star has a mass of 8 solar masses, means it has a dark companion with 12 times the mass of the Sun. No normal stars are that massive and invisible, so, in other words, you have a black hole. Also, as shown in Figure 8, most models of real black hole environments imply very complicated mechanisms that produce high energy radiation and particles very unlike what you get in any other astronomical body. These emissions can also provide us with the smoking gun evidence to figure out whether a black hole lurks there or not. [2461, 399, 78]

164 Where are the best candidates for black holes located?

Astronomers distinguish between two classes of black holes—stellar mass and supermassive. Stellar-mass black holes have masses from about 1 to 10 times the mass of the Sun and are the end products of the evolution of very massive stars. These are often found in binary star systems where they can be most easily detected as they affect the nearby star. Supermassive black holes contain millions or even billions of times the mass of the Sun and are found in the nuclei of galaxies and quasars, which the Hubble Space Telescope has confirmed in images, such as Plate 8, which shows the inner core of the quasar-like galaxy Messier 87 in the constellation Virgo. Table 10 is a list of the current suspected and confirmed black holes.

Black holes are the least exotic explanation we can offer for some of the energetic things we are seeing in the universe. No other object has proven to be as helpful in accounting for the great variety of data now accumulated. We will never be able to actually see a black hole, but we will come to know them well by their handiwork. We can never directly observe electrons or quarks either, but we know they are there nonetheless. In the court of Nature, sometimes circumstantial evidence is all we will ever have to judge our theories. [1572, 900, 645, 405, 253, 107, 78]

165 Does the matter that falls into a black hole come out as another big bang?

We will never know, because we can never look inside a black hole to see what is going on, and we can never look behind it to

Table 10 **Black holes that astronomers know about or suspect to exist.**

Solar-Mass Black Holes		Supermassive Black Holes	
Name of Star	**Black hole mass (Sun = 1)**	**Name of Galaxy**	**Black hole mass (Sun = 1)**
A0620-00	3–4	1E1740.9-2942[†]	100 thousand
Cygnus X-1	4–8	Sagittarius A*	2 million
Scorpius X-1	3–10	Messier 32	3 million
GS2000+25	3–10	Centaurus A	<14 million
GX339-4	3–10	Messier 31	30 million
V 404 Cygni	8–12	Messier 106	40 million
Nova Muscae 1991	3–10	NCG 3379	50 million
Nova Ophiuchi 1977	6–7	NGC 3377	100 million
		Messier 84	300 million
		NGC 4486B	500 million
		NGC 4594	1 billion
		NGC 4261	1 billion
		NGC 3115	2 billion
		Messier 87	3 billion
		Cygnus A	5 billion
		NGC 4151	Not known
		Messier 51	Not known

[†]This object is in the center of our Milky Way along with Sagittarius A*.

see what comes out in some other dimension or universe. Because there is no experiment we can conduct to test this hypothesis, it is not a scientifically interesting question, no matter how compelling it seems. [2285, 2207, 1067, 989, 953]

166 Do tidal gravitational forces near a black hole singularity distort the shapes of fundamental particles?

Inside a black hole is a region called the singularity where the curvature of space-time becomes infinite according to Einstein's general relativity. Other than theoretically, no one really knows what happens close to a singularity, but, in what is called quantum gravity theory, no singularities actually exist. This extreme condition in space is simply replaced by a region where the graininess of space and time becomes evident at the so-called Planck scale. Because all fundamental particles are believed to be some kind of loops of energy, also about the size of the Planck scale, 10^{-33} centimeters, individual particles just dissolve away into some kind of quantum froth at these scales. But we do not know for sure and have absolutely no way of finding out. [2866, 2495]

167 Is there really a black hole in the center of the Milky Way?

Yes. The data in hand seem to indicate very clearly that a very dense point mass containing several million times the mass of the Sun is located in the core of the Milky Way. The only logical candidate is a black hole, because an equivalent number of normal stars crowded into a solar system–sized volume of space would look very different than what we actually seem to be detecting in the core of the Milky Way in an object astronomers call Sagittarius A*. [2525, 1027]

168 Is it true that there is a huge black hole that has swallowed thousands of planets?

I am sure that this has happened in some distant galactic core containing a supermassive black hole, although, of course, we cannot know of a particular example where this has actually happened. Supermassive black holes, like the one in Messier 87 (Plate 8), do, however, swallow stars and gas, and it is not a big stretch of the imagination that some of these stars were accompanied by planetary systems. What a dreadful fate. To be able to look up at the sky and see a distant hole in space, knowing that in a few centuries you and your world would cease to exist, and there is not a single thing you could do about it. The laws of physics are cruel, and they can destroy worlds as easily as the fool who steps out a window on the forty-fifth floor. But to see your civilization's destiny literally written in the stars each night in this slow-motion death dance that lasts for decades must be simply awful. [2210]

169 Is there a black hole in the center of every galaxy or is this just science fiction?

You cannot *prove* that there are black holes in the cores of every galaxy, but the ones that are close by or show nuclear activity seem to show signs that there are supermassive black holes living inside them. Thanks to the Hubble Space Telescope, the list of black holes in Table 10 gets longer every year. It seems that in order to be a host for a supermassive black hole, a galaxy has to be large enough to have a rather well-developed nuclear region with lots of stars crowded together in a small volume. [2980, 2391]

170 When black holes evaporate and reveal their singularities, why don't they explode to make a new universe?

Except for some peculiar circumstances, the evaporation of black holes by the so-called Hawking mechanism doesn't remove the event horizon, so the universe outside the horizon never gets to see these naked singularities. Even if they did appear, they would not produce a new universe on top of our own, because they are the wrong type of singularity. Black holes are what physicists classify through their mathematical properties as spacelike singularities. They are not in the same mathematical category as timelike singularities, of which the big bang is the only known example. [2886, 2393, 2126, 2015, 1813, 1042, 205]

171 How can gravity escape a black hole?

This is a very difficult question to answer, because we need a better understanding of gravity. We think this better understanding will happen once we have a fully quantum mechanical explanation for gravity, perhaps in terms of the elusive particles called gravitons. Then, the answer will draw upon quantum mechanics for most of its explanation.

To explain how gravitons escape from a black hole in order to cause the gravitational field we see at great distances, quantum mechanics predicts that the event horizon is not an infinitely high energy barrier. The event horizon is just a region of space that has a particular gravitational potential. This can now be translated into a problem in quantum mechanics where you are asking what the penetration or tunneling probability is for quantum particles, such as gravitons and electrons. Outgoing quanta can therefore pass across the potential barrier at the spatial distance of the event horizon and tunnel across it. According to Heisenberg's uncertainty principle, the event horizon is poorly localized and is just like any other energy barrier across which quantum mechanical particles can tunnel, as through a leaky membrane.

There is another reason, and this one draws upon a nonquantum mechanical feature of black holes. As seen from a great distance, black holes look as though all the mass that went into them is still hovering on our side of the event horizon, thanks to relativistic time-dilation effects. The gravitational field from this matter can, therefore, escape from the black hole because the mass producing it is not yet inside the event horizon, as seen from our external vantage point. [2994, 2770, 2569, 2434, 2401, 2328, 1498, 1497, 756, 385]

172 What happens when two black holes collide?

When they are far apart, black holes interact just like any other bodies acting under weak gravitational fields. For black holes with about the mass of the Sun, their sizes are about 2.7 kilometers in radius. When they get within a few dozen kilometers, their shapes begin to deform, meaning their event horizons are distorted from a spherical shape (if they are not rotating). As they get closer together, they are under enormous acceleration, and because all accelerating bodies emit gravitational radiation, the combined black hole system begins to shed some of its energy. Because energy and mass are equivalent, this also means that the sum of the masses of the black holes during the collision is steadily decreasing, compared to the sum of their masses when they were far apart. Within a few minutes, the black hole event horizons begin to interpenetrate and resemble a peanutlike shape. By this time, the combined system is spinning at a fantastic rate, and at the same time emitting still more gravitational radiation until its shape settles down into something more spherical. The mass of this new hole would be about 10 percent less than the sum of the black hole masses before the encounter because of the loss of mass due to gravitational radiation. [859]

173 How do white holes work?

In general relativity, white holes are time-reversed black holes in which the four-dimensional lines representing the histories of all particles (world lines for matter) must emerge but not enter. World lines represent the locations of particles throughout their history from start (creation) to finish (destruction). For a black hole, all world lines at the event horizon may enter but not leave. In this way, black holes are seen as sinks for matter, which falls into them from our universe, while white holes are seen as sources for matter entering our universe from somewhere else. [1470, 1469, 1446, 513]

174 Are there any white holes in the universe?

None that we know of. It seems to be easier to detect black holes and even supermassive black holes than a single white hole. As far as I know, we don't really know if all the supermassive holes are truly black or if there are a couple of white holes in the mix. Gravitationally, they would look about the same from a great distance. The flows of matter near them, however, would be a dead giveaway, because the white holes would show matter or radiation being emitted from them with large blue shifts, and black holes would exhibit large Doppler red shifts from material falling into them. [2628, 2167]

175 What would happen if a black hole and white hole collided?

The details are rather complicated, and no one has modeled such an event on a computer, but you apparently still end up with an object with an event horizon that resembles a black hole. [2880, 2236, 1848]

176 What are worm holes?

A worm hole is a particular solution to Einstein's relativistic equation for gravity in which two parts of space may be joined together. Unlike black holes, they have no internal singularities, at least in the vacuum solution, but certain rotating Kerr-type black holes may serve the same worm hole–like function.

In relativity, all world lines either start on a singularity or end on one. The only way to ensure this kind of condition in rotating Kerr black holes is to make certain that when a world line passes from large distances to zero at the exact center of the black hole it can continue through zero and extend to negative radial distances. For Schwarzschild black holes, all world lines entering the event horizon absolutely must terminate on the singularity at R = 0. For Kerr black holes, the singularity is avoidable, and these other space-times required for completing the world lines in this way can be reached, at least mathematically, by a single world line from our own space-time. This is sometimes called the traversable Kerr worm hole solution.

Traversable Kerr worm holes do not exist naturally. No matter what the physical origin, as far as we understand the physics of real systems, real worm holes must have within them the physical object that formed them. As you enter a black hole, the object that formed it (a star) is still in front of you, filling the space-time with gravitational radiation, which makes the entire edifice of stacked, connected universes dynamically unstable. Worm holes are not born this way because there is always star stuff blocking the doorway. [2753, 2129, 1970]

177 Are there any paradoxes involved in using worm holes for faster-than-light travel?

Is it possible to travel back in time and kill your parents before you were born? This ghastly possibility seems to lead to a contradiction, because if you are here, then your parents were alive, but if you killed them before you were born, you could not be alive now to kill them in the past. These kinds of paradoxes only occur if a space-time, or portions of it, can have what are called closed timelike world lines. This would allow you to revisit some moment in your past and, presumably, allow you to wreak logical mayhem on your own future and existence. Curiously, general relativity allows such macabre opportunities to arise in certain exotic settings which preclude our universe existing in the first place. It is only when you bring the two ends of the worm hole back together that the possibility arises for a paradox to happen, because the local space-time gets so badly distorted that some world lines can be closed upon themselves. This is all just theoretical speculation, and I would not take it too seriously, but it makes for some great science fiction stories. [1141, 444]

178 What do astronomers know about the black hole in Cygnus?

Cygnus X-1 is the brightest X-ray source in the constellation Cygnus and appears to coincide with a faint, ninth magnitude, supergiant star identified as HD 226868, located 8,100 light years away. It is also known to be a binary star with an orbital period of 5.6 days. A careful study of the X-ray emission detected by the *UHURU* satellite revealed that Cygnus X-1 is highly variable. In addition to the regular 5.6-day period that is seen optically, variations as short as 0.001 seconds have been recorded in the system's X-ray emission. The available data suggest that the optically visible star HD 226868 is orbited by a black hole every 5.6 days, which draws in some of the matter from the visible star, converting it into X-rays. The mass of the unseen companion is estimated to be at least 3.4 solar masses, a number much more than the mass of either stable white dwarfs or neutron stars, both of which would be optically invisible at this distance. In addition, the X-rays that such objects produce would be much less energetic than those found in the Cygnus X-1 system. Considering this, together with the rapid, millisecond variability that suggests an X-ray source only 300 kilometers across, the evidence for a black hole orbiting HD 226868 is currently thought to be very convincing. Because the mass of the optically visible companion star is estimated to be about six to eight times the mass of the Sun, most stellar evolution models predict that within a few million years HD 226868 will end its life as a supernova, leaving behind either a neutron star or a second black hole. [1766]

179 Can black holes really suck things up?

Yes and no. If the distance between you and a black hole is more than twice the diameter of the black hole, the black hole acts just like any other mass and will only affect you if you happen to be suicidal enough to dive directly for it. If you are inside this limit, however, the mathematics show that no stable orbits are possible because of a phenomenon predicted in general relativity called frame dragging or the Lenz-Tirring effect. Your orbiting spaceship would quickly slide through the event horizon no matter how hard you tried to park yourself in a stable orbit. You could constantly run your steering rockets to keep in the same orbit, but as soon as you ran out of fuel, once again you would slide into the black hole and vanish from the outside world. If the Sun became a black hole all of a sudden, the Earth would continue to orbit at its present distance without missing a step. Black holes, in general, do not suck, unless you find them on your final exam. Then they can suck big time. [1682]

Chapter 10

The Milky Way and Other Galaxies

I enjoy talking about the Milky Way and other galaxies. They are, after all, some of the largest objects in the universe. Even a small galaxy has millions of stars. For decades we didn't think that galaxies did much that was interesting during their lives. We now know that there are many phenomena in the universe that can involve such enormous collections of mass. Galaxies harbor vast quantities of the mysterious dark matter. They can collide with each other and be consumed into vast growing giant galaxies by cannibalism. Their core regions can harbor some of the largest black holes in the universe, capable of quasarlike outbursts of energy. Even the Milky Way is still a mysterious system, because while we may know its dimensions and mass, we do not know with much accuracy just what it looks like from outside. Astronomers are still uncovering new information about its distant core, which is hidden from view by nearly 25,000 light years of dust clouds as seen from Earth. It is hard to answer such straightforward questions as "How many spiral arms does the Milky Way have?" or "What is at the center of the Milky Way?" I have been surprised by the sophistication of many of the galaxy questions at the Astronomy Cafe, some asking for specific information about such obscure galaxies as Dwingeloo 1 and the Draco system.

One of my favorite questions is "Do all galaxies have names?," which got me thinking that the answer is probably "Yes," because if there are advanced civilizations elsewhere in the universe, our combined efforts have probably named all of the 100 billion systems in the visible universe by now. Most people do not find this topic as *interesting as I do as an astronomer. The Milky Way is our home in the universe, and I thought for sure that nonastronomers would be a bit more curious. The number of original questions was pretty slim for this topic, which means to me that in as much as the Milky Way can be seen in the night sky from most locations, nonastronomers do not think about it very much and thus do not ask a wide variety of questions.*

180 What is a galaxy?

A galaxy is any large collection of stars outside the Milky Way, which is itself a galaxy. A galaxy can be recognized as a distinct physical entity. In terms of the exact number of stars, a small, dwarf, irregular galaxy, like the Small Magellanic Cloud, contains about 1 billion stars, but there are even smaller systems that are recognized as galaxies, such as the Leo I and II dwarf galaxies with a few million stars each and the Draco system with a few hundred thousand stars. The largest star cluster, a globular cluster called Messier 15, has about 6 million stars. Thus, for small galaxies, there is a blurring together of what we mean by a galaxy and a large star cluster. [2901, 2762, 2233, 2213, 1324, 1299, 1113, 959, 445, 71]

181 What is inside the nucleus of a galaxy?

A lot of things have been found in the centers of galaxies by astronomers, depending on the kind of galaxy. In the nucleus, there may be an almost continual rain of gas from outside the nucleus, which can settle into a disk-shaped, rotating maelstrom more than 1,000 light years across. We see such flattened disks of gas and dust in many galaxies including our own. What happens inside this disk depends on a lot of factors, but it seems common enough that stars can be formed there, and massive stars can explode as supernovae in tremendous numbers, leaving behind swarms of neutron stars and black hole corpses. Even supermassive black holes can be created, as individual stellar corpses collide into larger black holes over billions of years. All of this happens within a dense clustering of billions of stars that fill the sky far more thickly than anything we can imagine way out here in the boondocks of our own galaxy. In the centers of some galaxies, it must be both a glorious view and a terrifying thought that your next-door neighbor might be a monstrous black hole just waiting for your little star to plunge into its deathly maw. [2297, 2058, 632]

182 What is at the center of our galaxy?

Within 500 light years, there is a flattened, rotating disk of dense interstellar clouds that contain embedded star-forming regions. These stellar nurseries produce young, massive, B-type stars. This activity has been going on for the past 10 million years or so, and, in fact, astronomers using the Hubble Space Telescope recently discovered what appears to be a massive star perhaps 200 times the mass of our own Sun located in the core region. It has probably only been around for a few million years, given the rate at which it seems to be losing mass. Within a few light years of the so-called galactic center, there is a hole in this disk, and material seems to be getting stripped from the inner edge of the disk along two or three armlike extensions that resemble a miniature pinwheel spiral.

Within a light year of the galactic center, there are the shredded remains of a star that went supernova a few thousand years ago. There is a dense cluster of perhaps hundreds of stars, and there are dozens of red supergiant stars. The most mysterious object, Sagittarius A*, is located right at the heart of the galactic center. It seems to contain a black hole with a mass perhaps as much as 3 million times the mass of the Sun but a size less than the orbit of Earth around the Sun. [2785, 2626, 1983, 1982, 1952, 1632, 1027, 634, 346]

183 Does the Milky Way move in space or does it just stay put?

The Milky Way moves through space within the cluster of galaxies of which it is a member, and this cluster, called the Local Group, in turn moves through space toward yet another larger cluster of galaxies off in the direction of the constellation Virgo. An instrument called the differential microwave radiometer on board NASA's *COBE* satellite measured the brightness of the cosmic background radiation and confirmed that a prominent dipole component (see Plate 9) exists, which makes one-half of the sky appear cool (red) and the other half appear warm (blue). This shift is caused by the Doppler effect as the Sun moves in the direction of the blue-shifted region of the universe. The total speed in this direction is about 370 kilometers per second and is a combination of the Sun's motion around the center of the Milky Way and the Milky Way's motion relative to the rest of the universe. [2889, 2407, 2249, 1598]

184 Do all stars belong to galaxies?

Not all of them. Galaxies collide, and this process strips stars from their parent galaxy and hurls them into intergalactic space. The Hubble Space Telescope has detected a few hundred very bright, orphan stars between the galaxies in the Virgo cluster. Although stars most certainly form inside some collection of matter, such as a galaxy, their history after formation can include being ejected from the same galaxy, especially if the galaxy has collided with a neighbor, flinging millions of stars into the intergalactic void. [2486, 1925, 76]

185 How many galaxies are there?

The Hubble Space Telescope Deep Field Survey photograph shown in Plate 10 found enough galaxies in the small patch of sky it studied to be equivalent to about 2 to 3 million galaxies per square degree of the sky. With 42,000 or so square degrees in the sky, this means that there are at least 80 billion galaxies in the visible universe. There are probably many more than this by perhaps a factor of 10, because for every bright galaxy you see, there are many more faint, dwarf galaxies, like the Magellanic Clouds, which would be impossible to see at great distances. [2223, 2051, 1580, 1115]

186 Would a nebula look colorful if you traveled into it?

Interstellar space is filled with a thin gas, and in some places this gas forms clouds. When stars form in these gas clouds, they light up the cloud, forming spectacular nebulosities of colored light as the gases in the cloud are stimulated by the light from the individual stars. Although nebulas like the ones in Plates 2 and 7 are lovely and colorful, you would see nothing at all if you were inside one because the gases are so spread out in space and there is no blank sky against which to see the contrast. At a density of only a few hundred atoms per cubic centimeter, most nebulas are better than the best vacuums we can make on Earth, and as such, it would be impossible to see anything of their color if you were inside one of them. I am always amused by movies that portray a starship inside or near a very colorful nebula or with background skies swirling with color. In reality, nature is far less colorful, and even the Great Nebula in Orion, with all of its color, would be almost invisible from inside. [1929]

187 How do astronomers measure the distances to galaxies?

We use the distance ladder listed in Table 11. For nearby galaxies, where you can see individual luminous stars called Cepheid variables, their brightness changes depend on their luminosity. Knowing just how bright Cepheids appear to us in the sky, we can figure out very accurately how far away these stars are and the distance to their host galaxies. For very distant galaxies, individual stars cannot be seen, but you can measure distances based on Type 1B supernovae, which can be seen out to 1 billion light years or more. [2133, 1468, 1463, 1192, 680]

188 If you observed the Milky Way from a distant quasar, would it also look like a quasar?

Quasars are very luminous galaxies at the edge of our visible universe, billions of light years away. There are so few of them compared to other types of galaxies that they must represent a very uncommon phenomenon among only a few thousand galaxies in the entire universe. To answer the question, we have to know what the Milky Way looked like 10 billion years ago. We think it did not look like a quasar, because quasars seem to require the existence of a giant, supermassive black hole containing more than 1 billion solar masses of material. As recent Hubble Space Telescope photographs of quasars show (Plate 11), a quasar involves activity in the cores of galaxies that have recently experienced collisions with their neighbors or have even cannnibalized them completely. The Milky Way has nothing like a billion-solar-mass black hole in its core. It could, however, have been a Seyfert or a starburst galaxy, with an output of only one-

Table 11 Astronomers use many techniques to estimate the distance to objects in space, but these techniques are linked together in a distance ladder. Each rung depends on the previous ones to specify the distance accurately, and a slight change in our understanding of Earth's orbit distance has a significant impact on all the higher rungs in the ladder out to the most distant quasars and supernovae.

Object Used	Method	Distance Ranges
Earth orbit	Radar and celestial mechanics	0–10 AU
Nearby stars	Parallax	4–300 LY
Nearby clusters	Moving cluster	300–1,000 LY
Distant stars	Spectroscopic parallax	up to 10,000 LY
Cepheid variables	Period-luminosity relationship	up to 20 mpc
Supernovae	Maximum luminosity	500 mpc
Brightest galaxies	Tenth brightest have same luminosity	1,000 mpc
Hubble constant	Distance vs. red shift relationship	5,000 mpc

Distances inside the solar system are measured in terms of the Earth-Sun distance of 1 astronomical unit (AU), which equals 93 million miles or 149.6 million kilometers. A popular distance unit is the light year (LY), which is 5.7 trillion miles, although astronomers prefer the parsec, which is 3.26 light years. For intergalactic distances, astronomers use the megaparsec (mpc), which is 1 million parsecs or 3.26 million light years.

hundredth the power of a quasar, which is still mighty impressive. [1867, 1785, 1657, 1378, 1017]

189 What are the most distant objects in the universe?

The most distant objects known are still the quasars. Only about 6,000 have been cataloged, after very intensive searches using many different techniques. Astronomers estimate that the universe may only have created fewer than 100,000 of these very luminous objects in a total population of galaxies now thought to exceed 100 billion. Quasars are rare, and only a very small minority of all galaxies have gone through this phase; quasars are probably limited to the most massive galaxies.

The recent deep image of galaxies (Plate 10) provided by astronomers using the Hubble Space Telescope is spectacular in that so many different types of galaxies seem to be jumbled together along the line of sight. The most distant nonquasar objects we can see appear to be pieces of galaxies and small irregular clouds containing millions of stars. There are few if any pretty spiral galaxies, and we think we are seeing the smaller building blocks of conventional galaxies, merging together and colliding to form the larger systems we see around us today. [2449, 2139, 2016, 1253, 927, 593, 16]

190 What is the most distant object known to us as of December 1997?

The record holder goes to the quasar PC1247+3406, discovered in 1991 by astronomers Donald Schneider, Maarten Schmidt, and James Gunn. This quasar has a red shift of $z = 4.897$. This means the light we detect from this quasar has been so tremendously shifted in wavelength that the received light is nearly six times longer in wavelength than when it started its journey to us long ago. For a plausible cosmological model, the light left this quasar when the universe was 7 percent of its current age or less than 1 billion years old. The most distant known radio galaxy was recently discovered by Steve Rawlings and his colleagues at a red shift of $z = 4.41$. This object seems to be a massive elliptical galaxy with a powerful, radio wave–emitting, supermassive black hole at its core. The most distant young galaxy discovered was found by the Hubble Space Telescope. Astronomer Marijn Franx of the University of Groningen, the Netherlands, discovered this galaxy at a red shift of 4.92 as the distorted image produced by the gravitational lens effect of the cluster CL1358+62. The galaxy, located behind the cluster, had been amplified and distorted, but its light could be spectroscopically studied by the ground-based Keck telescope to arrive at a distance of about 13 billion light years. This is also about 7 percent of the age of the universe. A similar but more dramatic lensing event can be seen in the photograph of galaxy cluster CL0024+1654 (Plate 12), although the lensed galaxy (blue images) is not as distant. In all three instances, we are seeing that the universe formed very active, galaxy-sized objects within 1 billion years after the big bang.

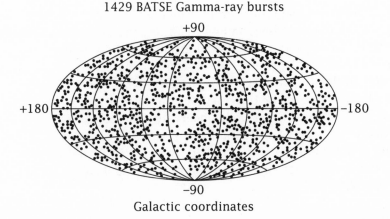

1429 BATSE Gamma-ray bursts

Figure 9 Location of the first 1,429 gamma ray bursts detected by the Compton Gamma Ray Observatory's BATSE instrument at about one event per day. Note their uniform distribution over the sky, which suggests a great distance for the bursts outside the Milky Way, because the flattened appearance of the Milky Way does not show through in the locations of these objects. Astronomers have used this difference to conclude that gamma ray bursts are not located inside our galaxy, because they do not follow the distribution pattern in the sky of objects within the Milky Way.

Astronomers, however, still do not know where the enigmatic gamma ray bursts come from. The objects producing these bursts may be the farthest objects yet detected. For years, their daily flare-ups have been plotted on maps, such as the one in Figure 9. Since the recent detection of one in action by NASA's orbiting Compton Gamma Ray Observatory and the Hubble Space Telescope (Plate 13), astronomers have become increasingly convinced that they may be among the most distant objects in the universe, perhaps as far (or even further) away than quasars themselves. [2192, 1468, 1450, 1029, 876, 706]

191 Are there any more big galaxies hidden behind the Milky Way in our local group?

The Milky Way is a very thick band of light on the sky, measuring 20 degrees in width. This translates into a significant amount of volume in the local group, and in the past 20 years, three galaxies have been found hidden among the murk and stars of our galaxy. In 1996 a new galaxy in our local group was discovered in the direction of the constellation Antlia. According to an article in the August 1997 issue of *Astronomy,* Alan Whiting and George Hau of the University of Cambridge and Mike Irwin of the Royal Greenwich Observatory detected this galaxy at a distance of 3 million light years. It contains only about 1 million stars and is only about 5,000 light years across, which makes it a dwarf spheroidal galaxy. [2946, 778]

192 What is the latest on the nature and existence of dark matter?

There is still a growing body of evidence that something is missing in our inventory of the contents of the universe. The big question remains: "What is it?" Some galaxies definitely rotate faster than they should, given the total mass of the stars we can count in them, so galactic dark matter seems real enough and perhaps outnumbers stars by two to one in mass. This is not a problem for cosmology, because there is easily enough room to accommodate these small amounts of galactic dark matter in the form of ordinary matter that does not produce much light, such as black holes, neutron stars, and dwarf stars. The key cosmological parameter affected is the abundance of helium and deuterium, and these require that all forms of baryonic normal matter made from neutrons and protons contribute less than 1 percent to the so-called critical density of the universe. More than this amount of matter would seriously alter the abundances of helium and deuterium in the universe.

Even more dark matter seems to be needed in some distant clusters of galaxies, based on X-ray and gravitational lensing observations, such as the ones shown in Plate 12. This kind of dark matter seems to be much more abundant than galactic dark matter and must be in a form that does not involve ordinary matter consisting of protons and neutrons, in order to avoid contradicting the cosmological helium and deuterium abundances that have been measured. This form of dark matter may be 100 times more abundant than ordinary matter, if you are compelled to believe that the universe has exactly the critical

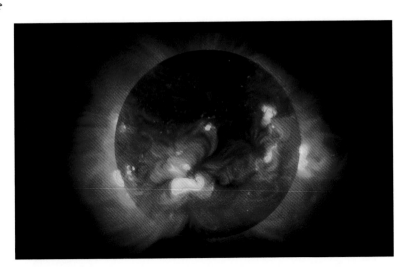

Plate 1 *Yahkoh* mission soft X-ray photograph of the Sun showing coronal activity.

Plate 2a *(left)* NASA's *Pathfinder/Sojourner* on the surface of Mars.
Plate 2b *(right)* The surface of Mars at sunset.

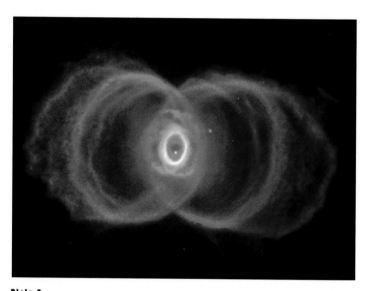

Plate 3 MyCn18 Hourglass Nebula showing ejected gas (a planetary nebula) from a dying star.

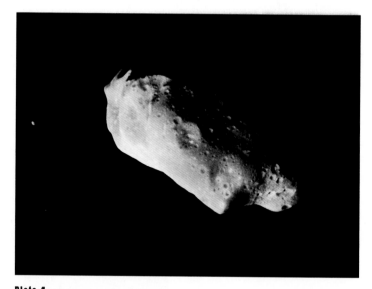

Plate 4 Photograph of asteroid Ida and its companion Dactyl, taken by the NASA *Galileo* spacecraft. Ida dimensions: 56 x 24 x 21 km; Dactyl dimensions: 1.2 x 1.4 x 1.6 km. Ida is as big as a large city. Dactyl is similar in size to a large city block.

Plate 5 A Chevy Malibu after a meteorite impact.

Plate 6 Image of an icy minicomet entering the Earth's exosphere discovered by Louis Frank using NASA's *POLAR* satellite UV imager. Background provided by ARC Science Simulations.

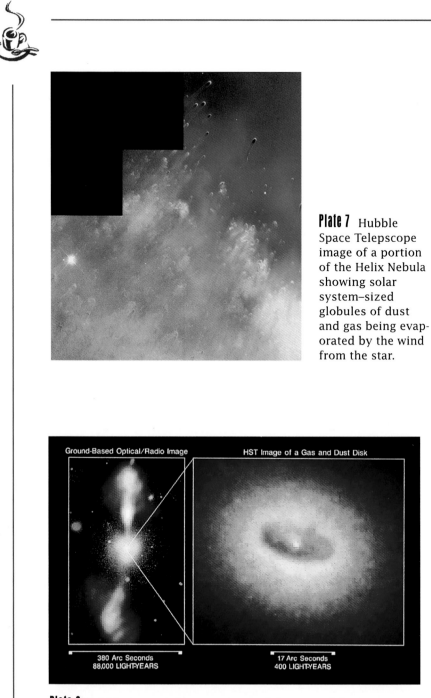

Plate 7 Hubble Space Telepscope image of a portion of the Helix Nebula showing solar system–sized globules of dust and gas being evaporated by the wind from the star.

Ground-Based Optical/Radio Image

HST Image of a Gas and Dust Disk

380 Arc Seconds
88,000 LIGHT-YEARS

17 Arc Seconds
400 LIGHT-YEARS

Plate 8 Hubble Space Telescope image of the core of the giant elliptical galaxy Messier 87, showing the disk of gas orbiting the central supermassive black hole.

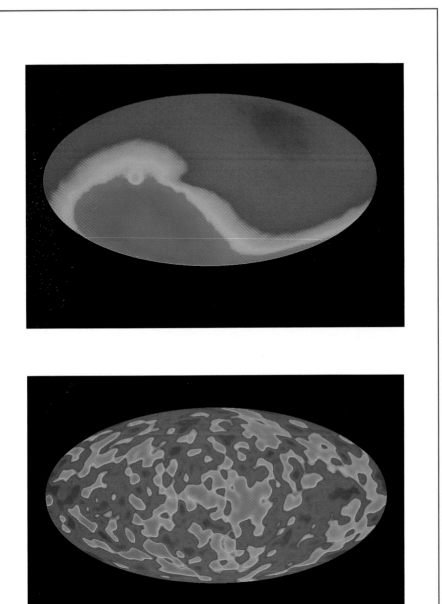

Plate 9 *NASA*'s *COBE* satellite image obtained with the Differential Microwave Radiometer. *(top view)* The blue (approaching) and red (receding) Doppler shift in the cosmic background radiation due to the motion of the Sun. *(bottom view)* The irregularities in the cosmic background due to irregularities in the expanding universe about 300,000 years after the big bang. The largest clumps are more than 300 million light years across.

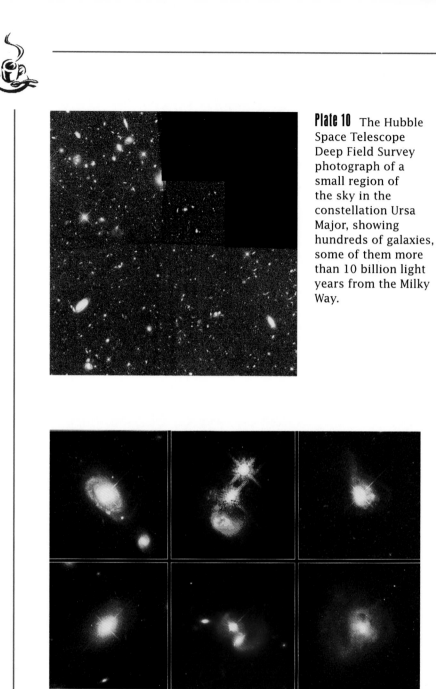

Plate 10 The Hubble Space Telescope Deep Field Survey photograph of a small region of the sky in the constellation Ursa Major, showing hundreds of galaxies, some of them more than 10 billion light years from the Milky Way.

Plate 11 Hubble Space Telescope montage several quasars, showing for the first time that they are located in the cores of distant galaxies and seem to be triggered or related to galaxies undergoing collisions with their neighbors.

Plate 12 Hubble Space Telescope image of the distant cluster CL0024+1654, showing the gravitationally lensed *(blue)* images of a distant background galaxy.

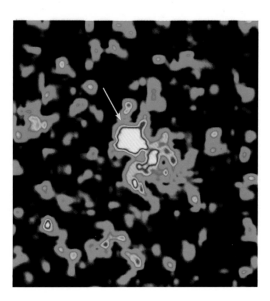

Plate 13 Detection by the Hubble Space Telescope of the fading glow *(arrow)* of an enigmatic gamma ray burst detected hours before by NASA's Compton Gamma Ray Observatory in orbit around Earth.

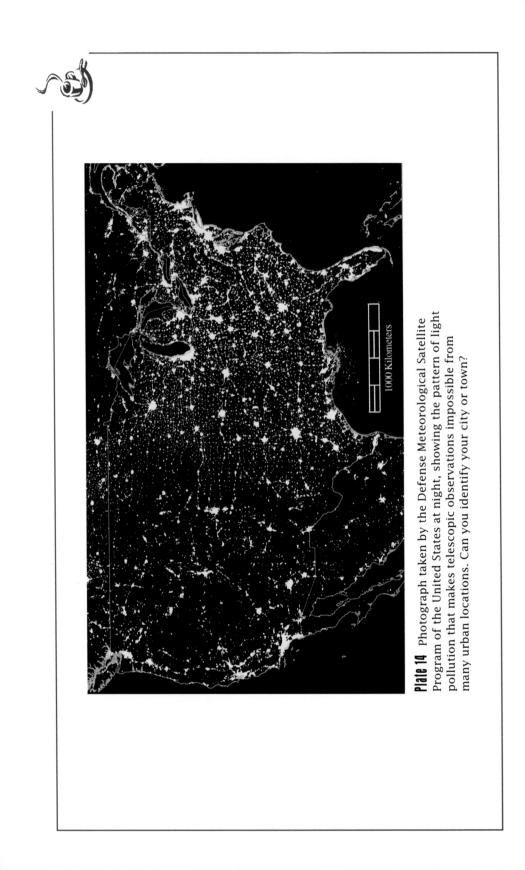

Plate 14 Photograph taken by the Defense Meteorological Satellite Program of the United States at night, showing the pattern of light pollution that makes telescopic observations impossible from many urban locations. Can you identify your city or town?

density put forth by some cosmological theories. But, enormous amounts of dark matter are not required by all versions of big bang cosmology, so the nature of dark matter, and even its very existence, remains something of a mystery for now. [2822, 2623, 2603, 2373, 2306, 1968, 1740, 1655, 1492, 1404, 1266, 1230, 783, 438, 404]

193 Do we know what the Milky Way looks like?

We only know its shape in very rough terms. We know it is a spiral-type galaxy, possibly of class SBc or Sc, and we know roughly where the major spiral arms are located, but as for details equivalent to photographic accuracy, we have none. All we know is the location of the major star-forming regions, nebulas, star clusters, and large gas clouds. There are several competing models of what the Milky Way looks like from outside, depending on which collection of spiral-arm tracers you care to choose. The arms are not clean features but have considerable detail and even fragmentary spurs and armlike pieces. In the past 10 years, new infrared observations by astronomers at the University of Maryland and the *COBE* satellite project seem to convincingly show that the Milky Way has a barlike central region extending many kiloparsecs into the disk, so we live in a barred-spiral galaxy, not a regular spiral-type galaxy, like the Andromeda galaxy, which is our closest neighbor. [1867]

194 Exactly how many stars are in the Milky Way?

This is a difficult, if not impossible, question to answer. The problem is that we cannot directly see every star in the Milky Way, because most are located behind interstellar clouds from our vantage point in the Milky Way. The best we can do is to figure out the total mass of the Milky Way, subtract the portion that is contributed by interstellar gas and dust clouds (about 5 percent), and then divide the remaining mass by the average mass of a single star. From a number of studies, the mass of the Milky Way can be estimated, to an accuracy of perhaps 20 percent, as 140 billion times the mass of the Sun. But even this number is not etched in stone, and several recent studies have suggested a mass for the Milky Way that may be two or three times this value, especially if the dark matter component is added to the tally.

Now, to find out how many stars this represents, you have to divide by the average mass of a star. If you like the Sun, then use 1 solar mass, and you get about 140 million Sun-like stars. But astronomers have known for a long time that stars like the Sun are not that common. Far more plentiful are stars with half the mass of the Sun, and even one-tenth the mass of the Sun. The problem is that we don't know exactly how much of the Milky Way is in the form of these low-mass stars. In textbooks you will therefore get answers that range between 140 billion and as high as 1 trillion stars, depending on what the author used as a typical mass for the most abundant type of star. This is a pretty embarrassing uncertainty, but why would you need to know this number exactly? [76]

Chapter 11

The Big Bang and Before

Here it is—by far the most popular topic area of all at the Astronomy Cafe, and boy have I received some amazing questions about the big bang. There have been so many good ones that it was hard for me to settle on the few that are included in this chapter. I am surprised that I receive so few questions with any obvious religious point of view. The public is more than happy to frame their questions in terms of the particular physics of the issue rather than demand some reconciliation between science and religion, particularly the Book of Genesis. That's fine with me, because as a scientist I prefer to frame answers in terms of concrete observations.

I have had a very hard time convincing nonastronomers that questions about what happened "before" the big bang are probably not posed correctly. I try to argue that humans can pose more questions than there are sensible answers in the physical world and that when dealing with extreme conditions in nature, some questions may not be proper at all. We speak about the big bang as a definite event in space and time, but what the theory of general relativity tells us is that it was the event that actually created space and time. It is not, therefore, possible to ask what happened before this instant in the same way we ask what happened last week, because there was no time present in which the question has a physical answer. Recent attempts to create a quantum theory of gravity only slam this door even more firmly. I have spent quite a bit of space repeating the same answer over and over again in slightly different ways, hoping to land on that magical combination of words that will bring these kinds of questions to an end, but still they come in one form or another. No one likes to be told that a seemingly sensible question has no possible answer.

It is surprising to receive questions about negative entropy, dimensional phase change, and the Weyl tensor, because these topics are usually reserved for graduate-level courses in cosmology. I haven't a clue about what has prompted these questions nor what the questioners have made of my answers. I was happy to announce that astronomers have not the slightest evidence for the supposed quantum production of the universe out of a primordial nothingness. Some people thought that an oscillatory universe was a foregone conclusion to the evolution of the universe, and I had to remind them that a necessary precondition for this to be a possibility is that the universe must appear closed today and that this is a long way from being proven. I have also answered not a few questions about whether other big bangs have happened and where in the universe the present big bang happened. It is very hard to think about the big picture without having to accept some pretty bizarre concepts in physics. I think the general public is still generally unaware of just how nonintuitive is much of the physical world.

195 What are the simplest things we know about the big bang?

We know that the galaxies, out to the most distant ones we can discern, are moving away from us, so the universe is expanding. We know that the universe is bathed in the microwave glow of a background radiation too smooth to be produced by nearby matter and stars. We know that there is a universal abundance of hydrogen, helium, deuterium, and lithium that doesn't vary much, no matter which old objects we look at. We know that there are no stars older than 20 billion years, even though these kinds of stars should be easily recognizable if the universe is truly older than 20 billion years. These are the basic facts we get to work with. There are also a number of other observational facts that are important but not as irrefutable as these are in asserting that the universe had a birth a finite number of years ago in a very hot state and is now expanding. [2131, 2069, 337]

196 Do you believe in big bang theory?

I think that the majority of evidence we now have from a wide range of independent investigations make it a sure thing that the big bang, or something like it, did happen. There are technical quibbles about age discrepancies and expansion rates, but I would be very surprised if these were not ironed out in a decade or so, after we have better data and more of it. I would be surprised if a real showstopper was found that forced us to reconsider whether big bang theory is correct. There are simply too many things that the big bang theory explains and successfully predicts, and conflicting data are still not of high enough quality to conclusively counter the theory at this time.

Personally, I have always had trouble with the word "believe." It has been used in pretty sloppy ways over the centuries. People "believe" in flying saucers, the magical properties of certain numbers, ghosts, and astrology. On the other hand, it is not the business of science to create new belief systems. We are trying to determine how the physical world works, and this has nothing to do with whether you believe it to work one way or the other. I do not believe in big bang theory any more than I believe in special relativity, the constancy of the speed of light, quantum theory, or Newton's law of gravity. I do not see these features of the physical world as matters of belief. They either represent the world as we see it to the limits of our present ability to measure and test or they do not. As far as I am concerned, they are not matters of belief but matters of fact, until such time in the future when new observations say otherwise.

The process of science does not require you to believe anything. If you were to jump off your chair, it is not a matter of belief that will change the outcome but a matter of the theory of Newtonian mechanics that dictates what will happen. Your destiny as a physical object can be computed to many decimal places by this theory, and that is the only standard we use in science to determine the value of a theory, that is, are its predictions compatible with the evidence. Even so, evidence varies enormously in quality as older technologies and techniques of measurement are replaced by better ones. You do not throw out a theory until results can be replicated and predictions checked in a variety of independent ways. This is the point that always gets lost when the nonscientist tries to evaluate the progress of science or new ideas. [1047, 916, 354]

197 Scientists keep hammering on the big bang theory like it is some kind of divine truth. It's only a theory, so why not give it up and find something else that better fits the data?

Whoa, just a minute there! Who says that scientists are treating the big bang theory like it is a divine truth? First of all, the only scientists who have any vote in the matter are physicists and astronomers. Only they devote a sizable fraction of their time, professional skills, and reputations toward making the necessary observations and refining theories of the physical world. Everyone else, including me, is a sideliner totally irrelevant to articulating what is or what is not big bang theory.

Astronomers and physicists are certainly not treating big bang cosmology like a religious truth. Why should they? Could you imagine how famous an astronomer would be if he or she found irrefutable proof that a major prediction (or assumption) in big bang cosmology is not supported by observation? A search through the refereed scientific literature reveals dozens of variants on big bang cosmology and a goodly number of anti–big bang theories. The central problem with virtually all of these carefully crafted alternate cosmologies is that they begin by making assertions like, "Given that Einstein's theory of general relativity is wrong," "Given that atoms and light gain mass over the course of billions of years," or even "Let's suppose that gravity is not the dominant force in the universe, but electromagnetism is." Those who are trying to formulate radical departures from big bang theory almost always have to go to enormous extremes outside what has been proven as factual to craft their models. At the present time, no one has yet created a competing cosmology to big bang theory that: is consistent with all available observational data to at least the same extent as big bang theory, doesn't ask us to violate previously established laws of physics that have been corroborated by independent investigations, and has been developed by individuals who have a proven track record with new ideas that work.

The argument most often used against big bang theory is that scientists, like sheep, flock to this theory and, in some grand conspiracy, suppress all evidence that refutes the theory. This argument works because very few nonscientists have a clue about the history of science. Do you really think that if some scientist could prove that quantum mechanics or Einstein's relativity theory were false that he or she would be vilified? Or do you think that such a scientist would receive a Nobel Prize? When it comes to the major ideas in science, there is tremendous pressure to innovate and find better explanations for the data at hand.

What the general public does not understand is that scientific progress is not a free-for-all where all ideas are equally credible and all theories deserve equal weight and respect. Science is not a democratic process. If a theory isn't supported by a preponderance of the data, it doesn't matter how many Nobel laureates support it. Such a theory is in bad need of revision, expansion, or outright rejection. The testing of a theory is not, however, like some court of law where a single contrary piece of evidence is all it takes to destroy the prosecution's case. This is the part that the general public and philosophers of science don't fully understand. No observation is etched in stone. Experimenters make mistakes in their labs and at the telescope in a variety of different ways, from calibration errors to simple computational errors, even as technologies and measurements improve in quality. It is not a good idea to throw out a theory that has worked well in the past just because a single new piece of information does not corroborate the theory. Instead, astronomers test a theory by asking it to make predictions for a number of different situations that ought to be covered by that theory. Many different observers then test all of these predictions in a number of independent ways. If the process takes 50 years, so be it.

For some reason, perhaps fostered by the "let's give equal time to every idea" philosophy in news reporting, many of you might think that there are lots of data that already refute the big bang theory and that scientists are just being narrow-minded and stubborn about getting rid of the theory and starting over. As we all know, news stories are sometimes reported this way. For example, even though 2,500 scientists specializing in atmospheric studies state that Earth is getting warmer, a reporter might write both about the majority view and a contrary view held by only five scientists, giving equal space to both views. This makes it look like the ideas are shared nearly fifty-fifty between the two groups and that there is a major controversy.

The bottom line is that big bang theory is not massively broken, and the data that we need in order to come to some better judgment about its details are still a decade or two away. What is dark matter? Is there a nonzero cosmological constant? The Hubble Space Telescope's careful analysis of the motions of one or two galaxies is *not* sufficient evidence to demonstrate a problem with big bang theory. Many more galaxies will have to be studied to make certain that our little 1 percent corner of the universe isn't some deviant region sitting on top of a much larger distribution of matter (or dark matter) that is behaving in a way consistent with big bang theory. The testing of a theory is not like the testing of guilt or innocence in a court of law. Every observation is fraught with error and uncertainty, and only by comparing a variety of predictions against a host of seemingly unrelated data knit together by that theory can a true test be performed. [1330, 1228, 1203, 1137, 55]

198 Why can't we see where the big bang started?

There was no unique center for the big bang anywhere in space. It was an event that theory says happened everywhere, in every corner of space. It did not happen in one location and then spread out like some kind of fireworks display. Figures 10 and 11 give you some idea of what the universe looked like when it was only 1 second and 1 100-billion-billionth of a second (10^{-20}) old. Our familiar, empty, and dark interstellar space was absent, but, more important, because the expansion happened everywhere at once. The distance to even the most far-flung matter in our visible universe today was located outside the light travel horizon of our location at those early times. One second after the big bang, the matter contained in a distant quasar today was only a light year away, but at that time light could only travel 1 light second! [2359, 2161, 1869, 1164]

199 Did the big bang happen in a medium or in a vacuum?

We do not know. The best speculation these days is that the medium *was* the physical vacuum, which in turn is just another name for the gravitational field of the universe. But there is much we do not know about the physical vacuum. Extensions of big bang cosmology developed by some physicists seem to attribute many very unusual properties and phenomena to this state. No

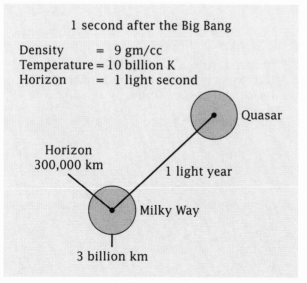

Figure 10 The predicted temperature and density of the universe 1 second after the big bang. The matter now in a distant quasar today located at 15 billion light years from the sun was only 1 light year away when the universe was this old. The shaded circles indicate where the mass inside the Milky Way and the quasar were once located. The Milky Way required the collection of matter within a sphere 3 billion km in radius while at the same instant the visible universe had a radius of only 300,000 km. Note the distances are not to scale.

one really understands enough about space-time and the quantum dynamics of the vacuum state in any true fundamental way to be able to predict what the implications are for cosmogenesis. How one goes about testing such predictions is equally unknown. [2400, 986]

200 What existed in space prior to the big bang?

Again, we do not know whether this question has a meaningful answer. Many cosmologists feel that it is very much like asking how many angels can dance on the head of a pin. It sounds like a sensible question, but in fact its physical basis and foundation may be utterly lacking.

Einstein's theory of general relativity, our premier theory of how gravity works, tells us that in the cosmological setting the

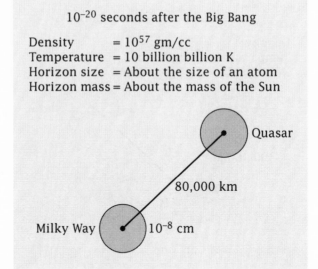

10⁻²⁰ seconds after the Big Bang

Density $= 10^{57}$ gm/cc
Temperature $= 10$ billion billion K
Horizon size $=$ About the size of an atom
Horizon mass $=$ About the mass of the Sun

Quasar

80,000 km

Milky Way 10^{-8} cm

Figure 11 The universe at about 1 100-billion-billionth of a second after the big bang, when the horizon to our universe (age of universe times speed of light) was only about the diameter of an atom. The matter in the Milky Way and the now-distant quasar were only 80,000 kilometers apart and located inside spheres only 10^{-8} cm in radius. The average density of matter in the universe was 10^{57} grams per cubic centimeter. This figure relates the various distances to each other and indicates the typical density and temperature of the universe at that time. Compare this with today's density of 10^{-30} grams per cubic centimeter and a temperature of 2.7 kelvins and with the quasar 15 billion light years distant.

concepts of time and space did not preexist the big bang. The big bang is seen as the defining event that created space, time, matter, energy, and gravity. You cannot ask what happened before the big bang because this state was both timeless and spaceless and lacked the concepts of "before" and "place." This is serious business and not just some stupid semantic game of hopscotch played by astronomers and physicists.

The one thing we have learned over and over again is that the way nature works is nothing like what our intuitions often tell us. Evolution did not prepare us to understand intuitively the laws of quantum mechanics and relativity. These are things we had to teach ourselves about the physical world. We fully expect that any investigation of the origin of the universe will force us to reconsider the very fabric of space and time in some blurry state that merges with the indeterminacy of quantum laws. [2049, 1543, 1515, 1514, 577, 508, 324, 119]

201 Was there really no time before the big bang?

All we can do is watch as our best current theories predict what "before" the big bang could have been like. Without including quantum mechanical effects, the standard big bang model predicts an incomprehensible singularity state of infinite density and zero space and time. Physicists and cosmologists during the past 20 years have in various ways attempted to paste quantum mechanical effects into this theoretical picture and have come up with an initial state called the Planck era, when the scale of the universe was about 10^{-33} centimeters at a time 10^{-43} seconds after the big bang. This is an absolute horizon to cosmology because "before" this era, all properties are presumed to have been determined by quantum fluctuations in some indeterminate vacuum state, a state that existed outside our space and time and for which these very concepts may not have had a compelling physical interpretation.

Our best theoretical guesses suggest that time and space as we know these concepts will become rather meaningless in the purely quantum mechanical state near the Planck era. Cosmologists, such as Stephen Hawking, suggest that the dimension of time is transformed via quantum fluctuations into a spacelike coordinate, so that instead of three space and one time dimensions, we end up with a fully four-dimensional space devoid of any timelike features. What this state represents physically is anyone's guess, because as humans trained to think in terms of processes evolving in time, our next question would be what came before the Hawking spacelike state. There is no possible answer to this question, because in the mathematics of this condition there is no time in which the concept of "before" can be said to have a meaning. The question itself becomes the wrong question to ask.

If we ever develop a truly unified field theory that includes gravity, we may have more to say about what this state may have been like. But that seems to be a very far-off goal, especially insofar as actually testing such a theory is concerned. If you can't test it or, in principle, falsify it, then it is not science that you are doing but philosophy. Still, speculating about this initial state is fun, and very few of us in the sciences can avoid thinking and writing about what it might have been like. [2313, 1754, 1455, 323, 294, 290]

202 What is the evidence that there was a beginning of time?

General relativity provides a framework for making precise calculations of what our expanding universe was doing in the past, and these calculations all require an origin of time a finite number of years ago. There doesn't seem to be any way out of this condition without doing great violence to other verified predictions that follow from general relativistic big bang cosmology. [2313, 1536]

203 How could a quantum vacuum state have produced our universe when the universe has such regular physical laws rather than random things just happening?

Investigations beginning in 1977 by H. Nielson and M. Ninomiya at the Niels Bohr Institute in an area now called chaotic gauge theory seem to show that various physical laws can seemingly emerge spontaneously from a hot, chaotic state. Also, the fact that we are here at all means that we have to exist in a universe with many built-in rules of operation, otherwise we could not exist to frame the question in the first place. Laws of nature exist because, in essence, we are here to observe them. In a perfectly chaotic universe, sentient life is impossible, and in such a universe, no one exists to marvel at its possible complexity. [2000, 1568]

204 What is the upper limit for the energy of the big bang?

You would think that a lot of energy had to go into blowing up the universe with all its atoms and far-flung matter. We can try to estimate how much energy was involved using what little we know of the origin conditions, and the answer turns out to be, well, astronomical! Because of what are expected to be quantum mechanical effects involving space-time itself, the maximum energy is believed to be about the equivalent of 10^{94} grams/cc or 10^{115} ergs/cc. The concept of the conservation of energy, however, is meaningless, because space-time will be so badly curved that even this sacrosanct law will be invalid for times within about 10^{-30} seconds of the big bang. [2881, 2329, 986]

205 If the big bang singularity dwarfed a black hole singularity, how did anything ever escape?

As I mentioned in Chapter 9, black hole singularities are classified as spacelike, and the big bang singularity is called a timelike singularity. The big bang singularity was a very different kind of singularity than what you find inside a black hole, at least that's what is predicted by the theory that gave us both these phenomena. The essential properties were entirely different. For the big bang there were no ingoing world lines, only outgoing ones in time. For black holes, you only have ingoing world lines. Also and more significantly, in general relativity, black holes are part of the local geometry of space-time and are embedded objects. The big bang, however, is part of the global geometry of space-time and is not an embedded object in our four-dimensional space-time. As to how matter escaped from the big bang singularity, it's simple. Matter had no choice. These were the only outgoing world lines possible at the time, and in many ways the initial big bang singularity resembled a white hole. [2718, 2668, 2368, 2268, 2024, 1357, 1104, 1062, 417, 322, 84]

206 With special relativity, how long did the famous 10^{-43} seconds after the big bang actually last?

The same amount of time, 10^{-43} seconds. Observers will see this as an indicator of the local graininess of time with this duration in their own reference frame. The concept of a true distant observer is almost meaningless, because the size of the observable universe is equal to 10^{-43} seconds multiplied by the speed of light, which gives you 10^{-33} centimeters. There are no distant observers. Special relativity also does not work in these highly curved spaces and is irrelevant to describing what is going on in any physical reference frame at that time. [2716, 1265]

207 Do you agree with the idea that the visible universe was once smaller than an atom?

This seems to be an inevitable conclusion to be drawn from the fact that light takes a finite time to travel. Figures 10 and 11 show what we think this very early time may have been like. When the universe was one 100 billion-billionth of a second old, light could travel only 3×10^{10} centimeters/sec $\times 10^{-18}$ seconds = 3×10^{-10} centimeters, or about the size of an atom. At that instant, the visible universe had a size as big as an atom. Our mathematics tells us what to expect, and without successful competing theories or supportive data, we are captive to what the current theory of gravity embodied in general relativity has to say about these conditions. [1326, 1196, 359]

208 Does Hawking's imaginary time idea have any impact on Guth's repulsive gravity theory for inflationary cosmology?

Inflationary cosmology is an add-on to big bang cosmology developed in 1980 by Alan Guth, then at the Stanford Accelerator Laboratory in California. It claims to describe events that happened 10^{-35} seconds after the big bang and suggests that the universe went through a brief episode of rapid expansion. Stephen Hawking's cosmological speculations have to do with a time long before the inflationary era. These are two different phenomena predicted theoretically. Hawking's process occurs near the Planck era, at a time 10^{-43} seconds after the big bang and involves space-time changing one of its fundamental characteristics due to quantum fluctuations. It is like being told that instead of the hypotenuse being the sum of the squares of the two sides, it is the difference in the squares of the two sides. Hawking says it is possible that a quantum fluctuation near the Planck era could change our familiar timelike dimension into another spacelike one, insofar as how these dimensions are mathematically defined. The mathematics of such transformations let you think of this as time becoming imaginary. Guth's inflationary cosmological theory describes a new field in the universe that temporarily produced repulsive gravity, which led to a period of rapid expansion about 10^{-34} seconds after the big bang, which is long after the era when the Hawking event may have happened. They have nothing to do with each other physically if they occurred at all. [2917]

209 If space increased faster than light moments after the big bang, why do we see anything at all near us in space?

Because space dilation does not occur at every scale. Nearby matter can provide a stronger local gravitational field than the rest of the universe so that galaxy motions are not affected by the cosmological dilation of the universe. We see this effect even today, because the cosmological expansion only "wins" at scales of several megaparsecs or larger. For smaller regions, the local gravitational fields of individual galaxies and stars are far more important in deciding what will happen next. [2724]

210 Isn't the question all advocates of big bang theory should answer is what caused the big bang?

Not at all. Although this is the question that all nonastronomers feel is the most compelling, astronomers have a more incremental outlook. We are interested in developing explanations for observations that encompass as many of the directly observable features of the universe as our observations can provide. Big bang cosmology, despite its portrayal by the news media, is alive and well, because it has proved itself over and over again to logically knit together many diverse observations of the universe into a single grand evolutionary model. Speculations about what caused the big bang are not part of the testable and falsifiable aspects of this theory. Physicists realize that the original big bang theory could never give us a logically consistent answer about this event, because the essential details of what really happens at such high energies are not available experimentally for comparison with the theoretical predictions. There is no present theory that unites quantum mechanics and general relativity.

The bottom line is that we can still use big bang theory as a starting point, because if a better theory comes along (which it surely will), it will have to explain *everything* big bang theory does. Newton's mechanics was replaced by special and general relativity, but we still can use Newtonian mechanics to predict the motions of planets and satellites, provided we understand that relativity theory has to be used for rapid motions and strong gravitational fields. We use big bang theory the same way but realize that it cannot be stretched to cover every aspect of cosmology, which is why it is undergoing refinement. But the purpose of this is not to explain where the big bang came from. The purpose is to better explain direct observations we are now making and that can be corroborated independently. [1227]

211 Why are the abundances of hydrogen and helium set to a constant value in the cosmos?

In the big bang model, once you specify the ratio of density of the universe to the amount of cosmic background radiation (often given as photons per quark) and the rate of expansion today (given by Hubble's constant), the big bang model predicts a hot dense state within the first 5 minutes after the big bang, when helium nuclei formed from the free protons and neutrons. After about 15 minutes, any remaining free neutrons decayed into more protons and some electrons, and you then end up with a fixed ratio of stable hydrogen (protons) to helium. For the observed expansion rate and density of the universe today, the abundances of hydrogen and helium follow from the big bang model. This is an absolutely fantastic prediction, relating two observable factors to the abundance of the lightest elements. [2576, 1479]

212 Is the expansion of the universe slowing down right now?

The expansion of the universe *is* slowing down. Astronomers are working hard to measure how rapidly the deceleration is happening to determine whether or not it will be large enough to cause a collapse of the universe in the future. [2847, 1743]

213 Have other big bangs happened?

We don't know. For a while, some cosmologists speculated that instead of one single big bang, there were many tiny big bangs long ago. The problem is that a universe created from many big bangs would be very lumpy looking. The cosmic background radiation is so smooth that only by some very bizarre fine-tuning could you get a lot of separate, tiny big bangs to end up producing something as phenomenally smooth as the background radiation.

Some theorists have speculated that our universe might be the spawning ground for other universes. At a scale near the Planck scale of 10^{-33} centimeters, pieces of space-time break off from our universe through worm holes, and their worm-hole connection to our space-time evaporates, but each piece that has broken off then experiences its own big bang and inflates to become a separate universe, completely disconnected from our own and totally unobservable. There is no way to test such a theory, so it is actually a nonscientific speculation. [2267, 577, 508, 480]

214 Of what is the universe a part?

We do not know. All we know is the portion of our universe from which we can see out to the limits of the so-called visible universe. Beyond that limit, we can only use our best theoretical models and extrapolations to speculate on what conditions lay beyond, based on what we see inside the visible universe. Virtually all of these extrapolations, using big bang cosmology, say that the rest of the universe looks very much like what we see all around us with the same types of galaxies and stars on average. It is only when you leave the portion of the primordial patch of space-time that emerged from the inflationary era that things can start to look very different. We will never know. [2768, 120, 54]

215 Why did nature produce a big bang at all?

We honestly do not know. The problem seems to be that we live inside the universe, and even if the big bang is an event that occurs with a probability of one chance in 1,000,000,000,000,000,000,000,000,000,000,000,000,000, we who live inside this rare event will perceive it as having a likelihood of one chance in one, by the mere fact that we exist. Assuming that quantum indeterminacy, or something like it, is a universal process that transcends the big bang, we can speak of probabilities for events to cross a threshold to trigger the big bang via quantum tunneling. But if you do away with space and time before the big bang, what do you hang your hat on to describe any phenomenon? What is the arena within which these mysterious quantum fluctuations are supposed to be operating? We have discovered quantum indeterminacy and chaos only as actors on the stage of space-time. How can they exist apart from the arena in which they are seen to operate? No one really understands how even quantum laws can be somehow encoded into a vacuum state that is beyond our three-plus-one-dimensional space-time. [1393]

216 What are the pros and cons for an infinite universe and for a finite universe?

This is a very complex question. Observationally, there is virtually no evidence that the universe is anywhere near being closed, because no accounting of the contents of the universe gives answers that exceed the so-called critical density. Taken at face value, observations consistently point toward densities that are less than critical and often by a handsome margin, ranging from 2 to 10. True, many galaxies show they have some kind of nonluminous dark matter, but the amounts are always consistent with ordinary matter (although some ordinary matter may be nonluminous) and have a total density of less than 10 percent of the critical value for an infinite, flat universe.

As for which kind of universe I would prefer to live in, it doesn't matter. In either case, the prospects for life continuing indefinitely are bleak. In a finite universe, collapse will be finished in about 60 billion years or so and that's the end of life in this universe. In an infinite universe, we have a bit more time, measured in trillions of years before all of the stars burn out and it starts to get real cold. Life is doomed in either kind of universe. [2986, 1026, 37]

217 Will better images than those of the Hubble Deep Field Survey ever show the edge of the universe?

What you will see, and what the best photographs like the one in Plate 10 seem to show, will be an increasing number of younger and younger objects until you reach a point where the individual objects are too faint to see and only their overlapping fuzzy images remain to form a diffuse background glow, like the billions of stars that make up the faint glow of the Milky Way. Eventually, you reach objects so young that you arrive at the 300,000-year marker, when all that existed was a dilute plasma, which is the glow seen by the *COBE* satellite in Plate 9. You never reach a true edge to space. You just run out of objects that are old enough and bright enough to be detected at distances from us that are less than the horizon limit, which is set by the age of the universe itself. We are seeing objects within 7 percent of this limit today, and we can't go much further. [2925, 806]

218 What are the speculations about the future of the universe?

If astronomers determine that the universe is destined to collapse, in something like 20 to 30 billion years from now the expansion will have slowed to a stop and begun to reverse in a collapse phase that will last until about 50 billion years from now, when the big crunch will happen. The universe will get much warmer, from its 2.7 K today to billions of degrees within the last few minutes. Galaxies will be torn asunder about 5 billion years before the big crunch. The stars themselves will cease to exist as the cosmic background radiation reaches thousands of degrees within a million years before the big crunch. Radiation will flow into a star's surface rather than be emitted from it as stars become the coolest intact objects in the universe.

If the universe is destined to expand forever, in about 10 trillion years all of the stars will go out with no new ones being formed, because the interstellar medium is consumed from ancient star-forming episodes and only degenerate stellar cinders are left. Beyond that era, nothing more can really be said, because the time scales for anything new and interesting to happen then become an order of 10^{30} to 10^{40} years, when protons may decay away into electrons and neutrinos, and 10^{60} years, when stellar-mass black holes evaporate by the Hawking process. In either case, the long-range forecast is pretty bleak for life. [2864]

219 What is the contribution of virtual particles to the mass of the universe?

Virtual particles are required in order to understand a variety of subtle processes in physics. The problem is, given the current state of the art in producing a truly comprehensive theory of everything, there seems to be no good idea about how nature avoids having the energy of the physical vacuum contribute mass/energy to the total energy budget of the universe. This weight is determined by the size of the so-called cosmological constant.

For decades, astronomers have been saying that their observations indicate that the cosmological constant, if at all present, contributes no more than about the same mass as the mass in all matter in the universe. Physicists calculating the same factor from their various versions of the theory of everything get predictions that are 10^{120} larger than the astronomical limits. Unless they fine-tune their theories very carefully, it is hard to avoid this catastrophe, but somehow nature manages to set this number to a very small number with an accuracy of 1 part in 10^{120} from zero. Theoreticians have various schemes for how this could be done, but none are experimentally provable at this time. [2603, 1066]

220 If gravity is so strong, why couldn't it keep the big bang from exploding?

Because some things are far stronger apparently than gravity. For decades, cosmologists simply accepted the fact that the big bang involved an explosive expansion of matter and energy and the production of space. No one had much of a clue as to what triggered the explosion. Then, in the early 1980s, Alan Guth and Andre Linde independently hit upon the idea that if a new kind of scalar field existed and had zero quantum spin, it would have some very unusual properties in the cosmological arena. For instance, it would have to undergo a phase transition as the universe cooled and the strong, weak, and electromagnetic forces began to split apart into distinct forces. This would get caught up in a false vacuum state in which the density of energy in the scalar field would remain constant, but as the volume of space increased, the product of its energy density and volume would lead to an increase in the effective mass of the universe. It would, in essence, lead to a powerful antigravity-like force that would amplify the expansion of the universe, making it an exponential process rather than a linear one. The time scale for the universe to double its size would be 10^{-35} seconds, and there would be somewhere between 10 to 30 of these doublings before the phase change in the scalar field had a chance to complete itself.

During this time, the energy density in the scalar field was vastly higher than that in the gravitational field of the existing matter and radiation in space, so even though gravity now dominates the motions of all galaxies in the universe today, during this fleeting inflationary era, it was the scalar field that dominated the dynamics of the universe. We have yet to find any evidence for such a new type of field in nature at any of the accelerator laboratories now in operation. [2718, 2329, 1062, 322]

Chapter 12

The Expanding Universe

What are the most common questions that people have about the universe? That's easy. First, they wonder whether big bang theory is the only one about the universe that fits the data, then they ask how it is that we can still be seeing distant quasars 15 billion light years away if matter can't travel faster than light. I have taken some liberties in rephrasing these two questions, but that is how they sound to an astronomer.

Many people are quite upset and indignant about astronomers accepting big bang theory like it was an indisputable fact. They seem to think that we are a bunch of sheep flocking to only one theory, or they think there is some major conspiracy going on, where astronomers are suppressing viable alternatives. I find these attitudes pretty bewildering and mysterious and can only believe that nonscientists still do not get it when it comes to the scientific method.

General relativity is a hard subject. It is our premier theory of how gravity affects bodies in space and incorporates, as limiting cases, Isaac Newton's physics, which we use every day, and Einstein's theory of special relativity, which we use less frequently. General relativity makes many testable predictions, not just cosmologically but here on Earth, and has had five of the most fundamental ones verified to high precision. But it asks us to accept that space can be bent and that, in the cosmological arena, space can dilate faster than the speed of light. Many people have trouble with this because these ideas are massively counterintuitive. If you do not accept these predictions, however, you end up with cosmological models that look *nothing like the universe we see around us. These wrong ideas then generate meaningless questions that require the universe to have exploded from a particular point in space like some fireworks display, when in fact this intuitive point of view is itself flawed as a starting point for visualizing the big bang.*

221 Is there an easy way to describe big bang cosmology?

Existing evidence suggests that the universe was once much denser and hotter than it is today. As it cooled and continued to expand, some galaxies and stars formed within a few billion years after the big bang; the rest took a while longer and are continuing to form today. The universe continues to expand and may do so indefinitely, if the gravity of all the stars and matter in our universe is not enough to halt the expansion at some distant time tens of billions of years from now. Astronomical research hopes to determine whether the universe will or will not expand forever by identifying and measuring all the major sources of mass in the visible universe. [2131, 2069]

222 Can you list 10 observational facts supporting big bang theory?

Sure!

1. The universe is expanding.

2. A background glow of electromagnetic energy is detectable at microwave frequencies and is measurably the same brightness everywhere in the sky to better than a few parts in 100,000.

3. This cosmic microwave background radiation is precisely that of a mathematically perfect emitter of radiation with a temperature of 2.726 ± 0.010 K.

4. There is a constant abundance of helium and deuterium compared to hydrogen seen in a diverse variety of objects.

5. There are only three families of neutrinos—electron, muon, and tauon.

6. The night sky is not as bright as the surface of the Sun.

7. There are no objects that have ages indisputably greater than the expansion age of the universe.

8. The degree of galaxy clustering we now see around us is consistent with an expanding universe with a finite age of fewer than 20 billion years.

9. There are no elements heavier than lithium that have a universal abundance ratio.

10. The universe is now dominated exclusively by matter and not a mixture of matter and antimatter.

I should point out that although some rival theories have proposed alternative explanations to a few of these observations, there are no rivals that provide a simple explanation for all of these remarkable observations. What could be simpler than a universe expanding from a hot, dense state to the present cool, rarified one that contains all of the listed features? No new physics is required, no mysterious forces, just gravity and hot matter doing their thing over billions of years. [401]

223 Can you name some things that contradict big bang theory?

This is a very fair question.

1. Big bang theory is based on general relativity (GR), which predicts how gravity and space-time operate. If it is found that GR is incomplete as a classical theory, then big bang theory could be doomed, because all current cosmological solutions or models are based on solving Einstein's original, general relativistic formula for gravity. So far, five tests have been performed and compared with GR predictions, and it has been found that Einstein's original version remains the simplest version of GR. For example, clocks run more slowly in a strong gravitational field than in a weak one, and gravity can deflect light in a way that is exactly required if space is warped. In the next few years, a completely new test of GR will be performed by the NASA satellite *Gravity Probe B,* which will search for gravitomagnetism. If this new effect predicted by GR is not found, GR and big bang theory will be in severe trouble.

2. A basic feature of big bang theory is that the universe has a specific age, given its expansion rate. The ages estimated for the oldest known stars are between 12 billion and 17 billion years, but if the Hubble Space Telescope estimates for the local expansion rate are correct, an age for the universe closer to 12 billion years is predicted. There are only three known ways to explain this disagreement: the distances to galaxies have been incorrectly calibrated; the galaxies used to measure the Hubble constant are too nearby to measure the true, slower expansion rate; or there is a new cosmological antigravity force present that is produced by the so-called cosmological constant. If it should come to pass that the expansion speed for the most distant galaxies holds fast to 60–65 kilometers/sec/megaparsecs *and* the ages of stars hold to 12–17 billion years *and* observations can eliminate the cosmological constant as being negligible, *then* big bang theory is in severe trouble, because you cannot have stars older than the big bang.

3. If some new process is discovered that can reduce the cosmological abundance of deuterium, then big bang theory would be predicting more deuterium than can be accommodated by the expansion rate and the known matter density of the universe.

4. If a new explanation for the cosmological red shift is discovered, the existing red shift, which leads to plausible solutions from GR, would be overestimating the cosmological effects that are already consistent with other types of observations.

5. If a new mechanism is found for producing a smooth cosmic background radiation, then the uniformity of the measured cosmic background would not be explained by big bang theory or plausible extensions of it.

6. If a new, long-range force is discovered, then big bang theory will have incompletely described the dynamics of the expansion process, because a new force would fill in for gravity at the greater distances.

7. If dark matter is found to be made of ordinary protons and neutrons and exceeds the amount on which the big bang nucleosynthesis calculations are based, then there is something severely wrong with big bang theory predictions about the first 10 minutes after the big bang, a time period that is recognized as a piece of cake because of its simplicity.

8. If galaxies are found to have formed earlier than the first million years after the big bang, this would conflict with big bang theory and plausible extensions of it, because the predicted amount of primordial clumping at galactic scales would be more numerous and intense than the theory allows.

9. If something like inflationary big bang theory is not vindicated, then there will be no simple solution to the problem of how the cosmic background radiation can be so smooth and at the same temperature at scales larger than a degree. At earlier times in the expansion, regions of the sky that were further apart than this would not have been in communication to coordinate their temperatures so exactly.

I want to warn you that these are weaknesses, but currently none has been established from the data at hand to be actual problems for big bang theory. This makes big bang theory a falsifiable theory of the highest caliber but still makes it the leading candidate for the premier theory of how our universe works. Thus far, big bang theory or versions of it have survived a number of important tests. Whether or not it continues with this track record for the next few decades, we will have to await the outcomes of ongoing and planned experiments. [1794, 1593, 1137]

224 How can we still see the birth of our universe in the cosmic background radiation when light travels faster than the expansion of the universe?

The cosmic background radiation is all around us all the time. Every cubic centimeter of space, about the size of a thimble, in our universe has about 400 photons from the big bang. These photons are constantly moving through space in random directions, but in any one instant, every cubic centimeter of space has about 400. The big bang, you see, did not start "out there" and eject us to where we are now, but instead it was a process that happened in every cubic centimeter of space and dilated space so that matter is now much more sparsely distributed. Of course, thanks to expansion, there are a lot more cubic centimeters of space in our universe than there used to be. The stretching of space has also caused the temperature of the fireball radiation to be shifted downward from its original billions of degrees after the first second of the big bang, to 2.7 K after about 15 billion years. [1919, 1918, 1472, 1305, 721, 551]

225 In the balloon analogy to the expanding universe, what is inside and outside the surface of the balloon?

Taking a deflated balloon and marking its surface with dots, then inflating the balloon, is often used as an analogy to the expanding universe, with each dot representing a galaxy. No one galaxy is at the center. In this particular analog to the expanding universe, all of three-dimensional space is within the surface of the balloon. What is inside and outside the balloon is the coordinate that is at right angles to the space axis, which is the dimension of time. When you use the balloon to think about the big bang, your perspective is a goofy one, because your mind's eye is not located in space to watch the universe expand. Instead, you are floating along the dimension of time, and none of us has any idea what that perspective is supposed to look like. [2257, 1717, 1384, 1016, 853, 837, 507]

226 Do galaxies move at the speed of light at great distances?

No. It is not the galaxies themselves that are in motion. It is the stretching of space that gives the impression that more distance has been covered between now and when the light first left the galaxy. For example, in a 50-yard foot race, if you moved the starting line back after the racer takes off, the distance the racer ran would have increased. You would end up with a race that seems to have been run further than 50 yards in the elapsed time. The runner didn't actually move across the new distance added to the track behind him, so this distance to the starting line cannot be used to determine the speed of the runner from the elapsed time to the finish line. General relativity says that something like this is also happening with the universe, and distant galaxies thus seem to be traveling at huge speeds. [2554, 1419, 825, 503]

227 Was the big bang purely dilation of space or was some kind of conventional explosion involved?

If by "conventional" explosion you mean that there could have been a preexisting three-dimensional space into which it expanded, no, because this is not a solution that is compatible with general relativity. I am also not certain what you would call an explosion that involves all of space all at once and where there is initially no matter present, just pure gravitational energy locked up in the curvature of space-time. There would be nothing conventional about any aspect of such an explosion, and to avoid incorrect analogies, I prefer not even to think of the big bang as an explosion at all.

One of the most peculiar aspects of modern astronomy is how the universe expands. Not a single one of us carries a different picture around in our heads than seeing this as some kind of titanic fireworks display taking place in a greater, infinite darkness. The expanding embers are thought of as the outward-rushing galaxies, and we stand inside one of these and see an expanding cosmos all around us. It is a very comforting image created by our mind's eye, and it has a rich parentage in the number of explosions and fireworks displays we have seen firsthand or viewed on television. What could be simpler than using this perfectly reasonable image when we try to think about the universe exploding into existence and expanding relentlessly through the eternities to come?

So convincing is this intuitive idea of what an explosion ought to look like that we use it to organize much of what we have heard astronomers say about the big bang and the subsequent evolution of the universe. The problem is that virtually every basic aspect of this intuitive image for the big bang is incorrect. Our mental image of the big bang, despite what the theory says, contains these basic elements: a preexisting "sky" or space into which the fragments from the explosion are injected; a preexisting time we can use to mark when the explosion happened; individual projectiles moving through space from a common center; and a definite moment when the explosion occurred. The way that big bang cosmology and general relativity challenge this mental image will astound you.

Preexisting space? There wasn't any! The mathematics of general relativity states specifically and unambiguously that three-dimensional space was created at the big bang itself, at time zero, along with everything else.

Preexisting time? There wasn't any of this either! Again, the mathematics of general relativity treats both space and time together as one object, space-time, which is indivisible. At time zero plus a moment, you had a well-defined quantity called time. At time zero minus a moment, this same quantity changed its character in the mathematics and became an imaginary quantity.

Individual objects moving out from a common center? Nope! General relativity says specifically that space is not a passive stage upon which matter plays out its dance but is a member of the cast. The reason is simple. General relativity does not distinguish the mathematics between the gravitational field of the universe and the properties of space-time itself. They are equivalent terms for the same mathematical symbol. When you treat both the galaxies and space-time together, you get a very different answer for what happens than if you treat them separately, which is what we instinctively always do.

Many have used the dotted expanding balloon an analogy to the universe for a mental anchor. As seen from any one spot on the balloon's surface, all other dots rush away from it as the balloon is inflated. There is no one center to the expansion on the surface of the balloon that is singled out as the center of the big bang. This is very different from the fireworks display, which does have a dramatic, common center to the expanding cloud of cinders. The balloon analogy, however, is not perfect, because as we watch the balloon, our vantage point is still within a preexisting larger space. But for the universe, this larger spatial arena did not exist, so general relativity tells us. The center of the big bang was not a point in space but a point in time! It is a center, not in the fabric of the balloon, but outside it along the fourth dimension—time. We cannot see this point anywhere we look inside the space of our universe out toward the distant galaxies, but we can see its ghostly image written in the histories of every particle of matter and every force in the universe. These histories all end, very thoroughly, at the big bang, some 10–15 billion years back in time.

Projectiles moving through space? Sorry! General relativity again has something very troubling to say about this. For millions of years we have learned from experience on the savannas of the African continent that we can move through space. As we drive down the highway, we have absolutely no doubt about what is happening as we traverse the distance between landmarks. This knowledge is so primal that we are incapable of denying the veracity of the experience. But, what if I told you that you could increase or decrease your distance by standing still and just letting space dilate and contract the distance away? General relativity predicts exactly this phenomenon, and the universe seems to be the only arena in which it occurs. Like spots glued to the surface of the balloon at fixed latitude and longitude points, the galaxies remain where they are while space dilates between them. There is no reason we should find this kind of motion intuitive.

If space is stretching like this, from where do the brand new millions of cubic light years come one moment to the next? The answer in general relativity is that they have always been there. To appreciate this point, I like to think of the shape of our universe as a cosmic watermelon. Every mathematical solution to the equations of general relativity yields answers that represent the entire past, present, and future of the universe all at once and predicts its entire four-dimensional shape. As we slice the cosmic watermelon at one end, we see three-dimensional space and its contents soon after the big bang. At the other end of the cosmic watermelon, we see the collapse of space and matter just before the big crunch. In between, our slices show the shape of space (spherical volumes) and the locations of galaxies (at fixed locations) as space dilates from one extreme to the other.

Where does space come from? As a particular slice through the cosmic watermelon, we see that it has always been present in the complete watermelon, the complete shape of space-time that general relativity solves for. Just as the pulp of a real watermelon is present as a continuous medium, we never ask where the pulp in a particular slice came from. Cosmologically, general relativity asks us to think of three-dimensional space in somewhat the same way. Space is not nothing, according to Einstein, and is merely another name for the shape of the gravitational field of the universe at a particular instant in time.

It is the changes in this shape from instant to instant that make up the curvature in space-time that we call the force of gravity. This shape at one instant is wedded to the shape in the next instant by the incessant quantum churnings of the myriad individual particles that make up the gravitational field.

If you wish to look for where the new space is coming from as the universe expands, paradoxically, the answer seems to be somewhere in the enigmatic hinterlands of the quantum world.

Was there a definite moment to the big bang? General relativity is perfectly happy to forecast that our universe emerged from a singularity at time zero, but physicists now feel very strongly that this instant was smeared out by any number of quantum mechanical effects, so that we can never speak of a time before about 10^{-43} seconds after the big bang. Just as Gertrude Stein once remarked about Oakland, California that "There is no 'there' there," at 10^{-43} seconds nature may tell us that there was no "when" there. The moment dissolves away into some weird quantum fog, and, as Steven Hawking speculates, time may actually have become bent into a new dimension of space. [2454, 2096]

228 If we looked far enough out in space, could we actually see the big bang?

We can only see, with electromagnetic radiation, the events that happened about 300,000 years after the big bang, and the *COBE* images of the cosmic fireball radiation in Plate 9 show us what there is left to see, at least at the largest angular scales many times the size of the full moon. This background seems to be mottled (Plate 9, bottom) because of irregularities in the gravitational field of the universe at these early times. These irregularities have probably evolved by the present time to become vast superclusterings of galaxies and matter. Smaller irregularities representing the clumps of individual galaxies are also expected to be present, and this is why new generations of telescopes are being designed to search for them. At earlier times, the universe was completely opaque, because matter was completely ionized at temperatures above 3,000 K. We can never receive electromagnetic images of the big bang earlier than this horizon. However, if we could use neutrinos, we could explore back to about 1 second or so after the big bang, and with gravitational radiation we could see back to the big bang itself. Presently, such imaging technology is beyond what we know how to create. Even if all we could do is measure the temperature off the neutrino background or the gravitational radiation background, this would indirectly tell us what the universe was like less than 1 second after the big bang, and it would literally be written all over the sky like cosmic graffiti. [1869, 806]

229 I was taught the universe was infinite. How can an infinite universe expand?

There is nothing about infinity that makes any intuitive sense. Don't even try to imagine that you understand infinity well enough to have an intuitive idea about what it represents. For instance, infinity is so big that you can stuff an infinite number of infinite manifolds (universes) into an infinite four-dimensional space-time and still have lots of room left so that they do not touch. How this is possible is an example of our limitations in reconciling seemingly conflicting logical concepts in an arena of experience with which we cannot have intuitive familiarity. [2457]

230 If the universe expanded from the size of a grapefruit to the size of the solar system by 10^{-10} seconds after the big bang, was matter traveling faster than light?

Ah, the wonders of relativity! According to general relativity, it wasn't the matter that was moving faster than light but the distance between various points in space that was increasing faster than light. No matter actually made the journey from one point to another at translight speed. In general relativity, space is free to do things that matter cannot, and one of these is to cause the distances between galaxies to increase without the galaxies themselves having enough time to traverse the distance. We do not like to think of this possibility, because we never see such things happen in our nonrelativistic world, and we have never had the pleasure of developing the right intuition about it.

Table 12 gives the times, scales, and the distances between the matter in the Milky Way and the matter in the most distant quasars we now see, along with the effective velocities in multiples of the speed of light. You don't have to go very far back in time before you seemingly run into problems. The distant matter didn't do any real traveling at all but was carried along by the expansion of the universe, which caused distances to expand faster than light speed. Expanding space is a new idea not found in special relativity and is only provided by general relativity. [2554, 2017, 1342]

Table 12 **How rapidly has the universe changed since the big bang?** This table shows that if you start with a distance of 14 billion light years between the Sun and a distant quasar today, this distance was quite a bit smaller when the universe was younger and was actually increasing faster than the speed of light during most of the universe's history. The table gives the scale, which is related to the inverse of the cosmological red shift and a rough estimate of the physical distance between a distant quasar and the Sun at each instant in time since the big bang.

Time (after big bang)	Scale	Distance (light years)	Speed (times light speed)
Now	1.0	14 billion	1
1 million years	1/1,800	7 million	7
1,000 years	1/56,000	240,000	240
1 year	1/1,700,000	78,000	78,000
1 second	1/10 billion	2	43 million

231 Is the age of the universe closer to 15 billion or 8 billion years, and why don't we know this exactly?

It's beginning to look like it is near the middle of this range, at about 12 billion years. We cannot pinpoint the age accurately right now, because we do not have enough independent, high accuracy "clocks."

The Democrats, Republicans, and the Congressional Budget Office once claimed that the U.S. budget was running a deficit of between $150 billion and $250 billion, but despite the fact that the annual budget is $1.6 trillion, they could not agree on exactly how many dollars this deficit actually amounts to by a range of plus or minus $50 billion. How can this be? Aren't there a fixed number of dollars in the annual budget and a fixed number of tax dollars collected? Why is there an uncertainty in the deficit by as much as 33 percent? Likewise, all the available evidence convincingly tells us that the universe came into being a finite number years ago, but the uncertainties in all of the chronometers we are using are about 10 percent, so it is hard to get a precise number for the actual age. Still, astronomers have not done such a shoddy job so far.

Astronomers have been trying to develop several different kinds of "clocks" that can be compared with one another to figure out the age of the universe. Most often they use the expansion rate of the universe and the age of the oldest stars. The expansion age range is between 8 billion and 15 billion years, depending on whether the expansion factor is closer to 50 or 100 kilometers/sec/megaparsecs. As for the oldest stars, theoretical evolution models depend on many input parameters, including the heavy element content of the stars and their current spectrum and luminosity. The latter depends on distance, which can again introduce errors. The range of ages for the oldest globular cluster clocks in the Milky Way is 12–14 billion years.

In 1997 the size and age of the universe changed because the *Hipparchos* astrometric satellite launched by the European Space Agency succeeded in measuring by trigonometric parallax the distances to more than 100,000 stars, including 50 Cepheid variable stars. This established a crucial luminosity calibration to the so-called Cepheid period-luminosity relation. The result is that the entire distance ladder used by astronomers for determining distances outside the Milky Way galaxy has been revised upward by 10 percent. This means that every object outside the Milky Way is now 10 percent further away, and the universe is thus 10 percent bigger. It also means that the Hubble constant (velocity/distance) is now 10 percent smaller and closer to 60 km/sec/mpc than it is to 70 km/sec/mpc. Thus, the age of the universe is also 10 percent older and is closer to 12 billion years. There is now less of a disagreement between expansion age and oldest-star age, which are now between 10 billion and 14 billion years. This is now comfortably lower than the various estimates for the age of the universe using observationally plausible models that have a Hubble constant near 65 km/sec/mpc and have a total density within 20 percent of the critical value defining the boundary between an open and a closed universe (what astronomers call an omega of 0.20). [2597, 2142, 2092, 1150, 1129, 836, 681, 581, 506, 356,1]

232 If the universe is finite, what is outside it?

Einstein's theory of general relativity is the only existing theory we have to guide us in thinking about physical space. General relativity shows that if we look at a space-time whose three-dimensional space sections are finite (the case of our universe as a closed, finite one destined to recollapse in the far future), we would discover that the paths of particles and light rays would be closed curves. There is no edge to such a space for much the same reason that if surveyors were to map the two-dimensional surface of Earth, they, too, would not find an edge to it.

There are many philosophical attitudes we can adopt about this question. None of these can be strictly proven on the basis of hard data, because the arena of interest lies outside our space-time. The first attitude is that our space-time, our universe, is absolutely all there is. It extends beyond our visible horizon, and there is no embedding space to account for because it simply doesn't exist. The second, Platonic attitude is that nothing is forbidden in nature, so, if a mathematician can imagine it, it actually exists. The embedding space is as physically real as our space-time, and in it all possible universes, even infinite ones, exist, including ones with drastically different physical laws, particles, forces, and dimensionality.

Astronomers only see and receive information from a small part of the universe we are actually living inside, because light has only had about 15 billion years since the big bang to do much traveling across the vast space of the present-day universe. We call this the visible universe just to keep in mind that the universe is actually much larger than the part we will ever be able to see. Our visible universe, however, expands at the speed of light, one light year per year, so that billions of years from today, we will be able to see a much larger part of the entire universe that came out of the big bang. There is, however, no edge to space like the edge to a piece of paper. At least no theory we know of predicts such a situation. [2527, 2460, 2439, 2254, 1741, 1585, 737, 37]

233 Is it your view that the universe is finite or infinite?

My personal opinion is that I don't have much of an opinion either way. Technically, the question is whether the universe contains more or less than a critical mass density of gravitation material. If it has more, then the gravity of everything pulling on everything else will slow the expansion of the universe so that recollapse can occur.

Just by counting up how much luminous matter there is in stars and galaxies, we can only find about 0.5 percent of this critical matter. For decades, astronomers have been weighing clusters of galaxies in space and often find that the luminous matter is only a few percent of the total gravitating mass of some clusters (an omega of 0.01). The amount of dark matter, if present in all clusters, would bring the total gravitating mass to about the critical amount (omega = 1.0) and perhaps a tad more, so that the universe would be finite. The jury is still out on all of this, but it is very troubling to know that the universe might be filled by dark matter of which the luminous kind in stars is only 1 percent. [26]

234 Why do galaxies collide if they were all ejected from a point at constant speed?

Because they were *not* ejected from a single point in the big bang. This is the classical, and pernicious, mistake nonastronomers make in thinking about the big bang. As the big bang continued for millions of years, small collections of matter began to feel their own gravity more strongly rather than continue expanding with the rest of the universe. This caused the flow of matter to become irregular, and the motions started to become very complicated, with small cores of matter the size of large star clusters collapsing. Overall, the largest systems are still sailing along with the big bang, but their constituent galaxies may be moving in complex local orbits of which some intersect, causing collisions. [2661]

235 Are we really near the center of the expansion, or are we off to one side?

According to big bang theory and the data and images from the *Cosmic Background Explorer* (*COBE*), we appear to be at the center of the local expansion of the universe, because the cosmic background radiation is very smooth in its brightness to better than one part in 100,000. This is predicted by big bang theory, which also says that no matter where you are in space, you will see the matter around you appear to move away as a result of the expansion of the universe. Imagine yourself somewhere on the surface of an expanding balloon looking at dust motes on the balloon. The dust will appear to be moving away from you regardless of where on the balloon you are located. The physical universe seems to be very similar to this simple heuristic model. [2201, 2045, 741, 562]

236 Could our universe be a quark in a bigger universe?

Quarks are the building blocks of more familiar particles, such as protons and neutrons, and are second cousins to electrons. Long ago, science fiction authors, but not scientists, imagined that our solar system was simply an atom in a larger object vaster than our universe—perhaps a dust mote on the nose of some mosquito in a superuniverse. It is impossible to ever know what the universe is like at a scale larger than the current horizon to the universe, some 12–15 billion light years distant. The universe we see certainly doesn't behave like a quark or any subatomic particle, because the motions of the galaxies and stars we see are not dictated by the laws of quantum mechanics. Some cosmologists believe that our universe is a part of an unimaginably vaster thing and that what we now see around us may be just a small point in a vast tapestry of structure extending to infinity. This unimaginably vaster landscape is not expected to take the shape of a pimple on a dragon. We will never know what the truly big picture looks like beyond our visible universe, because these issues are beyond scientific analysis and observation. [203]

237 What fraction of the universe is made up of antimatter?

Familiar forms of antimatter include the positively charged twin to the electron and the negatively charged twin to the proton. Combining matter and antimatter annihilates both particles into a burst of pure energy. Observations tell us that there is very little free antimatter in today's universe. The best estimates place antimatter at much lower than one part in a million of the matter we see. Because matter and antimatter look absolutely identical insofar as the light they emit, we cannot tell by way of direct observation whether a particular star in the sky is made of matter or antimatter. However, we do know that all stars in our galaxy and all the galaxies in our corner of the universe are tied together by an interstellar medium and an intergalactic medium of stray hydrogen atoms and ionized plasma. This material comes into contact with all scraps of matter by way of a long chain of connections. If antimatter was present in large quantities, such as 1 percent of all matter or 0.001 percent, we would be able to detect the annihilation radiation at gamma ray wavelengths of electrons colliding with antielectrons and protons colliding with antiprotons. We do not see any large-scale evidence of this.

When the universe was very young, less than one-trillionth of a second after the big bang, there may well have been nearly equal amounts of matter and antimatter, but virtually all of this was annihilated, leaving behind only a small amount of matter and a lot of annihilation radiation, which we now see as the cosmic background radiation. [1872, 594, 591, 491, 374]

238 What is the universe made of?

Well, all of the universe we can see is made from matter of the kind we find near us and in about the same abundances of the elements everywhere. Most of this matter is at the temperature of the surface of the Sun. There is also quite a lot (several percent), of cool matter, often found in interstellar clouds. We think there is a large reservoir of dark matter, which may not even be matter (protons, neutrons, electrons) at all. Some astronomers believe this makes up anywhere from 20 to 99 percent of the total mass of the universe. If that is the case, the stars and galaxies we actually see in the sky are only a few percent of what the universe actually contains.

And don't forget that the largest single constituent of the universe is empty space. Physicists and astronomers are only now beginning to understand what space is, and someday someone will write a book about this subject. [2151]

239 Whatever happened to the rival theories of big bang cosmology?

In the past 70 years, there have been many seriously considered alternative theories to describing the universe. Here is a partial list of theories and their definitions and what happened to them:

DeSitter cosmology, c. 1917 The universe is presumed to be entirely empty of matter but expands exponentially in time because of the presence of a nonzero cosmological constant. But the density of matter in our universe is not zero because we are here and so are a lot of other stars and galaxies.

Einstein static cosmology, c. 1917 The universe does not expand, and is unchanging in time. Edwin Hubble showed the universe was in fact expanding.

Oscillatory big bang cosmology, c. 1930   The current expansion will be replaced by a collapse phase, then an expansion phase, and so on. Despite the fact that non-astronomers love this idea, because it neatly does away with the need for an origin or a final state for the universe, there is no evidence that there was ever a prior expansion-collapse phase. More important, the universe does not appear conclusively to be closed and capable of recollapsing to start the next cycle.

Steady-state cosmology, c. 1950   The universe has been expanding for eternity and new galaxies are created, atom by atom, in intergalactic space out of empty space. This theory was never able to explain convincingly where the cosmic background radiation comes from or why there ought to be a universal abundance for helium and deuterium relative to hydrogen.

Alfven's antimatter cosmology, c. 1960   The universe contains equal parts of matter and antimatter. The problem here is that no large-scale background annihilation radiation has ever been detected to suggest that there are equal amounts of matter and antimatter anywhere within the visible universe at galactic scales. And you cannot hide antimatter stars in matter-dominated galaxies.

Cold big bang cosmology, c. 1965   Something like a big bang occurred, but the initial state was at absolute zero and consisted of pure solid hydrogen. This theory is based largely on thermodynamic arguments but provides no explanation for where the cosmic background radiation came from, why it is so uniform in brightness, and why it has a temperature of 2.7 K and not something else.

Chronometric cosmology, c. 1970   Space-time has a different mathematical structure than the one that forms the basis for general relativity and from which big bang cosmology derives. It predicts an expansion law that, unlike Hubble's Law, has galaxies receding at apparent speeds that change as the square of the distance to the galaxy. This is not observed.

Plasma Cosmology, c. 1970   The matter in the universe, on the largest scales, is not neutral but has a very weak net charge that is virtually undetectable. This causes electromagnetic forces to dominate over gravitational forces in the universe, so that all of the phenomena we observe are not the products of gravitation alone. This invalidates general relativity as the correct starting point for cosmological models. No explanation is given for the cosmic background radiation, its smoothness and temperature, and the abundances of helium and deuterium.

Old inflationary big bang cosmology, c. 1980 The inflationary era at 10^{-34} seconds after the big bang spawned innumerable bubbles of vacuum that merged together to form a patina of matter and radiation in a very lumpy configuration. The cosmic background radiation, however, shows that the universe is very smooth to one part in at least 10,000.

So, who says that astronomers are suppressing alternative ideas to big bang cosmology? The problem is that none of these other ideas satisfies all of the observational evidence at the same time as well as big bang cosmology. [1044, 407]

240 Why doesn't the actual location of galaxies right now make any difference?

All relativistic cosmological models let you predict where galaxies are at any instant in cosmological time. In principle, given the model that fits our data the best, we could predict what the universe looks like today, some 15 billion years after the big bang, and predict where the most distant galaxies are located right now. But this information is not needed for any astronomical purposes. First, because forces only transmit their influences at the speed of light, the thing that matters is where a galaxy *appears* to be right now, not where it actually is. Gravitational and electromagnetic effects are retarded in time and do not happen instantaneously. It doesn't matter to us that a galaxy we see 10 billion light years away is now 50 billion light years away; it is only its gravitational field at a distance of 10 billion light years that affects us at this moment. The cosmological model takes all of this relativity into account. [2375, 2102, 2060, 1743]

241 What is space itself made of?

According to general relativity, "space" is just another name
for the gravitational field of the universe. As such, we stand in
relation to space the way photons of light stand in relation to
the electromagnetic field. Space is just another physical field in
nature, and at its smallest scales, it dissolves away into some kind
of quantum haze where our ideas of time and space no longer
have much meaning. [2330]

Chapter 13

Special and General Relativity

T he questions having to do with special and general relativity received at the Astronomy Cafe have been so numerous and varied that they demand their own chapter. When they hear about relativity, most people are prepared for a rough ride through some of the most amazing and perplexing phenomena in the physical world. The only way to fully understand these theories is by working with them in their natural language—mathematics. Only by attacking hundreds of problems in relativity do you begin to understand how all the parts fit together. Popularizers are ranked according to how well they can explain such imponderables as the famous twin paradox or where the mass comes from that particles gain as they accelerate to relativistic speeds. I suspect I will fail miserably on such a test, because I do not subscribe to the idea that a couple of clever paragraphs will make relativity understandable. There is nothing intuitive about relativity, and virtually all of the questions I receive on relativity demand an explanation for how such phenomena can be possible. Frankly, I don't know. All I know is that special and general relativity work. They are capable of accounting for an amazing variety of phenomena beyond anything that Newton ever imagined, and they do so with unfailing accuracy. Why nature has elected to set the speed of light as a fundamental limit to motion in this universe or why in so doing nature then permits the mathematics of relativity to follow are questions better left for philosophers.

General relativity always attracts its share of confusion. Where do you go after describing space as something that can be bent? How does space manage to dilate between the galaxies to cause the *phenomenon of the cosmological red shift? These are not questions that will be resolved by debating particular descriptive choices of words. For decades, physicists and astronomers have attempted to find alternative ways of describing these phenomena, originally predicted by general relativity, but no theory as mathematically complete and as simple as Einstein's original vision has been able to muster the range of confirmed predictions provided by general relativity. That said, we now have another issue to ponder. Einstein developed general relativity and based it on the assumption that space-time was a feature of the gravitational field. All that we see around us, all empty space, is just the gravitational field of the universe looking back at us. Matter, in many ways, is just a knot of empty space that has been assembled electron by electron, quark by quark, into atoms, interstellar gas, stars, planets, and life. This is a rather unsettling idea, because it provides no anchor that we can grab onto. We are mere dust motes embedded in Jell-o, and from this vantage point, we look at the world around us as having more or less substance.*

The most common questions posed by nonscientists frequently have to do with travel near the speed of light, the possibility of faster-than-light velocities, and the nature of space-time. Many wonder why it is that your rate of speed should have anything to do with the way that time passes or are curious about how it is that a body can physically warp space-time. There has even been a question asked about whether time is intelligent. I have also received a request or two to read detailed manuscripts with claims to have found a better theory than general relativity to explain just about everything in physics. I have politely declined, because most of the authors lack formal training in either physics or mathematics and a familiarity with the existing body of experimental data. Manuscripts are often long strings of "If A, then B" statements, which seem to make logical sense but that can experimentally be shown to be false. Scientific reasoning is more than logic, because it mixes in only statements that can be tested to be correct, no matter what the logical intent.

242 What is the speed of gravity?

All present experimental evidence indicates that it is the same as the speed of light. This is based on the agreement between the predictions of Einstein's theory of general relativity, which requires it, and a variety of key experiments. If the speed were other than the speed of light, there would be a disagreement between theory and experiment, which is not seen at a precision high enough to rule out gross differences of a percent or more. [2915, 2226, 1652, 1510, 671]

243 What is it like to be in a place with no gravity?

Most people think of weightlessness as the state astronauts are in while orbiting Earth, but, in fact, there is gravity there; it's just that it is exactly balanced by the centrifugal force of the spacecraft orbiting Earth. You can still detect the gravitational field because it produces a tidal effect even within the spacecraft.

It is impossible to shield gravity, so no matter where you are in the universe, it can never go away. Gravity acts on and is generated by both matter and energy, and the very objects or containers you try to use to build a shield would themselves produce their own gravitational fields. And it's a good thing, too, because, according to Einstein's theory of general relativity, "gravity" is just another name for the geometry of space and time. If you could eliminate gravity, then space and time also would vanish, and such an experiment would, at the very least, require an environmental impact statement to be filed by the experimenter with the Environmental Protection Agency. [2896, 2442, 2184, 1941, 1497, 610]

244 What the ding-dang are gravitons?

Physicists expect that because gravity is a force that shares many technical similarities to the other three natural forces (electromagnetism and the strong and weak nuclear forces), it must also have a quantum particle that mediates it—the graviton. Gravitons are predicted to travel at the speed of light, have no rest mass, have an unlimited range of influence, and have a quantum spin of 2 quantum units. Gravitons, if they exist at all, are far too weak to study individually. It is very unlikely that we will ever detect individual gravitons, because they interact about 10^{40} times weaker than the electromagnetic force produced by photons. This makes gravitons so weak and elusive that it is a major task for experimenters to verify that they even exist. [2869, 1707, 1669]

245 How does a body bend space-time?

Einstein developed general relativity, which, among its many
applications, describes the gravitational field. One of the most
bizarre aspects of general relativity is that apparently empty
space can be warped by matter. This was confirmed in the 1919
solar eclipse by looking at the deflection of star images and
spectacularly confirmed for enormous systems, such as clusters of
galaxies, as seen in Plate 12, which shows an entire cluster acting
as a gravitational lens to distort the image of a distant galaxy (blue
smudges) billions of light years *behind* the cluster.

The underlying mathematical idea of general relativity is
that there is no technical difference between the mathematical
role played by the gravitational field and the role played by the
geometry of space-time. That being the case, whenever we ask
how space-time is curved by matter, we are simply asking an
equivalent question: How does the gravitational field change,
subject to the presence of matter? Presumably, a body produces
a gravitational field the same way that other bodies produce the
other fundamental forces, but we have no experimental proof that
a quantum description for the gravitational field is a reachable
goal any time soon.

Theoreticians believe that gravity is, at its heart, a quantum
field, just like the fields associated with the other three
fundamental forces. It could thus be thought of as a shimmering
cloud of gravitons which come and go according to the dictates of
Heisenberg's uncertainty principle and are exchanged by matter
and other forms of energy. Other than this expectation, physicists
have no independent observational evidence that gravity really
does act as a quantum field. At least with electromagnetism, the
realization that this field was quantumized was obvious from the
data about 50 years before the first successful quantum theory
of electromagnetism was finally put together in the mid-1940s.
[2758, 2506, 2371, 2027, 1715, 25]

246 Is antigravity possible?

No one really thinks so, because unlike the other forces, gravity
does not act on matter in different charge states; gravity acts
on the total energy of an object. Electric forces attract or repel
because charged matter can be either positive or negative.
However, gravity acts only on the total energy of an object, which

includes its rest mass energy, its kinetic energy, and the energy contained in its various component fields. [2922, 1941, 921]

247 Do other dimensions exist?

All of the evidence is of the theoretical kind, but none of it has been put to the test because we don't know how! All we know is that our space-time is four-dimensional, to about a few parts per 100 billion, based on how well gravity follows four-dimensional general relativity inside our solar system. There has also been quite a lot of talk in the past decade or so about hidden dimensions, which are needed to unify the four forces in nature. But some feel this is just a bookkeeping problem, and, in fact, nature doesn't really have any more than the four dimensions we already know. No one has the faintest idea how to go about proving that other dimensions exist in the microcosm by some kind of direct observation. All the evidence seems to be indirect, but even indirect evidence, as in the case of quarks, can be compelling to scientists if there is enough of it and it is self-consistent. [2916, 1828, 1068, 1049]

248 What is nothingness?

We do not know, other than that it can be described very precisely by mathematics, which says it is a state represented by the negation of all physical quantities and attributes. It is even less than a vacuum, which can still possess dimensionality and extension. Nothingness would have no extension, no dimensions, no structure, no time, no politicians, and so on. Mother Nature may never realize this one in the physical world with perfect fidelity. Interstellar space is the closest it gets, and even this is positively filled to the brim with lots of things that make it a far cry from perfect nothingness. [2651]

249 What is time?

We don't really know. Physically, time is an essential parameter that we seem to need to sort out spatial configurations of matter and energy in our universe. For thousands of years, four dimensions have circumscribed how we classify and link together external events in nature. Some physicists in search of the theory of everything have suggested that, at a scale trillions of times smaller than a proton, many more dimensions are needed to mathematically sort out how particles interact and account for the various patterns seen at these scales. Like the numbers we throw away in long division to get our answer, we don't really know if the hidden dimensions in the mathematics of quantum field theory are real or just bookkeeping tricks we need to carry out our calculations with the theory.

The direction of time seems to have no real physical meaning for subatomic systems. It is only with large ensembles of particles that a direction emerges for time. This is very much like the concept of temperature, which is meaningless for systems consisting of only a few particles. Like temperature, time may be an emergent quality of nature only defined for large enough systems. Time may have no real existence in the quantum world of individual particles and systems. [2174, 1245, 1105, 735, 711, 710, 603]

250 What is a space-time continuum?

In 1906, soon after Albert Einstein announced his theory of special relativity, his former college teacher in mathematics, Hermann Minkowski, developed a new scheme for thinking about space and time that emphasized its geometric qualities. In a public lecture on relativity, Minkowski announced: "The views of space and time which I wish to lay before you have sprung from the soil of experimental physics, and therein lies their strength. They are radical. Henceforth, space by itself, and time by itself, are doomed to fade away into mere shadows, and only a kind of union of the two will preserve an independent reality."

This new reality was that physical space and time have to be combined into a new physical entity, space-time, because the equations of relativity show that both the space and time coordinates of any event must get mixed together by the mathematics in order to accurately describe what we see. Because space consists of three dimensions and time is one-dimensional, space-time must therefore be a four-dimensional object. Physically, contrary to many popular descriptions, space-time is not a fabric. Space and time are not tangible things like water and air. It is incorrect to think of them as a medium at all. No physicist or astronomer versed in these issues considers space-time to be a truly physical medium, but that is the way in which our minds prefer to visualize this concept, as we have since the nineteenth century.

The theory of general relativity, as developed by Einstein, states (and this is a direct quote from Einstein): "Space-time does not claim existence in its own right, but only as a structural quality of the [gravitational] field." Added to that are comments by theoreticians, such as Nobelist Steven Weinberg: "Space and time coordinates are just four out of many degrees of freedom we need to specify a self-consistent theory. What we are going to have [in any future theory of everything] is not so much a new view of space and time, but a deemphasis of space and time." A similar view is expressed by a coinventor of superstring theory, Michael Greene: "In the theory of gravity, you can't really separate the structure of space and time from the particles which are associated with the force of gravity [such as gravitons]. The notion of a string is inseparable from the space and time in which it moves." Finally, as Einstein noted: "Space and time are modes in which we think, not conditions in which we exist." This view was also expressed in A.D. 900 by Arab physicist Ikhwan al-Sufa: "Space is a form abstracted from matter and exists only in consciousness." Thus, the question about what space-time is of itself is a very complicated one indeed. Physicists think of it as a field in some ways analogous to the electromagnetic field, but when they leave the office after a long day, I'm certain they think about it just like the rest of us do, including astronomers. [2381, 2330, 1832, 1748, 909, 411]

251 Because we see stars the way they were thousands of years ago, could some of them already be gone?

The stars we see in our own galaxy are too close for them to be greatly different than what we see in their millenia-old images, except for the many massive red supergiant stars, which are on the verge of becoming supernovae. Although given the galaxy's current appearance, this possibility is unlikely, the supergiant star Betelgeuse in the constellation Orion may already have gone supernova, but we won't know for another 1,500 years. The Hubble Space Telescope is studying Cepheid variable stars in galaxies 10 million light years away. In 10 million years, such stars can change a lot, and it is very likely that some of the ones that have been carefully studied may no longer exist, because they have evolved into white dwarf stars. We also see very distant supernovae in galaxies hundreds of millions of light years away. These individual stars have already exploded and have been black holes or neutron stars for millions of years. The supernova 1987A seen in the Large Magellanic Cloud 160,000 light years away actually detonated 160,000 years earlier. We only just received news of this explosion in 1987 because of its great distance from Earth. [2985]

252 What is it that physically prevents faster-than-light speeds?

We really do not know why it is that nature has decided that the speed of light, 299,792 kilometers/sec, or 186,287.9 miles/sec, is to be the fastest speed allowed in our particular four-dimensional space-time. But experiment after experiment shows that if you take electrons and boost their speeds faster and faster, they behave as though they are gaining mass the faster they are accelerated. As you approach the speed of light, the amount of energy required to boost them a fraction of a micron per second faster outstrips the energy available in your local power utility, then your nation, and so on. Why this happens can be accurately explained by the equations of special relativity to a zillion decimal places, but as to why it should be so, no one has a clue. There have been many interesting proposals to exceed the speed of light by using certain features of general relativity, such as black holes or worm holes. Most recently, University of Wales physicist Miguel Alcubierre proposed in the May 1996 issue of *Classical and Quantum Gravity* that by using "exotic matter" to contract space-time ahead of a rocket, you could produce any amount of acceleration you want locally. But there are problems with this idea, which I mention in a later question. For more details on surfing space-time, visit www.islandone.org/Propulsion/Alcubierre.html. [1984, 1730, 1522, 1518, 1407, 909, 424]

253 Is there such a thing as hyperspace?

Science fiction writers since E. E. "Doc" Smith have invoked what they call hyperspace as a means of short-circuiting normal space and allowing their heroes to travel to the stars in the time it takes to scramble eggs. It is such a commonplace idea that it has now grown to be accepted by many as a given in the physical world as well.

Physicists have long speculated, based on the mathematics they need to describe the forces in nature, that the physical universe must have some other dimensions attached to it, other than the familiar four that make up ordinary space-time. But it is pretty well agreed that these added hyperspace dimensions are a billion billion times smaller than the nucleus of an atom, and only subatomic particles can experience what they have to offer. Given how large these other hidden dimensions are, 10^{-33} centimeters by some estimates, your journey through them will be very short and uncomfortable. [939, 653]

254 How does gravity travel through space?

According to general relativity, gravitational forces are defined as the curvature of space-time, but this curvature in four-dimensional space-time is specified by 20 distinct mathematical terms. Only 10 of these terms are defined by the local distribution of matter, which is mathematically found by solving Einstein's equation of gravity. The other 10 terms in the full Riemann curvature tensor define how the space-time outside the massive body responds to the presence of the mass and define a source-free solution for gravity. This only happens in space-times with four or more dimensions, which is why gravity does not exist as a force in three-dimensional space-time. In space-time with fewer than four dimensions, gravity as a force does not extend beyond the body producing the force, which means it is not a long-range force at all. That is the complicated mathematical reason why gravity can "travel" through space. In general relativity, gravity and space-time are exactly the same things by definition. It is impossible, within general relativity, to separate gravitational fields from the fundamental properties of space-time. This is like trying to define what a computer is without its hardware. Gravity travels through space because it is simply another name for space itself. [2869, 2758, 2226, 1707, 1618, 1510, 1497]

Chapter 14

Space Physics

space physics is a large catchall category I have created that includes all of the nonrelativity questions that have been posed at the Astronomy Cafe. I have been amazed by the variety of topics that have nothing to do with relativity that are collectively familiar to many individuals. Some questioners are not aware that gravity travels at the speed of light rather than instantaneously, and this has led to many questions about gravity that start out on the wrong foot. Antimatter is also a popular topic, with many questions about what it is and whether physicists have created any of it. Some of my favorite questions include: "Does time stop at absolute zero?" "Is Schroedinger's cat dead or alive?" "How is Zeno's paradox resolved in modern physics?" I had to spend time with my old, dusty physics textbooks to find a simple explanation for how the famous slingshot effect works. Many people are also confused by how it is that a symmetric gravitational field can produce a net increase in velocity for a passing spacecraft. One person even asked if the space inside particles is the same as that inside atoms.

Modern physics is a complex tapestry of issues, many of which require explanations involving very subtle and technical concepts. Take the familiar quantity of spin in atomic physics. Spin is what defines the types of particle you are talking about, such as an electron and a quark (0.5 quantum unit of spin) or photons and gluons (1 unit of spin). The problem is that this property of fundamental particles has nothing whatsoever to do with the familiar concept of rotation. Spin is a new feature of nature at the same level as a new dimension to space-time. One may just as well have

*adopted some other name for this feature, one akin to "color,"
which is a term used to describe the charge of a quark and has
nothing to do with the color we see in our everyday lives. Every new,
successful theory presents us with new and exotic phenomena, most
of which cannot be intuitively understood unless you are a physicist
who has literally lived with the new ideas for decades. Even so,
physicists may visualize a particle like an electron as some kind of
tiny sphere of electromagnetic charge, but they know full well that
electron structure has nothing to do with such a shape. So, for the
general public attempting to make sense of physics, there are many
hidden traps lurking along the road to understanding. Probably
the worst thing you can do is ask how a particular phenomenon
is possible. The bottom line is that we don't know, but we do have
detailed explanations anyway, and these explanations seem to work
astonishingly well. Progress in science is not gauged on the basis of
how well it continues to validate our intuitive beliefs about how things
ought to be, but by how well it confronts ingrained beliefs and shows
us what the objective world is really like.*

255 What happens to matter at absolute zero?

According to predictions by Einstein some 70 years ago and
experiments at the Massachusetts Institute of Technology and
Joint Institute for Laboratory Astrophysics at the University of
Colorado, you end up with a new state of matter called a Bose-
Einstein condensate. According to Michael Anderson and his
colleagues, in a paper published in the July 14, 1995, issue of
Science, the quantum shapes of the individual atoms begin to
spread out as their speeds plummet in a near absolute zero trap
cooled to only 170-billionths of a degree above absolute zero.
Their collection of rubidium atoms started out at a healthy 4
million, but after evaporative cooling continued, they wound up
with only a few thousand atoms that actually took up residence in
the Bose-Einstein condensate state. Eventually, the wave functions
blend together so that you can no longer determine the positions
of any individual atoms no matter what you try. In essence, the
new system is no longer a collection of individual atoms but is an
entirely new form of coherent matter describable by a new wave
function. The nuclei remain distinct, but the electron clouds blur
into one entity. [2451, 1827, 1750, 1660, 804, 382]

256 Do antiparticles produce antigravity?

This is unlikely, because, unlike the other forces, gravity does not act on matter in a way that is determined by the different charge states for matter. Electric forces attract or repel because charged matter can be either positive or negative. Gravity acts only on the total energy of an object, which includes its rest mass energy and its kinetic energy, along with the energy contained in its various fields. There are, however, planned experiments to see which way antiparticles fall in Earth's gravitational field. Some physicists think that antimatter may fall up relative to normal matter, or at least not fall down as fast as normal matter. Antiprotons and antielectrons, when they are produced in atom smashers, usually live only 100-millionths of a second. During this time, gravity would cause them to fall or rise by only $1/2 \times 1,000 \times (10^{-8})^2 = 5 \times 10^{-14}$ centimeters. This is an extremely small distance, about the diameter of an atomic nucleus. Stay tuned—the results will definitely be on the front pages of the major newspapers. [2922, 1032, 921]

257 Can the structure we see in the physical world be simply a projection of how our brains work?

I don't think so. For example, it doesn't matter how your brain is put together when it comes to the outcome of jumping off a cliff. Gravity will affect humans, lemmings, and frogs in the same way. All that humans have done is predict what these outcomes will be. I think there is a genuine, objective, outside world that exists independently of whether humans are present or not. The particular way in which we describe this world may have a certain degree of arbitrariness to it. We can develop an entire physical theory on the Newtonian concept of force and obtain a consistent system of description. We can also develop a theory that describes everything in terms of energy and Lagrangian mechanics, in which force is never mentioned, and still develop a completely consistent way of describing the world. These two descriptions were developed by humans about the same time in the eighteenth century. There are also other systems of interpretation that suggest there may be several self-consistent ways of describing the physical world. The key thing that unites all of these approaches, however, is mathematics. Each system can be mathematically transformed into the other in a definite way, just as English can be transformed into French or German.

Until we meet nonhuman beings who have become equally competent in exploring the physical world, we will never really know how different these interpretive frameworks can be. One thing is certain, however. Even among the human systems of physics, some are definitely better at interpreting aspects of the world than others. Quantum mechanics and quantum field theory have their natural expression in terms of Lagrangian mechanics, not Newtonian mechanics. There may be yet-to-be-discovered frameworks that will prove to be better in explaining key aspects of quantum theory that are better than Lagrangian mechanics.

258 Do all elementary particles have spin, and where does it come from?

Quantum mechanical spin is not to be thought of as equivalent to the spinning of a top or a planet. Heisenberg's correspondence principle states that to find out what a particular quantum mechanical feature corresponds to in the world at large, you increase the quantum number associated with that feature to very large values. This works for energy, but for quantum spin, you may not vary this quantum number beyond the range from zero to 2. Quarks and leptons all have a 0.5 unit of quantum spin and are called fermions. There is a second family of particles, called the bosons, which includes the electromagnetic photons, the weak force carriers (the W and Z particles), and the strong force carriers (gluons). They all have 1 unit of spin. Gravitons may also exist with spins of 2, but that's it. There are no higher-spin fundamental particles possible, at least theoretically. Quantum spin is strictly a feature of the quantum world and has no analog in our macroworld.

We don't know where spin comes from. This is like asking why there is gravity in the universe or why electrons exist. Spin just seems to exist and is another one of those imponderable features of our world that philosophers get to worry about. [1554, 221]

259 Can things be infinitely small?

We do not know for certain, but there are strong arguments that say that this is not so. It has been known for decades that if you combine Newton's constant of gravity, the speed of light, and

Planck's constant in the right way with the right powers, you can create a Planck length, which has a size of 1.6×10^{-33} centimeters. This is 100 billion billion times smaller than an atomic nucleus. Physicists believe that at this scale the quantum indeterminacy we have come to accept in the atomic world and in the description of matter and energy finally carries over into how we must describe space and time. Space no longer has a nice, smooth geometry but becomes an uncertain froth of geometric and gravitational distortion, with quantum black holes and worm holes shredding up space-time, making it into something resembling Swiss cheese. If the Planck scale is fundamental, then there are no physical objects, fields, particles, space, or time that can be infinitely subdivided below the scale set by the Planck length. [1503, 1493, 432]

260 How is Zeno's paradox resolved in physics?

The ancient Greek philosopher Zeno conjectured that motion is impossible, because to reach a given point by walking, you would have to travel first one half the distance, then one half of the remaining distance, ad infinitum, and this would take an eternity. We know that in the atomic domain, particles are defined in terms of wave functions that connect all points in space-time by a probability that a particle will be found there. We also suspect that space-time itself cannot be subdivided below a scale of 10^{-33} centimeters, at which point space-time becomes a quantum mechanical thing lacking a definite shape. Both of these ideas differ from Zeno's assumption that space and motion were subdividable infinitely, and it is in the true character of space, time, and motion that the mathematical paradox is resolved once and for all. Quantum indeterminacy means that parts of a particle can be found at many neighboring points in space and span many intervals of time so that nothing may be cleanly subdivided with infinite precision, especially a particle's location and speed, which are joined together by Heisenberg's uncertainty principle. [1267, 520]

261 What is energy?

It isn't anything real in the sense of a sunset or a rock. It is just a convenient bookkeeping index that scientists use to compare many different kinds of systems in terms of their ability to do interesting things. It can be quantified in terms of ergs or joules, which are the common energy currencies. Systems that have or can produce the same number of joules are said to be similar and can be converted one into the other, given the right circumstances. [2867, 1670, 1424, 754]

262 How do astronomers weigh the planets?

From a simple equation in physics based on Kepler's Third Law. The mass of a planet is related to the orbital period and distance of its satellite. Except for Mercury and Venus, all planets have satellites and can easily be weighed. For Mercury and Venus, flybys of spacecraft in the 1960s were able to make the equivalent gravimetric measurements. [2910, 2081]

263 Does chaos really occur or exist in nature?

Chaos seems to occur almost everywhere in nature whenever the final outcome of a process is very sensitive to the initial conditions prevailing at some earlier times in the system.

In 1989 Jack Wisdom and Gerald Sussman at the Massachusetts Institute of Technology used a specially designed computer, a digital orrery, to calculate the orbit of Pluto for the next 845 million years at 40-day intervals. As described in the August 1989 issue of *Sky and Telescope,* what they found was that the orbit of Pluto is chaotic, which means that its long-term shape depends very sensitively on the exact input parameters used to start the calculations. Not knowing today where Pluto is located to a precision of less than 1 kilometer adds up over thousands of orbits and makes the predictions vary over a wide range of possibilities. They were able, however, to show that for many reasonable choices of input parameters, Pluto will never get closer than 100 million miles to Neptune, because Pluto and Neptune are apparently locked into a resonant condition between the orbital periods of the two planets. [858, 364, 355, 190]

264 Are all particles and fields just vibrations in an energy field?

It seems that something like this is the case, but we still do not know the details. The folks working on the theory of everything reduce particles to vibrating strings of energy. When a unification theory including gravity is finally developed, we will see through tedious mathematics that all particles and fields are related to the gravitational field of the universe by a series of mathematical operations. Gravity is in some sense the ultimate field. Even now, when we study the structure of the electron, all we see is that it is smaller than 10^{-20} centimeters and has all of the properties of a knot in the electromagnetic field. This field, in turn, is related in some mysterious way to the gravitational field of the universe itself. [2669]

265 Does gravity produce gravity?

Yes, it does, and this makes the mathematical treatment of this force a nightmare of nonlinear effects comparable only to the interactions between quarks that are mediated by gluons. Gravitational fields possess energy, and energy generates gravity just the way matter does. Hence, gravitational fields self-interact. For Earth, the energy stored in its entire gravitational field has the mass equivalent to a large mountain, such as Mount Everest. It's not much, but only Einstein's theory of general relativity was able to anticipate this contribution to Earth's total mass. [2027]

266 What exactly is a subatomic particle's structure like?

We don't really know yet. Take the simplest particle we know about, the electron. Experiments show that it is just a knot in the electromagnetic field with no solid surface or internal structure. As you scatter more and more energetic particles off it, all you see is a region of increasingly higher electric field strength. The theory of quantum electrodynamics (QED) has been tested to a phenomenal number of decimal places, 10 or more, and still agrees with experimental data on the electron and how it behaves quantum mechanically. The theory stipulates that the electron is a pure point particle with absolutely no internal structure. If you added internal structure, the theory would violate special relativity. Recently, experimenters have found that in certain kinds of experiments, there may be a weak departure from the predictions of QED and experiment, but the scale at which this happens is about 10^{-20} centimeters or so and at energies above 100 GeV. Future experiments will check this. Also, some recent results at Fermilab seem to indicate that quarks may have some internal structure, making them less than fundamental, but these experiments are far less conclusive and controversial, given the statistical significance of the results.

On the theoretical side, it has been widely expected for decades that at a scale of 10^{-33} centimeters, the structure of space-time will cease to be the implacable, smooth "surface" we use in modern quantum theory and become something quite bizarre, perhaps an unimaginable froth of mini–worm holes, quantum loops, or strings wiggling about in some strange kind of hyperspace with a dozen or more dimensions. At these scales, all particles lose their pointlike character. All quantum fields are reduced to some more complex topological structure, as the superstring theorists advocate. Conceptually, I have not the slightest idea how to interpret the mathematics, but if the mathematics lead to testable and verifiable predictions, how we think of the mathematics becomes a moot issue. Although it is difficult to accept quantum indeterminacy, duality, and special relativity as commonsense ideas, this is the way nature seems to work. [1358]

Chapter 15

Space Travel

E veryone wants to know why the speed of light is a physical
barrier, and, by analogy with the speed of sound, when they can
expect to hear that the light-speed barrier will be surmounted by
our technology. Questions involve everything from worm
holes to Alcubierre warps, and I find myself increasingly in the
role of Scrooge, having to throw massive amounts of cold
water on the speculations of several generations of Star Trek
followers. I really hate this part of science popularization,
because it always seems to pit science against our most
cherished dreams about what the future could be like. All I can say
is that we have yet to see a single chink in physics that permits
faster-than-light travel without also requiring some impossible
goal, such as finding or creating a navigable worm hole or
black hole.

Two of the most interesting questions received at the Astronomy
Cafe were "Why is the sky always black in photographs from
spacecraft?" and "Will humans ever travel to the stars?" The first
question was a surprise, because, although I know the reason why,
I hadn't bothered to ever mention it to my nonastronomer friends
because it seemed so obvious to me. Now, when I look through
pictures taken by NASA satellites from space I have to smile and
appreciate that this is indeed a very clever question. Where did all
the stars go to make the sky look black from space? Concerning the
second question, let me expound in some detail about how I feel space
travel will evolve in the distant future. I have read science fiction all
my life and am now obsessed with the TV series Babylon 5, which I

rank as the greatest science fiction television series of all time. Still, I have to admit to being quite cynical about our prospects for leaving the solar system.

The expenditure of resources needed to build a single interstellar spacecraft is probably in the several-trillion-dollar range, and there are many engineering problems that need to be resolved in the areas of propulsion and operating reliability. Psychologically, I cannot imagine a single human being wanting to submit to leaving Earth forever, with the daily fear for decades that something may go wrong in the spacecraft. Think about it! The first interstellar ships will probably fail unless we work out many subtle technical issues, so the volunteer passengers will almost certainly understand that the trip will probably be a deathwatch. We will probably first send many robotically operated probes, but these will never be able to fully test the conditions under which humans will live and work. Each starship will be hideously expensive, and to send a test ship with a fully-functioning but robotically staffed biosphere, would be a hard cost to defend. Still, there will be plenty of opportunities to send robotically controlled, fast spacecraft to the stars. They are a factor of 1,000 times less expensive, and we have done some amazing things with the exploration of the solar system in this way during the past 30 years. Stay tuned. I think that in the next century we will indeed send our first probes to visit nearby stars.

267 Why does the sky look black from space?

You may have noticed that in all the pictures taken by astronauts or interplanetary spacecraft, Earth or the planet in the picture looks great, but there are no stars in the surrounding sky. This is not some attempt by NASA to censor information but is a consequence of the fact that the cameras are used have been stopped-down because of the great brightness of the primary object in the field. Stars are much fainter and require fast optics and long exposures to be rendered in the way we expect to see them. Go into an illuminated parking lot on a clear night and look at the sky. You will see the same effect as your eye is flooded by bright lights and its pupil gets smaller. This renders it less able to see faint stars, which requires the pupil to be almost at its maximum size. The same explanation applies to such photographs as Plate 4, of the asteroid Ida and and its companion, Dactyl. [2887, 2693, 1511, 606]

268 Why can't the space shuttle visit the Moon or the other planets?

There simply isn't enough fuel or provisions carried for the trip. [2570, 2891]

269 What do astronauts do in space?

They all live by strict schedules jam-packed with monitoring the health of the spacecraft subsystems and operating experimental equipment according to the guidelines established by NASA and ground-based experimenters. They probably get some recreation time, but it must be like trying to rest on a crowded bus. There is a fair amount of studying technical manuals and keeping close records of air quality, fuel, spacecraft attitude, and environmental factors. There also must be a number of daily checklists to go through. But the view is incredible! [2148]

270 How fast does the space shuttle have to travel to leave the atmosphere?

Even at an altitude of 200 kilometers, the space shuttle is still inside the outer reaches of Earth's atmosphere. The velocity at Earth's surface that the shuttle needs is practically the same as the Earth escape velocity of 11.2 kilometers per second, or 25,800 miles per hour, which is about Mach 30. [1167, 758, 757, 725]

271 How much radiation exposure do astronauts get in space?

Table 13 shows some dosage estimates for various missions. For orbits at 250–300 km at 65-degree inclinations to the equator, you get about 10 millirads a day. These numbers are from volume 2 of *Foundations of Space Biology and Medicine,* NASA SP-374 (1975). Passes through the Van Allen radiation belts give you 10–20 rads/hour, but most manned flights avoid the belts, even though passages through them only last about 10–20 minutes. [2906]

Table 13 Space is an environment filled with charged particles from Earth's Van Allen radiation belts and from the solar wind and occasional solar storms. This is a compilation of the radiation dosages that astronauts have received while orbiting Earth or on journeys to the Moon. For a comparison, on the ground you receive about 350 millirads of natural radiation, and a chest X-ray is worth about 70–90 millirads. Even during sunspot minimum, *Skylab* astronauts received large accumulated doses because of their 80+-day stays in space.

Mission	Date	Dosage (millirads)	Altitude (kilometers)	Duration (days)	Sunspot Cycle
Gemini 3	March 1965	23	240	0.2	Minimum
Gemini 4	June 1965	46	280	4	Minimum
Gemini 5	August 1965	176	303	8	Minimum
Gemini 7	December 1965	164	290	15	Minimum
Skylab	1973–1974	2,500	433	84	Near minimum
Apollo 11	June 1969	173	—	—	Maximum

272 Has anyone ever had sex in space?

Not that I have heard. Then again, who would tell? There are cryptic rumors about something called the Three Dolphins Club, but no official word on whether any human experiments have ever been attempted or even sanctioned. [2510, 1609]

273 Can you see satellites or the space shuttle from the ground?

Yes, depending on your location and the time of the year. For some of the shuttle flights, when their orbits come far enough north of the equator, you can see them as a bright, rapidly moving star in the west in the very early evening. I have personally seen a few satellites. They are always visible within an hour or so after sunset. Any later, and the satellite is completely in the shadow of Earth and is unobservable. The brightness range for satellites can extend from slightly fainter than the brightest star you can see to roughly the limit of your vision at a magnitude of about 6. It depends on how large the satellite is and how reflective. [7]

274 What would happen to you if you stepped into space without a spacesuit?

To experience the vacuum is to die but not quite in the grisly manner portrayed in the movies *Total Recall* and *Outland.* The truth of the matter seems to be closer to what Stanley Kubrick and Arthur C. Clarke had in mind in *2001: A Space Odyssey* or even the ghastly accident in the 1997 movie *Event Horizon.* According to the 1966 edition of the *McGraw/Hill Encyclopedia of Space,* when animals are subjected to explosive decompression to a vacuum-like state, they do not suddenly balloon up or have their eyes pop out of their heads.

When the ambient pressure falls below 47 millimeters of mercury (0–9 psi, about 6% of the earth's atmosphere at sea level), the water inside all tissues passes into a vapor state beginning at the skin surface. This causes the collapse of surface cells and the loss of huge amounts of body heat via evaporation. After 6 seconds, the process of cell collapse involves the heart and lungs and causes circulatory interruption, followed by acute anoxia, convulsions, and the relaxation of the bowel muscles. After 15 seconds mental confusion sets in, and after 20 seconds you become unconscious. You can survive for about 80 seconds if a pressure higher than about 47 mm mercury is reestablished; otherwise you turn into freeze-dried dead meat on a stick. [62]

275 Are there things in the universe that travel faster than light?

Yes, there are things that travel faster than light, but there is no matter or energy or information involved. For example, if you point your scissors at the sky and open them quickly, the mathematical points that lie along the lines formed by the jaws of the scissors travel faster than light at a distance of several million miles from the scissor. Quantum mechanics and Heisenberg's uncertainty principle allow particles to fleetingly travel faster than light, but any observation of this is completely hidden from view, and you cannot use this phenomenon to transmit information. The expansion of the universe caused the separations between galaxies to increase hundreds of times the speed of light when the universe was only seconds old. Pieces of some distant quasars seem to be moving faster than light when you compute the apparent distance traveled divided by a time interval. In all these instances, no information, matter, or energy moves this fast. [1859, 1611, 192]

276 Will travel at light speed ever be possible?

Never. To accelerate one gram to the speed of light, you would need to burn up all the stars in the universe. Objects with finite rest mass can never travel at the speed of light, but they can get close to this limit if you are willing to throw vast amounts of energy at them to accelerate them. [2458, 2240, 1993, 1920, 1824, 1731, 1522, 785, 561, 559, 306]

277 Will we ever be able to use worm holes for travel?

There is not a single scrap of evidence that navigable, stable, macroscopic worm holes exist in the real world. Until we can confront the mathematics with some real data, you can imagine worm holes doing just about anything. [2753]

278 How feasible are *Star Trek's* warp drive and matter teleportation?

I do not see any way in which the laws of physics as we have observed them can seriously allow either faster-than-light travel or the transportation and reassembly of matter as in *Star Trek*. Faster-than-light travel only seems possible under certain very specific or rare circumstances, which are completely hidden from view by the quantum nature of matter. As I mentioned in Question 252 in Chapter 13, Miguel Alcubierre proposed a novel way of surfing curved space-time by creating a warpage of space ahead of the spacecraft, but a recent calculation seems to kill this idea rather thoroughly. Mitchell Pfenning and Larry Ford of Tufts University published the calculation in the July 1997 issue of *Classical and Quantum Gravity* and showed that the energy needed would equal 10 billion times the energy locked up in every star in our observable universe. Nature has, yet again, suggested a way to beat its own speed limit but only at a prohibitive cost.

As for transporting matter, putting talk of pattern buffers, transporter beams and Heisenberg suppressors aside, we can already transport matter at nearly the speed of light in our accelerators and in our TV picture tubes. But entire people are more than atoms—they involve an enormous amount of information to specify the quantum states, locations, and velocities of every fundamental particle in the body. Shortcuts could be found, but then information would be lost, which could be fatal for organic systems and certainly fatal for specifying the locations and states of the trillions of neuronal connections in the brain that control memory and behavior, among other things. [368]

279 Is the kind of artificial gravity used in *Star Trek* possible?

It is not feasible at all. The only credible versions of antigravity devices are those used in the Earth Force spaceships in the TV series *Babylon 5*. You can simulate gravity in a rotating cylinder with your feet magnetically clamped to the floor. [1769, 1704, 899]

280 At what speed does the interstellar medium become lethal to high speed flight?

We do not really know what the interstellar medium looks like up close at a scale of a few kilometers. If it is just stray hydrogen atoms and a few microscopic dust grains (micron-sized is common), then at their expected densities you are probably in for a rough ride once you pass 50 percent the speed of light. The dust grains become lethal, interstellar BB shots that pummel your spacecraft like rain. At the higher velocities needed for interstellar travel at 95 percent the speed of light, these dust grains may be infrequent, but each will puncture your spacecraft and leave a very impressive hole many times the size of its own diameter across, like small bombs. But the situation could be worse, if the interstellar medium contains lots of ice globules from ancient comets and other things we cannot begin to detect in interstellar space. Impacts from objects even at 0.1 centimeter would be fatal. We just don't know what the size spectrum of matter is between interstellar micron-sized dust grains and small stars in interstellar space. I would be delighted if science fiction authors would write stories with a more physically realistic interstellar space. It could make for a hair-raising story line! [2720]

281 What are the known problems with human spaceflight?

Doctors report that prolonged exposure to low gravity causes loss of bone mass, and major changes in the cardiovascular system. After 100 days, we know that Russian cosmonauts from the *Mir* space station returned to Earth in pretty bad condition, close to the threshold where irreversible changes may occur. The body does not respond well to low gravity, and studies on the space station in the next decade will tell us more about this and if there are any ways to avoid damage. After 200-plus days en route to Mars and 200-plus days to return, the astronauts would not be able to return to Earth without fatal damage to their bones and hearts. There is also the problem with cosmic rays and the high energy particles produced by solar storms. Without significant spacecraft shielding, these would be lethal to astronauts caught in interplanetary space. There are also a whole range of psychological problems to worry about, especially if a crew is selected from multiple cultures, where differences in eating preferences and socialization techniques may lead to friction in close quarters. Also, as long as astronauts have been able to see Earth out the windows of their spacecrafts, they have maintained a sense of connection and contact with a familiar environment. In interplanetary space, Earth looks like another star and you are really *alone.* No Earth-based experiments can simulate this condition, because every subject knows they are still on or near Earth, even in the bottom of a cave. [2095, 483]

282 Have any artificial objects left the solar system?

Yes. In September 1995, *Pioneer 11* was 6.5 billion kilometers from Earth; in February 1996, *Pioneer 10* was 9.5 billion kilometers from Earth; on June 13, 1997, *Voyager 1* was 10.0 billion kilometers from Earth, and *Voyager 2* was 7.78 billion kilometers from Earth. The *Voyager* distances from the Sun are increasing by about 35 kilometers/sec or 3 AUs per year. Recall that 1 AU is the distance from Earth to the Sun, and Pluto's orbit is 39.4 AUs. For updates on the *Pioneer* positions, visit the site pyroeis.arc.nasa.gov/pioneer/PN10&11.html. For the latest on the still-operating *Voyager* missions, visit vraptor.jpl.nasa.gov/voyager/voyager.html. [1698, 1007]

283 If cosmic rays are a big problem for travel to Mars, why aren't they a problem for shuttle astronauts?

Earth's magnetic field shields astronauts from most of the harmful cosmic rays, but there is no such shielding in interplanetary space for long voyages to even nearby planets. [2953]

284 What technology developments do we need to get to Mars?

We need a self-contained life support system involving plants and other renewable sources of food. We also need to solve many nasty biological issues related to how humans degenerate in space over long spans of time in very low gravity conditions and devise a lightweight or low-cost shielding system to protect the astronauts from exposure to solar flares. We will also need to address issues of crew psychology and the need for constant contact with Earth. [2975]

285 How long would a trip to Mars take?

It depends on the details of the orbit you take between Earth and Mars. The typical time during the closest approach of Mars to Earth every 1.6 years is about 220 days. Again, the details depend on the rocket velocity and the closeness of the planets, but 220 days is the number I hear most often, give or take 10 days. [2811]

286 Will humans be able to land on Jupiter or Saturn in the next century?

No. We would be crushed if we landed on the surfaces of these planets. Besides, we will be very lucky if we make it to Mars in the next century. Jupiter's radiation belts are filthy and lethal, and they encompass most of that planet's inner satellites, some of which, such as Europa, might be worth visiting. [2824]

287 Will astronauts ever be hit by orbiting debris?

Probably. The space shuttle has already been hit by an object a millimeter in size. In November 1995, inspection of the cargo bay door showed a crater 2 centimeters long and 6 millimeters deep caused by a piece of electronic circuit board traveling at 5 kilometers per second. If the door had been open at the time of impact, the fragment would have hit oxygen tanks in the cargo bay, which would have exploded.

In 1998 construction will begin on the space station. A bumper will be installed on the leading edge of the station to vaporize harmlessly any particles up to a centimeter in size. NASA's Haystack radar has been monitoring radar signals from a small spot in the sky and has detected more than 400,000 pieces of debris about 5 millimeters or larger passing overhead. The U.S. Space Command routinely tracks more than 8,000 objects 10 centimeters across or larger. It is expected that the space station will have a 1 percent risk per year of being hit, and holed, by a debris particle or meteor. Over its 10-year lifetime, this is one chance in 10. Pretty bad odds. This does not include dozens of hits per month that are expected to be shielded by the bumper system. I do not know if I would want to work in a room where there is a good chance that a cosmic bullet will penetrate the walls and perhaps hit me or cause a catastrophic leak before I could scramble into a spacesuit. You can be sure that the first time this happens, there will be a major congressional investigation into who is at fault, but, of course, "the fault is not in ourselves, but in the stars." For more information on space debris hazards, visit the site sn-callisto.isc.nasa.gov/newsletter/v2i2/v2i2-3.html, and read issues of the *Space Debris Newsletter.* [1158]

Chapter 16

Strange Sightings

A stronomers are frequently asked for their opinions about UFOs, astrology, and ESP, and many of the questions I receive at the Astronomy Cafe continue this tradition. Still, the questions that are of the most interest to me are the frequent ones from individuals who have seen something unusual in the sky. For the most part, these unusual sightings were fireballs, which are bright meteors, and I have received questions with a frequency that pretty well matches the expected annual rate of meteors, based on studies by astronomers. About once a month, someone in the United States will happen to look up in the sky and see a bright fireball streak across the sky. Other sightings, however, are more unusual. The number of times that people report seeing a star grow in brightness and fade away or change its color has been more than I expected, but I still don't think these sightings are anything more than atmospheric phenomena. I have also seen the atmosphere do weird things to the shape of the Moon. Questions about mysterious bright flashes of light in the night sky or raging fires seen on the Moon are hard to answer, because the details are usually so sketchy that I cannot even speculate about what might have been seen. One individual insisted that the dancing lights seen in the direction of a military airfield could not have been the running lights from jet planes but had to be something more cosmic.

Most of my answers seem to be accepted by the people that pose the questions, and I never hear from them again. But quite a few people wanted to argue with me, because my possible answer didn't satisfy their feelings that they had seen something bordering on *the supernatural. The sky is a complex screen upon which nature treats us to some very rare and spectacular phenomena from time to time. When we only look at the sky one night a year, we can expect to see many seemingly exotic phenomena that have very natural explanations. Our predilection seems to be, however, to select the exotic explanation over the commonplace one. Fireballs, which are rare but natural, are dismissed in favor of satellites or alien spacecraft burning up in the atmosphere. The changing colors of stars by atmospheric refraction and dispersion is less believable than a signaling UFO. We all want to feel in awe of the world around us. The problem is that some people feel that they have to work hard at it. There is so much to marvel at if we only take the universe for what it is rather than what we wish it to be.*

288 My mother said that between 1947 and 1949 there were stars moving all over the sky. Any ideas what this was?

No, but on October 9, 1946, there was a very spectacular Giacobinid meteor shower, with up to 100 meteors per minute, which was hailed as very dramatic. A sky full of moving stars might have been one way to describe the experience. [2897]

289 I saw a planet looking like a full Mercury in the direction of Sirius at 8 P.M. GMT from France. Any ideas?

I have no idea what this could be all about. Mercury cannot be seen as a disk, full or otherwise, with the naked eye, and it would never be found near Sirius, which is too far from the ecliptic plane where Mercury moves when it is near the Sun. [2853]

290 Why does the color of bright stars oscillate from red to green through a telescope?

Because Earth's atmosphere acts as a lens to refract the light from the star into a minispectrum. Blue, green, and red light refract to different degrees, and your images will be colored as the transparency of the air column you are looking through changes due to turbulent eddies at high altitudes. This effect is most noticeable at low elevation angles near the horizon or on nights soon after or before a storm system has passed through. [2809, 2712, 2349, 1948, 1861, 1310, 48]

291 I saw a double rainbow with the colors of the inner one reversed. Was I imagining this?

Not at all. In the double-rainbow phenomenon, which is not that rare, the inner, primary rainbow is the brightest and forms first, followed by a secondary rainbow located above it. The reversed ordering of the colors is the rule, not the exception. [886]

292 What is the green flash seen at sunset?

This is an atmospheric phenomenon caused by sunlight when it is refracted by different angular deflections at different wavelengths by the atmosphere. I am not an expert in such matters, but I presume that it is caused when much of the light at wavelengths that are shorter than the green color we see in a rainbow is scattered out of the sunlight from the Sun close to the horizon. This leaves the light only at wavelengths of green, yellow, orange, and red, which combine to give a predominantly green color. Quite a lot of diffraction is needed to accomplish this feat, which means a very large path through the atmosphere is needed near the horizon. It would occur only in the last few seconds before the Sun actually sets. [222]

293 How do you tell the difference with the naked eye between a star, a planet, and a satellite?

Under typical observing conditions, planets do not twinkle but stars do. This is because the atmospheric cells that cause stars to twinkle when they pass across the star's position subtend about an arc second or two from the ground. For planets with disks several tens of arc seconds across, the effect averages out, so that even though the eye cannot resolve the planet's disk, it can average the intensity of the light over hundreds of these atmospheric cells, leaving a nearly constant intensity. This doesn't happen for stars because the cells are as big as the star images. Also, planets are found along a thin band in the sky called the ecliptic, which passes through the constellations of the zodiac. Satellites have a perceptible movement relative to background stars and are seen near or soon after twilight as the satellite passes into Earth's shadow. They move much slower than meteors, and it can take several seconds for them to cross a distance equal to the diameter of the Moon. [1590]

294 Why do you believe spook lights are real but not that UFOs are spacecraft?

There have been numerous reports of odd, ghostly spook lights in some parts of the United States. The Marfa Lights in Texas seem to appear on a particular highway and resemble headlights from distant cars. Others are glowing balls of light that move rapidly and vanish. Some call them swamp gas or other similar natural phenomena. I am very sympathetic to these observations, because it was essentially the very same kinds of persistent reports that led to the eventual detailed investigation of ball lightning, a rare plasma phenomenon that produces balls of luminous gas during severe lightning storms. Spook lights are intriguing and, if I do say so, a bit thrilling to study. There is much about them that one would think ought to be discoverable, if only someone would take the time and be persistent. I can think of a dozen experiments I would like to attempt to learn more about them. But until someone or some group comes forward to do such a study, I am perfectly willing to leave them alone and just enjoy the element of mystery that they introduce into my world. I have no time to think about them in any detail, but I am delighted that I might share this increasingly small planet with them.

As for why I "believe" in spook lights and not UFOs being spacecraft, I guess it is a matter of how much common sense I am willing to suspend for poorly observed phenomena. Spook lights are the second cousins to other light-producing natural phenomena. UFOs as spacecraft, on the other hand, seem to be quite illegitimate as plausible interpretations of another phenomenon. [2650, 2275, 1979, 1729, 1241, 1238, 1236, 963]

295 If astronomers feel that life can exist elsewhere in the universe, why don't they believe in the possibility that UFOs are from other worlds?

Science is not about feelings and beliefs. A scientist, as a human being, can believe that organic life exists in one form or another on millions of planets in the Milky Way. They can even arrive at this opinion by citing statistics. But it is almost impossible to talk about UFOs in any scientific terms because *all* of the purported evidence that tries to show that UFOs are spacecraft from other planets is anecdotal and, in most cases, based on flawed human perceptions and outright deceit. The implication that some UFOs might be spacecraft is so profound that we must demand hard physical evidence, not merely 1,000 reports by well-intentioned people. Scientists demand a level of integrity in data collection that nonscientists simply do not fully appreciate. We are not stubborn out of spite or narrow-mindedness. We are stubborn because we know full well how easy it is for humans to create belief systems that have no rational underpinnings, based on a few pieces of ambiguous information. We are not trying to uncover laws and facts that make us feel good. We are trying to understand how nature works. [1131, 326]

296 Have you ever seen or heard something you could not explain scientifically?

Yes. In a remote canyon in Yosemite Valley near Merced Lake, California, I was fixing dinner after a long hike, when in the distance I saw a thunderstorm approaching. It never passed overhead, but the eastern horizon was pretty cloudy. Then, in the distance and seemingly out of nowhere, I heard a pair of deeply resonating, low tones, about two octaves below middle C and about a semitone apart. The sound switched between the two tones about four times, then stopped. I imagined that winds from the storm may have excited some kind of resonance in something but could never figure out what. The effect was captivating and absolutely eerie. I did not sleep very well that night, given my penchant for an overactive imagination.

As for UFOs, in a backyard in Oakland, California, around sunset, I happened to be looking up at the sky when I saw a formation of what appeared to be seven or eight unresolvable lights flying westward in a V-shaped constellation. They moved at a rather high angular rate of speed and traveled from directly overhead to the horizon in about 10 seconds. The only thing I could think about was a flock of birds, but this explanation didn't seem to fit in with their high angular speed. They would not have been very high up, considering how fast birds fly, to be traversing the sky so quickly. Jets would have made a noise and left behind contrails. [2948, 1242]

297 What is your opinion about the thousands of people who say they have been abducted by UFOs?

Carl Sagan's book *The Demon-Haunted World* (Random House, 1995) is excellent for those of you who want to read about the scientific view on this issue. I fully agree with his analysis. The only people that report these "abductions" are the victims themselves. Despite accounts of abductions that occur in residential communities by the thousands, no next-door neighbors have come forward to say they have seen someone else carried off. I think that the general public simply has no understanding of just how badly they can be fooled by their own minds. This sounds arrogant but consider that the entire advertising industry exists because consumers can be easily seduced by movie stars hawking products on TV. We are told again and again by various surveys that TV influences us and our children, but despite the billions of dollars invested every year, advertisers claim that TV doesn't influence our children to be more violent or buy certain products. We accept this "pretzel" logic and fail to regulate TV advertising and programming.

It is well known that humans believe what they wish to despite any reasonable evidence, especially if what they experience meshes with some prior belief in how the world ought to work. We selectively remember events that reinforce our prejudices and ignore contrary evidence. This is why astrology is still believed to be valid by billions of people around the world, even though every study shows that it doesn't work any better than flipping a coin. Abductions, with all due respect to the thousands of people that have reported them, are simply misunderstandings of a very common phenomenon that occurs to many individuals when they are in a state halfway between full wakefulness and sleep. It has been scientifically documented that in this state we experience many curious and fleeting things as the brain is waking up the body. Paralysis is very common, as are reports of mysterious figures, vague sexual experiences, and feelings of some malevolent agency at work. This is science, not superstition. Why the brain does this is not known. A casual observer who doesn't believe in the scientific explanation will create elaborate stories about the event and may become famous. Our society does reward lunacy by making it economically profitable, while scientists are increasingly portrayed as stodgy curmudgeons disconnected from the real world. [1776, 987]

298 In Pennsylvania on October 20, 1996, I saw what looked like a star flare up at 5:00 A.M. about 50 degrees from the southern horizon. What do you suppose it was?

From the information you gave, the sighting must have been somewhere in the direction of the constellations Taurus and Auriga, but without any more specific information about the particular sky region you were looking at, I am afraid that what you are describing sounds more like a human-made object or perhaps a rare meteor streaking toward you and burning up to make a tailless fireball. There are no reports of any stars flaring up like that. [1948]

Chapter 17

Telescopes and Stargazing

Believe it or not, telescopes and stargazing are among my least favorite topics. Coming from an astronomer, who is supposed to use telescopes, this might sound like heresy, but it's true. Yes, I was once an amateur astronomer, and I built two good telescopes, but I never found the process very pleasurable. Had computers and the Internet been widespread in the 1960s, I would probably never have owned a telescope. My earliest memories were of struggling to get my telescopes to give me even mediocre views of distant galaxies, and my journey into astrophotography was pretty much a failure, despite the years I worked at it. Thus, in answering many of the questions on these subjects, I have had to draw from personal experiences that were perhaps not what you might imagine. My advice? Buy yourself the biggest telescope you can and drive into the countryside on a regular basis so that you can see what a dark sky really looks like. You will need a major dose of success in seeing the night sky the way it really is, before light pollution gobbles everything up into a paltry, milky white veil. It is difficult for me to get my two young daughters excited about the universe, because, even on the best of nights, you barely see a few dozen stars in the sky.

Many people have asked me for specific recommendations about books to get started in astronomy. If you visit your local bookstore or library, you will find a rich assortment of good titles. There is little mystery in what you need to do to become fluent and conversant in astronomy. You need to become familiar with the shapes of the constellations, the vital statistics of the planets in the solar system, *and the characteristics of the major classes of objects in deep space. This takes an amount of time and effort akin to what many children and adults are willing to expend in following their home team, a sports event, or a TV soap opera. The purchase of a telescope should be the last thing you do as the culmination of your love affair with the universe, because what you will see through the eyepiece will in most instances be disappointing. Except for the planets and a few star clusters, everything else in the universe will look like smudges of light, even with the largest telescope you can afford. Only photographic techniques eventually give you recognizable images of galaxies, and only after you have devoted some serious and significant time in working out the technical details. Meanwhile, visit the Hubble Space Telescope web site (www.stsci.edu) and enjoy the real universe. It may not be as personal because you didn't take the picture, but life is short and you owe it to yourself to get on with the true business of enjoying the view. As my daughters say, it's awesome!*

299 Why does the Hubble Space Telescope show green and yellow pictures of Saturn?

Sometimes the separate images of an object taken in several different filters are shown individually to bring out the differences in the surface details that are color dependent. Mars, Jupiter, and Saturn are good examples of where this is likely. [2899]

300 Can the Hubble Space Telescope see a human face from orbit?

At visible light wavelengths, the theoretical resolution of the Hubble Space Telescope is about 0.04 arc seconds. At an altitude of 200 kilometers, this angular resolution translates to a linear scale of 4 centimeters or about 1.5 inches. This is enough to see your eye sockets, mouth, and ears. Of course, atmospheric turbulence would reduce this acuity significantly, so it would probably not be able to do more than identify the gross anatomical features of a human body. Spying on sunbathers would be at the limits of what the instrument could do, but why bother? [2479, 2104, 379, 378]

301 Why can't we see more of the universe with a more powerful telescope?

Because the universe has not been around long enough for us to see objects much farther away than a few billion light years, and, with the exception of a few thousand quasars, most galaxies are very faint, which makes them hard to detect at great distances. The Hubble Space Telescope can see individual galaxies with multiday time exposure out to a red shift of 3 or so (Plate 10), but the kinds of objects it sees are still pretty bright compared to nearby small galaxies, like the Magellanic Clouds. Even if the universe was 50 billion years old, we would probably not be able to see much more than we do because it takes a lot of luminosity for a galaxy to be seen as an individual over such distances, and this is what limits even the biggest Earth-based telescopes in what they can see. Also, because of the red shift, a nearby bright optical galaxy will have its spectrum shifted into the infrared region of the spectrum, and you have to design telescopes differently to be sensitive to infrared light rather than to optical light. The universe hides distant galaxies by shifting their light out of the normal operating bandpass of telescopes used to study nearby galaxies. [2581, 2038, 2026, 1344]

302 Can we see any of the *Apollo* artifacts left on the Moon from Earth?

Not a chance. Even using the Hubble Space Telescope, with a resolution of 0.04 arc seconds, at the distance of the Moon, some 224,000 miles, you could only resolve objects 230 feet across. [2264, 1183]

303 Is everything you see with a small telescope a part of our Milky Way galaxy?

All of the bright stars, star clusters, and nebulas in the night sky are part of the Milky Way. Only the occasional faint smudge of a galaxy, such as Andromeda, or the Magellanic Clouds can be seen beyond our Milky Way and are separate systems of stars in the universe. Quasars are starlike objects, but the brightest one is 3C273 at a magnitude of +13, which is too faint for most amateur telescopes to see. [1101]

304 Why are Newtonian reflectors more popular than other kinds of telescope designs?

The most important single feature that determines how well a telescope will work is the size of its mirror or lens. Bigger is always better. Newtonian reflectors are the cheapest telescopes per inch of aperture compared to any other kind of telescope. They are very simple to make and require only one main optical surface to "figure," making them the favorite for amateur astronomers. [2981, 2412, 2219, 1933, 1437]

305 Do you think an 8-inch telescope is a good choice for general observing?

I think it is an excellent choice. When I was starting out as an amateur astronomer, I first built a 4.25-inch telescope, then an 8-inch. There was no question that an 8-inch gave me a far richer experience than with the smaller telescope. If you can afford an 8-inch, I strongly recommend getting one. [871, 814]

306 Can you network telescopes together to make one bigger telescope?

Yes, but it has to be done very carefully so that you do not end up combining the electromagnetic waves out of phase. Pairs of telescopes can be used in this way, greatly increasing their resolving power. Telescope interferometers, such as the Very Large Array in New Mexico or the transcontinental Very Long Base Line Interferometers connecting telescopes in Europe, the United States, and Great Britain, operate in this way at radio wavelengths. At optical wavelengths, the Keck I and II telescopes will be used in interferometer mode. There is also an optical interferometer operating at Mt. Wilson Observatory in California and run by scientists from the U.S. Naval Observatory. [2821, 1892, 1277, 335]

307 What basic things should a beginner look for in buying a telescope?

First, I would look for a solid mounting that does not wobble. No matter how small the telescope is, it can still give you very exciting views of the heavens, the Moon, and star clusters if the mounting is not rickety. Second, the optics must be of the highest quality you can afford. This is a difficult issue because you have to trust the word of the manufacturer. Poor optics will show star images as comet-like shapes at the edges of the field or show them to have colored halos. Third, you need a finder or guide telescope, which is a low-power 6x telescope with a wide field of view. This helps you point the telescope so that an object appears in the eyepiece field of view. The better telescopes also come with such accessories as a selection of eyepieces, a Barlow lens, and perhaps a wedge for observing the Sun. Do not use a solar filter, because it can crack and cause the telescope to focus a blast of sunlight on your retina that will burn a hole in it in a millisecond! You also need to decide whether you will want to photograph objects with the telescope, because this will determine whether you can use an inexpensive Dobsonian mounting or if you need a high-precision equatorial mounting with a clock drive to track the stars. [1974, 1575, 1307, 814, 673, 672]

308 I have a 10-inch reflector and can see ninth-magnitude stars but cannot see the eighth-magnitude cluster Messier 68. How come?

Because the brightness of the Messier 68 cluster refers to the total light from its constituent stars. You cannot see the individual stars but will see a diffuse glow with a surface brightness equal to a single eighth magnitude star spread out over the same area. But because the light is spread out over a large region of the sky, its apparent contrast to the background sky is probably so low that the sky brightness is killing you from your observing site. The ninth magnitude stars you see have far more concentrated light, and they literally punch through the sky background. For the best views, you have to go to locations where urban light pollution is minimal. As Plate 14 shows, it is getting more and more difficult to find such locations. This photograph was taken by the Air Force Defense Meteorological Satellite Program over the United States at night, and the white splotches are the combined light from street lights in hundreds of cities and towns. [2995]

309 I don't understand how to use right ascension. Can you help?

Objects in the sky have fixed addresses, much like the way cities and other features on Earth's surface are described by their latitude and longitude. Astronomers call these the equatorial coordinates. Declination corresponds to latitude on the Earth and decreases from +90 degrees at the north celestial pole, about which the sky appears to rotate, to zero degrees at the celestial equator. It then continues to −90 degrees at the south celestial pole. So far, so good, and few people have much problem with this coordinate. The problem is the second coordinate, the right ascension or simply RA. The RA coordinate of a star is fixed, but because Earth rotates, the direction you must look in the sky to find the proper RA coordinate changes from second to second. The circles of constant RA run from the north to the south celestial pole, like the longitude lines on the surface of Earth. To find out what RA passes north to south across the sky and intersects the zenith point directly over your head, you have to know your local sidereal time (LST), which tells you the RA through your meridian. From this and the RA of the object you are looking for, you can easily determine how many degrees to the east or west of your meridian at the moment you have to look and find the object.

You can get your LST by visiting the U.S. Naval Observatory's web site (tycho.usno.navy.mil) and by knowing your longitude. Once you know the LST for a particular date and time, subtract it from the right ascension of your object to determine the current hour angle of the object to the east or west of your local meridian. For every hour of difference, add 15 degrees. You have to repeat this calculation *every second* because the sky rotates. [2796, 2752, 2075, 1460]

Chapter 18

Internet Resources

I opened the Astronomy Cafe in May 1995 and since then
the quantity and quality of the resources on the Internet
have simply exploded. I receive many inquiries about where
to find certain specialized information, and there are many
places I discovered as I searched around for answers to some
questions. Here is my list of favorite sites, but given the nature
of the Internet, I can only promise that at the time this book
went to press the web addresses were correct and the sites
active.

310 Where can I find ideas for science fair projects?

The Internet is a wonderful source of unusual information.
Remember, the best topics come from the simplest questions you
can think of. Try to write down one or two questions that come
to mind from each of the sites you visit. Have a look at the ones
that display image data, and study the images until something
catches your eye. You can also visit the NASA IMAGE/Poetry
Space Science site (image.gsfc.nasa.gov/poetry), where I give
suggestions. Keep in mind that much of what you see at some
recent astronomy data sites has not been investigated in
detail by professional astronomers. [2804, 2333, 2310,
2077, 2070, 1603, 1597, 798, 552, 246, 228, 168, 164,
131, 61]

311 Where can I get more information about purchasing a telescope?

Check out Ronnie Kon's Purchasing Amateur Telescopes: Frequently Asked Questions site (www.mindspring.com/~aleko/scopefaq.txt).

312 Where can I find out how to observe earth satellites?

There is a web site called SatPasses (for Satellite Passes over North American Cities) that gives visibility forecasts for the space shuttle, *COBE* satellite, and *Mir* space station, among others (www.bester.com/satpasses.html).

313 Where can I find a three-dimensional map of the Milky Way?

You can have a look at a navigable multiwavelength image of the Milky Way at the Astronomical Data Center (adc.gsfc.nasa.gov/mw/milkyway.html). My friends there say they are working on a virtual reality version that will let you tool around the solar neighborhood out to 100 light years or so. It should be available on this Milky Way site in 1998. [2843]

314 Where can I get the latest count on the number of extra-solar planets (exoplanets)?

Visit the Searching for Extrasolar Planets site (cannon.sfsu.edu/~williams/planetsearch/planetsearch.html) and the Exoplanets page (www.physci.psu.edu/~mamajek/exo.html). [2740, 1075, 108]

315 Where can I get a picture of the star 51 Pegasi?

Visit the Space Telescope Science Institute's Digitized Sky Survey (stdatu.stsci.edu/dss/). Fill out the online form with the sky coordinates of the object and wait a minute for delivery of an image. [1555]

316 Where can I get more information about Comet Hale-Bopp?

Just visit the Sky Online site (www.skypub.com). They have a page on the comet. Also, the NASA Jet Propulsion Laboratory has a good site on the comet (www.jpl.nasa.gov/comet/). [2059]

317 Where can I get more information about the Mars fossils?

Visit the Center for Mars Exploration (cmex-www.arc.nasa.gov) at the NASA Ames Research Center. There is also the Life on Mars page (www.reston.com/astro/mars/life.html), which provides links to relevant web sites. [1520, 1427]

318 Where can I find color pictures of solar system objects?

Try visiting the Nine Planets (seds.lpl.arizona.edu/nineplanets/nineplanets/nineplanets.html). There is also Views of the Solar System (www.hawastsoc.org/solar/homepage.htm) and Welcome to the Planets (pds.jpl.nasa.gov/planets). The Astronomy Picture of the Day site (antwrp.gsfc.nasa.gov/apod/astropix.html) also has some great planetary images. Don't forget to try the NASA Johnson Space Center Digital Image Collection (images.jsc.nasa.gov). [2902]

319 Where can I get information about lunar phases, moonrise and moonset times, and the position of the Moon in the sky?

There is a web site at the U.S. Naval Observatory for finding moonrise and moonset (tycho.usno.navy.mil/srss.html) and lunar phases (tycho.usno.navy.mil/vphase.html). [1435, 1337, 113, 18]

320 Where can I find comet information and images?

There are many sites. My favorites are the Comet Observation Page (encke.jpl.nasa.gov) and the National Space Science Data Center comet page (nssdc.gsfc.nasa.gov/photo_gallery/photogallery-comets.html). [2876]

321 Are there web sites that give aurora forecasts?

Try the Aurora Home Page (www.pfrr.alaska.edu/~pfrr/AURORA/INDEX.HTM), which gives daily forecasts and links to other resources.

It also provides geomagnetic index plots that tell you how active Earth's magnetosphere is each day. Also visit the Marshall Space Flight Center (uvisun.msfc.nasa.nasa.gov/UVI/current_uvi_image.htm), which gives a daily snapshot from space of what Earth's auroral belt looks like. They also have an archive of past images. The *TIROS* satellite (www.sel.noaa.gov/pmap/index.html) provides images of the global auroral power. [2904]

322 Where can I get information about the local conditions in near-Earth space?

If you are planning to leave Earth for a jaunt to Mars, or just want to find out when to shut down your satellite to ward off a serious electrical disaster, visit Today's Space Weather site (sec.noaa.gov/today.html). You can have a look at what the solar surface is doing on any day to anticipate if any bad solar storms may be brewing for the near future by visiting Solar Images at the Solar Data Analysis Center (umbra.gsfc.nasa.gov/images/latest.html). Also visit WeatherNet4, the NBC space weather site (wxnet4.nbc4.com/spacenscience.html), which provides forecasts, solar images, and current events in space.

323 Where can I find out what Earth sounds like?

One of the creepiest sites I have ever visited is the POLAR Sounds of the Magnetosphere (www-istp.gsfc.nasa.gov/istp/polar/polar_pwi_sounds.html). You will find the eerie recordings of Earth's electromagnetic voice, including whistlers, chorus, and saucers! You will need a sound card and the proper software to handle the large sound files that can be downloaded to your computer.

324 Where can I get information about a particular artificial satellite?

Visit the online Satellite Encyclopedia (www.TELE-satellit.com/tse/online/) and enter the name of the satellite or browse their index.

325 Where can I get sunrise and sunset times?

There is no better place than the U.S. Naval Observatory's web site (tycho.usno.navy.mil/srss.html).

326 Where can I get an image of any part of the sky ?

Visit the Space Telescope Science Institute's Digitized Sky Survey (stdatu.stsci.edu/dss/) and enter either the name of the object or its sky coordinates. In a few minutes an image will be delivered that you can click on and download to your hard drive for further enhancement.

327 Where can I read about the latest developments at NASA?

Visit NASA Today (www.hq.nasa.gov/office/pao/NewsRoom/today.html), where you can read the day's postings and browse highlights from previous weeks.

328 I want to use my setting circles. Where can I get my local sidereal time?

Most telescopes come equipped with disks on each of their axes that are graduated into degrees for the declination axis and hours and minutes for the polar, or right ascension, axis. These are the setting circles that most amateur astronomers find very enigmatic and usually ignore, but they look pretty spiffy. To use them, however, you need to find your local sidereal time at the moment. The U.S. Naval Observatory gives this to you once you specify your location on Earth (tycho.usno.navy.mil/sidereal.html), but make sure you know your latitude and longitude to an arc second accuracy if you want a precise answer.

329 Where can I find out what the moon's phase was on a specific date?

The U.S. Naval Observatory has a wonderful virtual reality lunar phase calculator (tycho.usno.navy.mil/vphase.html). By selecting the year, month, and date plus your local time, it will give you an image of the Moon with the right illumination. You can also use it to extract by trial and error when the full moon will occur at your location. Another lunar phase calculator can be found at lion.ece.clarkson.edu/sunmoon/index.htm

330 Where can I find out where an eclipse will be visible on Earth at a particular date and time?

NASA has a good eclipse track viewer (umbra.nascom.nasa.gov/eclipse/predictions/eclipse-paths.html) and don't forget

Dr. Fred Espenak's beautiful and informative pages at planets.gsfc.nasa.gov/eclipse/eclipse.html.

331 Where can I find someone?

If you know their name, you can look up their street address anywhere in the United States at the People Finder site (alabanza.com/kabecoff/Inter-Links/phone.html). If you are looking for an astronomer, try the StarHeads site in France (vizier.u-strasbg.fr/~heck/sfheads.htm).

332 Where can I find unusual astronomical software?

Try Zephyr Services Astronomy Software (www.zephyrs.com/astro.htm).

333 Where can I get images of the Messier Catalog objects?

The Messier Catalog is a list of 110 nonstellar objects, such as galaxies, bright nebulas, and star clusters that many amateur astronomers like to use to find the brightest and most interesting objects for telescopic study. The Students for the Exploration of Space has a good archive (seds.lpl.arizona.edu/messier/).

334 Where can I get information about telescopes for amateur astronomers?

You might try the Amateur Telescope Making site (web0.tiac.net/users/atm/) or the one run by D. Murry (www.calweb.com/~dmurry/scopes.html).

335 Where can I get star maps of the constellations?

Visit the Students for the Exploration of Space site (seds.lpl.arizona.edu/messier/map/). Also see Science Net Starmaps (www.campus.bt.com/public/ScienceNet/astron/nightpatrol/starmap.html).

336 Where can I get an update on the *Voyager* satellites as they leave the solar system?

The NASA Jet Propulsion Laboratory runs a Voyager status site (vraptor.jpl.nasa.gov/voyager/voyager.html), which gives the satellite speeds, distances from the sun, and the health of each spacecraft as it journeys ever further away from the Sun in search of the heliopause boundary region.

337 Where can I find out how planets and stars get their names?

It's not much of a site, but you can visit the U.S. Geological Survey Nomenclature page (wwwflag.wr.usgs.gov/USGSFlag/Space/nomen/nomen.html). Also take a look at the IPS-Guidelines for Star Naming (ftp.oit.unc.edu/ips/Starnaming.html) and *Scientific American*'s Ask the Experts (www.sciam.com.askexpert/astronomy/astronomy8.html) page.

338 How can I find out what the sky looks like at any wavelength?

NASA has a site called SkyView (skyview.gsfc.nasa.gov/), which lets you select various satellite archives obtained at specific wavelengths, from gamma ray to radio, and extract data of specific areas and objects.

339 How can I help the Search for Extraterrestrial Intelligence (SETI) program find signals from aliens?

The SETI@home program (bigscience.com/setiathome.html) is an opportunity for personal computer owners to search for extraterrestrial signals. The program hopes to have 50,000 people use their PCs for a few hours using the data from the Arecibo radio telescope in Puerto Rico and software they provide to search for nonnatural signals. The project will launch in Spring 1998 and I plan to help!

Chapter 19

Miscellaneous Topics

his chapter is a grab bag of questions that were hard to classify but were a lot of fun to receive at the Astronomy Cafe.

340 Why does an egg stand on its end on the day of the vernal equinox?

It doesn't. If you do this experiment carefully, you will find no correlation with time of day, time of year, or anything else. A few lucky eggs may do it if their yolks are low enough toward the table, but in a fair sample of tests conducted over many days this effect washes out. (This would be a great science fair project.) [1003, 742]

341 Can you date the crucifixion of Jesus Christ using astronomy?

Many people have tried. Colin Humphreys and his colleagues at the University of Oxford reviewed all of the previous attempts and reported their conclusions in *Nature* (22 December 1983). They came up with a date of Friday, April 3, 33 A.D., as a very likely candidate. The basis for their conclusion hangs on several pieces of information in the New Testament. Crucifixion took place during the 10 years that Pontius Pilate was procurator of Judaea, which was between the years 26–36, according to independent historical records, particularly the writings of the Roman historian

Tacitus. All four of the Gospels, Matthew, Mark, Luke, and John, agree that Christ's crucifixion happened a few hours before the beginning of the Jewish sabbath, which would be nightfall on a Friday, and within a day of Passover, which is celebrated at the time of a full moon. The Last Supper was a Passover meal, which would have happened on the evening at the start of the festival calendar 15 Nisan. The Crucifixion occurred later that day. This, however, disagrees with John's date of 14 Nisan and those of the other Gospels.

Humphreys and his colleagues then assumed that both 14 and 15 Nisan are possible dates and consulted predictions of lunar motion to determine for which dates between the years 26–36 either 14 or 15 Nisan fell on a Friday. These are the only dates possible for the Crucifixion as set by the biblical evidence. The result is a set of five possible Friday dates: for 14 Nisan, April 11, 27, April 7, 30, and April 3, 33; for 15 Nisan, April 11, 27, or April 23, 34.

The April 27 date may have been affected by atmospheric conditions that would have affected the visibility of the lunar crescent, which established the first day of the Jewish lunar month. The year 27 is too early, because Luke carefully states that John the Baptist began his ministry in the fifteenth year of the reign of Emperor Tiberius Caesar. Humphreys also concludes that John's baptism of Jesus would have happened in the autumn of A.D. 28–29 or spring A.D. 29–30. Also, most scholars believe that Pontius Pilate had been procurator for some time before the Crucifixion. The year 34 is probably too late, because it would have conflicted with Paul's conversion, which is believed to have happened in the year 34. This means that 15 Nisan is excluded, leaving only 14 Nisan as a candidate and that the interpretation of the Last Supper as a Passover meal cannot be correct. Jesus died at the same time that Passover lambs were being slain, which is consistent with New Testament statements that "Christ our Passover is sacrificed for us."

There are now only two plausible dates—April 7, 30, and April 3, 33. John's Gospel states that three Passovers occurred during his ministry, which began in the year 28. This would eliminate April 7, 30, leaving only April 3, 33.

To this debate, Humphreys added a new factor that previous scholars had not included. In Acts 2, 14:21, it is reported that the Moon would be turned to blood and the Sun turned to darkness at the time of the Resurrection. This observation also appears in the so-called Report of Pilate, which was written by Pilate to Tiberius. If this is taken as a lunar eclipse, then the Crucifixion can be dated exactly. Lunar eclipses were frequently described in exactly this way, even verbatim, by contemporary historians. Predictions show that there was only one lunar eclipse visible from Jerusalem at the time of Passover in the period 26–36 A.D. It occurred on April 3, 33. The Moon already in the midst of eclipse, rose above the horizon and would have progressively "turned to blood" as the eclipse continued.

Thus, a combination of astronomical detective work and independent historical accounts confirms much of the details in the Gospels as being accurate and, moreover, lets us state with considerable certainty when the Crucifixion occurred. In the annals of world religious records, it is the most accurately dated key event of any known religion. A similar astronomical approach for the birth date of Jesus involving the Star of Bethlehem is far more complicated and ambiguous. [867]

342 What is going to happen when the calendar changes to the year 2000?

Chaos. Of course, as any self-respecting astronomer will tell you, the new millennium will not begin until January 1, 2001, but many people, if not most people, including myself, will put logic aside and have one blowout of a party on the evening of December 31, 1999. I have to admit that I feel very strange about joining the crowd on this matter, because the correct day to celebrate the turn of the new century is not a matter of belief, fashion, or opinion. Historians have looked over how humans have celebrated the beginning of a new century for the past two or three times and have found that we have always done the right thing in the past. This time we will not. We will be celebrating the new millenium on the morning of January 1, 2000, rather than on January 1, 2001. It is a troubling example of how facts can sometimes be mandated by popular vote rather than by logic. I think an excellent exercise for students would be to review this issue and council their parents that they are doing the right thing a year too early. You can be certain that the television networks will be filled with experts explaining in careful terms why celebrating the arrival of the new millennium on January 1, 2000, is wrong. There will be countless articles explaining what to do. You will even have an endless number of surveys asking what the public thinks, as though somehow truth can be arrived at by a show of hands.

More seriously, computer programs will start to screw up royally. Even now, computer consultants are beginning to make tons of money telling big companies how to modify or rewrite portions of their ancient software so that paychecks and pension payouts don't suddenly start dishing out 100-year benefit payments on January 1, 2000. This is serious business. Just look at the date line on your checks. There are two blanks for the year, but "19" has been printed, because for 99 years it has been understood that all transactions took place in the twentieth century. It also saves lots of computer memory and database size by hardwiring the first two digits and performing the math on the last two digits of the year. But when 2000 rolls around, those last two digits will be 00 and all of a sudden the math gets fouled up.

An increasing number of articles are now appearing in journals, such as *InfoWorld,* describing all of the problems that will start to happen when older programs begin to encounter the millennium year—the "Year 2000" problem, as it is called. There will be literally billions of dollars of software problems that will have to be surmounted before the new year rolls in. Some companies are beginning to work on the problem now, especially the Social Security Administration, which stands to lose huge sums of money if they don't get on the ball. There are probably other companies that won't bother with this problem until the year before the changeover. The Year 2000 consultants say that the cost of correcting and validating software to work properly is measured in the tens of millions of dollars, and this added cost could be enough to drive some companies into bankruptcy.

I imagine that there are lots of other programs out there that we think will work well but have built-in time bombs waiting to go off to crash the program when December 31, 1999, becomes January 1, 2000. That 24-hour period will be a very exciting one to watch. I just hope all the fancy military software doesn't have any glitches in it. It was, for the most part, written by the lowest bidder, and during a time when computer memory was expensive. This is just the kind of situation that would make the Year 2000 problem a veritable nightmare. Stay tuned.

By the way, I will be celebrating December 31, 1999, as the last day of the millennium, and will also celebrate December 31, 2000, as the last day (I really mean it this time!) of the year 00. [275]

343 How do stars and comets get named?

If you are the first to report the comet to the official bureau at the Smithsonian Astrophysical Observatory, run by Dr. Brian Marsden, and can provide detailed coordinates, then you are first in line for getting the comet named after yourself. This is the only way comets are named—by their discoverers. If more than one discoverer observed the comet and got their telegram to Brian Marsden at the same time, then the comet gets two names. As for stars, only astronomers who study stars get to name them, if the star is not already in a catalog. Sometimes, astronomers observing at different wavelengths will identify stellar objects by a name they select. In rare instances, astronomers discover new clusters or galaxies and are allowed by the International Astronomical Union to name them after themselves, such as Maffei I or Liller 1. Most of the time, however, an astronomer just publishes a catalog of objects and gives them such labels as FIR-1 and FIR-2. [1343]

344 What major astronomical discoveries have been made in the last 100 years?

That's a great question and has a lengthy answer, but let me take a crack at it in Table 14. These events are just a few that come to mind. I'm sure I have left out many other significant events. [1139]

345 I have an astronomical theory. What do I do with it?

First, I am delighted that you wish to spend your time thinking seriously about astronomy. Nonscientists sometimes believe that astronomy and physics are somehow seriously flawed for philosophical reasons, because they do not have the training to properly evaluate all of the evidence that has accumulated over the years to support various scientific ideas. I should warn you, however, that we are long past the time when it is possible to make significant scientific discoveries without first understanding the full breadth of the current investigative process. This is analogous to jurors thinking that they, too, can be a lawyer just because they sat in on one trial and listened to lawyers. Even the individuals who overturned or radically altered certain aspects of physical science by introducing new ideas were not newcomers to science and mathematics. Einstein knew a lot of math and physics in a very deep way. Don't be confused by the fact that he worked briefly as a patent clerk.

In science, there are standards of evidence that must be adhered to in order to ensure that human imagination does not run wild with experimental evidence. It is improbable that nonscientists studying physics or astronomy can hit upon any genuinely new ideas. I have seen many manuscripts written by very earnest individuals, but they are all seriously flawed. Without exception, the authors of the unsolicited theories I have received all suffer from one or more of the following failings:

1. They willfully deny the existence of evidence that refutes central tenets of their new theories. In doing so, they claim that this is what scientists do anyway, so what's the big deal.

2. They are unwilling to try to couch their explanations in language that is not inflammatory. I don't mind being described as an [expletive deleted] by a professional scientist if my logic and attitude have lapsed in a technical discussion, but I absolutely resent being called the same thing by an armchair cosmologist who doesn't have my mathematical and research background.

3. They do not follow accepted norms of logical deduction. None of the discussions has any mathematics in it, so it is impossible to follow the reasoning from start to finish in an unambiguous manner.

4. They are convinced that their ideas are correct and that professional scientists are bent on stealing their ideas. As a result, every manuscript that I have ever seen has been copyrighted.

5. They think that science is just another language and that if they use the verbs and nouns of science in a theory, that makes a theory scientific. By this reasoning, we should be able to create warp drive by just listening to what science fiction authors have to say about its operating principles. [738, 716, 403]

Table 14 **Major events in the history of astronomy.**

Year

1891	Arizona meteor crater first recognized as a meteor impact crater
1904	Johann Hartmann discovers gas in interstellar space
1910	Ejnar Hertzsprung and Henry Russell develop the HR diagram to classify stars
1912	Victor Hess discovers first cosmic rays, from a high-altitude balloon
1917	Harlow Shapley discovers the Cepheid luminosity-distance relationship
1919	Einstein's theory of general relativity tested during a solar eclipse
1920	Shapley determines the size of the Milky Way using globular clusters
1924	Edwin Hubble proves the existence of other galaxies in the universe
1926	Lindblad and Oort discover that the Milky Way rotates differentially
1928	Hubble discovers the expansion of the universe
1929	Thermonuclear fusion established as the energy source for the Sun and stars
1931	Karl Jansky detects radio waves from beyond the solar system
1933	International Astronomical Union adopts 88 constellations in modern era
1938	Fritz Zwicky proposes that galaxies come in clusters
1944	Walter Baade discovers distinct stellar populations in the Milky Way
1946	Hot big bang theory predicts cosmic background radiation
1949	X rays from space discovered by National Research Laboratory scientists
1951	Discovery of emission from hydrogen gas in interstellar space
1957	USSR launches the first artificial satellite
1958	George Abell confirms the existence of superclusters of galaxies
1964	Alan Sandage discovers quasars
1965	Arno Penzias and Robert Wilson discover the cosmic background radiation
1967	The first pulsar is discovered by Jocelyn Burnell and Anthony Hewish

Table 14 (*Continued*)

Year

Year	
1968	First gamma-ray bursts detected
1968	Water and ammonia detected in interstellar clouds
1969	*Apollo 11* astronauts set foot on the Moon
1976	*Viking 1* lands on Mars and finds the soil lifeless
1987	First supernova observed in modern times
1994	Comet Shoemaker-Levy 9 impacts Jupiter
1995	Confirmation of the first planet detected in orbit around another star
1996	Possible microfossils detected in Martian meteorite fragment
1997	Discovery of the origin of gamma-ray bursts in distant galaxies
1997	*Sojourner* probe lands on Mars surface and finds evidence for ancient waterway

346 Are there any questions that you are surprised were never asked at the Astronomy Cafe?

Between the Astronomy Cafe's Ask the Astronomer, and the NASA *IMAGE* satellite's Ask the Space Scientist (image.gsfc.nasa.gov/poetry) sites, I have fielded more than 4,000 questions from students, teachers, and, especially, the general public. I have been surprised that people can pose so many interesting questions about astronomy with very few duplications.

I am also amazed that I have received so few offers to read manuscripts written by amateur cosmologists. I find it hard to understand why I escaped being inundated by indignant visitors protesting my hostile, narrow-minded, arrogant, scientific attitudes about ESP, UFOs, and creationism. For some reason, my site has attracted a huge number of people supportive of science and reason and not those more interested in pseudoscientific discussions.

I have also been surprised by so few questions about the Sun's neighborhood in the Milky Way or about the Milky Way itself.

There also have been few questions about the life cycles of stars, about the details of how in the world astronomers know what they do, and the scientific methodologies behind important discoveries. Even recent discoveries of planets orbiting nearby stars has prompted very few questions about how the discoveries were made or what these planets might be like. As an astronomer, I find these kinds of questions fascinating, because they reveal how we have come to know the workings of the physical world with such amazing clarity and accuracy. Clearly, the general public is interested in results much more than procedure.

I am amazed that I have never been directly asked whether I believe in God. As a practicing and devout agnostic, I am relieved at not having to come out of the closet on this point!

Very few people have asked me to describe NASA's future or our future with space exploration. No one has asked how many rocket launches occur every year (26 by the United States alone), how large is the U.S. commercial commitment to space (more than $20 billion), or what are the main impediments to colonizing the solar system and beyond (money). [2999]

347 What will astronomy be like in the twenty-first century?

I see astronomy completing its survey of the diverse contents of the visible universe and the inventory of how the universe has changed since the big bang. We will have a definitive inventory that shows all the ways that gravity can shape matter on stellar and galactic scales. There will be no significantly new undiscoverable categories of stars or galaxies. The twentieth century was unique in having developed most of such a listing, but you can only do this once per universe.

Astronomers will extend the mapping of the structure of the universe, galaxy by galaxy, out to 1 billion light years and beyond 1 billion light years for some small parts of the sky. From this, they will conclusively establish whether the universe is open (omega less than 1) or closed (omega greater than 1). The structure of the universe at greater distances will be a constantly expanding horizon, and this cataloging and red shift surveying will end when we almost literally run out of galaxies that can be seen. It will be harder and harder to get grant money to continue such a survey, because in a finite visible universe, we must eventually run out of questions worth the money and manpower to answer.

Astronomers will establish what dark matter is and just how much of it there is in the universe. They will determine the nature of the galactic dark matter component, which is widely thought to be underluminous or nonluminous matter, perhaps in black holes, dwarf stars, Jupiter, and the like. This type of dark matter will explain the dynamics of individual galaxies and their constituent stars but may not explain the large-scale motions of galaxies inside clusters, or clusters in the larger universe. This second type of dark matter will be quantified by X-ray satellites and the like, and we will know by the end of the first half of the twenty-first century just how much of this kind of dark matter is present and whether it is even matter at all.

No mystery can remain so for very long. Even as this book was going to press, the decades-old mystery of gamma ray bursts was buckling as astronomers captured the fading glow of one of these events (Plate 13) and found that it coincides with a faint, distant galaxy, as many people expected. Many more of these events will be tracked down, and in the twenty-first century there will be new satellites that will study the physics of these events, obtain the ever-important spectra of their emissions, and so on. Such has been the history of every mystery astronomers have uncovered, from quasars to pulsars to black holes; dark matter is the last refuge of novel physics in astronomy.

We already know of more planets outside our solar system than inside it—a historic moment in astronomy. The study of extrasolar planetary systems will explode as new instruments supported by NASA's Origins program come online. By the end of the first half of the next century, we will have catalogs of hundreds of these worlds and a complete inventory of the planetary systems within 50 light years of the Sun. We will discover just how typical or unique our solar system really is and what consequences this has for life on other worlds. We will also have spectral data on many of these worlds, even a few small enough to be Earth-like twins.

We will have an active program of reconnoitering Mars, Titan, and Europa, with crust-penetrating probes to search for ecological niches and conditions where bacteria may have established a toehold. We will have soil and mineral samples from missions to many of these garden spots of the solar system, either en route or on the drawing boards.

We will discover how to stop the deterioration of human bones and health in long-duration missions, and with newer generations of heavy-lift rockets, we will reach out and set foot on the Moon again, beginning where we left off in the 1970s. There will be all-or-nothing missions to Mars. You do not spend 400 days on a round trip to Mars, just to spend three days on the surface, like we did with the Moon. We will have to send in advance lots of resources, which will take up parking orbits around Mars to wait for a crew of astronauts to assemble them and set up a colony on Mars. The colony will stay there for several years before returning at the next Mars-Earth opposition, when relief crews will arrive. This will take place in the twenty-first century, unless there is a worldwide referendum to abandon space.

The commercialization of near-Earth space will continue to expand rapidly. Every nation that now has "two dimes to rub together" is developing a satellite or a launch-vehicle system. Commercial communication satellites will be augmented by getaway specials for people who want to take $50,000 joyrides into Earth orbit for a day.

Gravity wave astronomy will finally come of age as the new nonelectromagnetic frontier in observational astronomy. Detectors will monitor the collapse of matter into black holes and neutron stars anywhere within 100 million light years of the Milky Way or even beyond as detector sensitivities increase. We are still at the Galileo-stage of building sensitive gravity wave detectors. In the next century, these instruments will allow cosmologists to examine what went on in the universe at times far earlier than what the *COBE* satellite has revealed (300,000 years after the big bang). We will begin to explore conditions before the first second after the big bang with these instruments.

Neutrino astronomy, which has expanded enormously in the past 10 years, will become a major new frontier as more sensitive detectors are built. The contents of the neutrino universe will be imaged, and, although no new physics is expected, we cannot be sure as we explore this second nonelectromagnetic energy spectrum.

A career in astronomy will still be hard to get as population pressure continues to make more humans every year. In 1982, 96 Ph.D.s in astronomy were conferred. By 1996, more than 130 were awarded, as young astronomers threw caution to the wind and followed their dreams with little thought given to employment prospects. Since the number of "Einsteins" in humanity seems to be a fixed-per-capita phenomenon, we will have many more brilliant "Einstein-caliber" people entering the physics and astronomy professions, which will take these fields in directions we cannot now imagine.

New technologies will become available, and amateur astronomers will reap the benefits of a whirlwind of amazing over-the-counter equipment that will dwarf the technologies now available to professional astronomers. Amateur astronomers in the twenty-first century will aggressively colonize the radio frontier as optical astronomy becomes old hat. Amateur radio telescopes will be as common as home-built optical telescopes were in the 1950s. With hundreds of amateur radio astronomers combing the skies for adventure, who knows what odd transient events they will find. Even radio interferometers may be attempted by amateur astronomers.

Professional astronomers will no longer have research published in journals, but will use all-electronic media, such as the Internet or its twenty-first century equivalent. This means that historians 200 years from now will only have electronic forms of research papers to work from and no backup paper copies, which could be a problem if you worry about permanent electronic data storage for 50–200-year lifetimes. VHS tapes of family movies degrade badly after 10–15 years, and the best CD-ROMS last only 50–100 years before the medium itself begins to break down. More important, the software and platforms needed to retrieve the information change every five years. Historians of post–twentieth century science will have their hands full trying to figure out how we discovered all that we did during this pivotal age in astrophysics.

Astronomy as a profession will also begin to wane as we run out of fundamental questions to ask and answer. We live in a finite visible universe, with only a finite number of interesting questions of the first rank. There will be millions of questions of the second rank, but you can answer some questions one time only, such as "Is the universe going to collapse or will it expand forever?" or "Is our solar system alone?" After that, questions are in the realm of "Why does the brightness of the star SAO 190456 vary the way it does?" Many astronomers will still like to answer those kinds of questions.

In 1996 physicists confirmed that the quantum mechanical vacuum state is not empty but produces a repulsive force between conducting plates less than 0.5 microns apart, as predicted by

Casimir in the 1940s and by quantum electrodynamics. This force will be harnessed by cheating Heisenberg's uncertainty principle, one electron at a time. With this as a local power source, computers in the next century that use the quantum processors now being developed will no longer require outside power sources to drive them. The first applications will be novelty toys that draw energy out of empty space rather than solar energy. Eventually, larger systems will be designed. We may never be permitted by nature to do more than give single electrons a minuscule kick, but a million of these kicks on a single chip might be able to do some useful work for nanotechnology.

Many astronomers will turn to reflective writing aimed at popularizing or integrating in simple terms the body of astronomical knowledge. The twenty-first century will be the century of science popularization, as governments and citizens ask for even more payback for their investments in astronomy and as many astronomers who have become restless with pure research begin to find increasing enjoyment in telling nonastronomers about the universe.

Although some astronomical research will take place on the lunar surface and beyond, the major resources of astronomers for scientific discovery will still come from Earth-orbiting satellite observatories and ground-based systems. The number of small optical telescopes below 4-meters in size will severely shrink as it becomes cheaper to build large 10–20-meter-class instruments. Most active research will be done in Chile and Hawaii, with virtually all North American optical research observatories being forced to close down because of light pollution and for a lack of interesting projects worth the cost of keeping the observatories active. The exceptions will be optical observatories using optical interferometers.

Last, because of the inevitable increase in the raw intelligence and curiosity of the average citizen, which has increased steadily for centuries, we will see greater demands placed on the entertainment media for thoughtful stories about astronomy in the genre of science fiction. [3001]

Chapter 20

A Career in Astronomy

I love to talk about my job, and this chapter is a pretty good overview of what you might expect from a career in astronomy. It is not all fun and games, but most of the time it is an amazing day job. Young would-be astronomers will not like what I have to say about the job market, and, in fact, I am glad no professional astronomer went public with some of these comments when I was in junior high and high school. I feel comfortable about making some of my comments now, only because people seem to be a bit more realistic (cynical?) and willing to confront bad news than they were in the gung-ho 1960s. We are, however, living through some mighty amazing years in the history of astronomy. Although there are only 6,000 or so professional astronomers in North America, many of them fight tooth and nail to stay in this profession, because they do not want to wander too far from the frontier of human knowledge. Astronomers like to go to work every day and look at the new journal issues, with their announcements of exotic new discoveries. Virtually all of these discoveries never make it into the news media, so leaving astronomy is an unthinkable option for many of us.

348 Why did you become an astronomer?

At a very early age, I became fascinated by space. My father once showed me the three stars in Orion's belt, and I can honestly say that before then I had never paid any attention at all to the stars. I recall that from that day onward, I visited the library often to fetch every book available about astronomy and space and spent many evenings outside with my father's binoculars having a look around. My older brothers chipped in to buy me my first telescope—a 3-inch Tasco reflector. When I was in the sixth grade, the science fiction series *Outer Limits* premiered on TV, and from then on, if I wasn't studying astronomy and following the dawning of the space age, I was reading science fiction. By the time I entered the seventh grade I had a pretty good understanding of how stars evolved, but it wasn't until high school that I began to explore big bang cosmology and the evolution of the universe. I became an astronomer largely as an outgrowth of my long-standing fascination with the night sky and the steady stream of exciting discoveries that have been made in recent decades. In fact, the way I conduct my research today is not very different from how I explored astronomy when I was 10 years old. I think the trick to becoming an astronomer is not to grow up and not stop asking "silly" questions. [1975, 1817, 760, 462]

349 Is astronomy fun?

Sometimes, but sometimes it is just hard work. It depends on where you are in your career and what you are working on. I think successful astronomers who have managed to secure long-term employment by winning tenure or a civil service position have the most fun. They can enter into research projects knowing that their jobs are secure until they retire. This removes the dreadful task of having to worry about finding your next job every one to two years and where in the country that job will be.

For me, I have had a lot of fun doing research, going to different observatories to study stars and distant galaxies, and working on many exciting space projects, such as the NASA Cosmic Background Explorer (*COBE*). I am very happy where I have been in my research. I have had lots of joy in teaching others how wonderful astronomy is and writing articles and books on the subject. [1773, 627, 626, 469, 169]

350 What is your favorite part of astronomy?

The thrill of the hunt. I love the rush you get when you make a discovery. This can be a real discovery of something new in the universe or simply the thrill of finally understanding some fine point in physics or mathematics that someone else created decades ago. I love going to meetings to talk to people I have not seen in years and going to some observatory and getting "down and dirty" with new observations that no one has ever done before. [1778, 468, 466]

351 Do you like to look at stars?

Yes, I do. I like to look at them on a perfectly clear, dark night, away from city lights, where you can see the Milky Way and get a sense of just how big our universe is. It always gives me a thrill, and a chill down my spine, when I think of what it is all about, how stars are born and how they die, and how all of this happens over millions and billions of years. Cosmology is my particular favorite topic. [2968, 1239]

352 Is there a lot of stress in your career?

Yes, there is. You worry about the security of your career and whether you will be able to do your own research, which depends on whether your grant proposals are accepted. There are now so many proposals for research that it is harder to get research funding every year. Some years you don't get to do any of your own work and have to rely on other projects your company is doing in space-related areas to carry you through until your next grant. Colleges require their faculty to teach more if they bring in less grant money. Even now, as I enter middle age, my concerns seem to be slowly turning away from making new and often obscure discoveries to teaching the public about science and astronomy. I have become restless about writing research articles that are read by only a few dozen astronomers, when millions of people still do not understand the difference between a star and a planet or think that all theories are of equal value in science. This adds stress to my professional life as I search for new ways to redefine just who I am as an astronomer. [2997, 937, 934]

353 How much mathematics do astronomers need to know?

For every area of astronomy, you need algebra and calculus, and I mean complete mastery of the subject, not just the belief that you know this material. For theoretical work, you need even more mathematics, including tensor analysis, especially if you are going into cosmology or general relativity, among other topics. You may not need these every day if you are an observational astronomer working with data collection and analysis, but a knowledge of calculus has to be right there at your fingertips, because there are times when you need to use it for calibration work and to compare your data with theoretical expectations. Algebra is a work-horse, because you are never very far from having to manipulate quantities in a way that you learned in algebra. I know of no astronomers who did not excel in algebra and calculus, getting mostly top grades in both forms of mathematics. For example, my theoretician friends all got virtually straight As in physics and mathematics. In addition to mathematical proficiency, you need to have insight. You can get high grades grinding out answers to problems in a textbook, but your success as a physicist and as an astronomer is in being able to formulate your own problems and have the insight to solve them. [2952, 1831, 1237]

354 How do astronomers get paid?

Government research grants, proposals for which we either write as individuals or as groups, provide our main source of income. Also, some are paid by colleges and universities to teach students and to enhance the research departments of colleges. Some also are paid by planetariums, museums, or private industry. We make up a very complex workforce with lots of different ways of getting paid. Sometimes in our lives, we move from one system to another, from academia to government contracts to private industry. Every few months in *Parade,* which accompanies U.S. Sunday newspapers, there is a survey of the salaries of people working at different careers. I have yet to see anyone ask a scientist what they make, so here goes! Depending on where you get your first job after receiving your doctorate, beginning salaries are near $35,000. After 15 years, you can earn $50,000 or even $100,000, depending on whether you get tenure at a major university (not me) or a stable lifelong job at some private aerospace corporation with contracts to NASA research labs (my situation). Including all overhead costs, the yearly salary that my company figures as my total cost to NASA on a contract is about $105,000. My actual paycheck is substantially less than this. Given the current climate of keeping costs down for government contracts, I will probably never earn more than $100,000 before taxes, but I sure hope to get as close as I can. [2637, 1053, 137]

355 Do astronomers work a lot at night?

Virtually all astronomers work in the daytime and sleep at night.
The exception for some astronomers is when they go observing
at optical or radio telescope observatories when the situation
demands that they stay up at night. [1135, 1134]

356 What are the benefits of being an astronomer?

You get up in the morning knowing that for the next 8 to 10
hours you get to think about a subject you love, and you have
opportunities to make wonderful discoveries if you are good at
what you do and you have the right data to start with. No other
physical science has the holding wonder of astronomy, so you
are caught up in a tidal wave of excitement about the wonders of
the universe and what you can learn about it every day. Sure, this
sometimes gets lost in the day-to-day details of crunching data,
but it is a small price to pay for one of the greatest exploration
opportunities humans have ever known. Even I have my off days,
weeks, and months, but when I consider how fortunate it is that I
have just the right skills to make my own small contributions to
this exploration, I remain thrilled.

There is the knowledge that once your research on a particular
topic is published in the technical journals, it will be there as a
resource for someone 100, 200, or 300 years in the future. You
never really know what will happen to your papers. You watch
your papers like stocks on the stock market and celebrate when
they take off. [1054]

357 What are the pros and cons of a career in astronomy?

The good things about astronomy are too numerous to count. For
many astronomers, it is a pleasure to be studying the universe.
The pluses are that you get to do this as a day job! You are
actually paid by your college or a government contract or grant
to investigate some very exciting aspects of the universe and the
objects in it. You are doing work that is truly fundamental and
contributes to the sum total of human knowledge. Your research
papers and findings will live on for hundreds of years after you
are gone. During off-times, you can even write for the layman and
try to communicate some of the exciting discoveries about the
universe.

The down side is that the quality of jobs in astronomy is decreasing as more temporary positions, lasting one to two years at low salary, are offsetting the traditional secure, tenured or civil service, positions. Most of us are constantly under stress about whether or not we are in our last job in astronomy. Many young astronomers get a postdoctorate degree at a leading institution after a long hard battle to get a Ph.D., and then find their careers stalled because there are no openings. Even us middle-agers have these stresses, because after 10 or 15 years as active researchers, some of us may find ourselves too expensive for what we do, compared to younger astronomers with less experience willing to do nearly the same work at 20–30 percent lower salaries. Another stressful thought is the repeated forecast that the NASA space research budget will decline by more than 30 percent in the next seven years. For many astronomers, NASA grants are the difference between astronomy as a career and as a hobby.

Would I get into astronomy again if I had it all to do over? Yes, absolutely, but I sure would have conducted myself a bit differently in graduate school. I would have made certain that I got into a very active research group doing projects that consistently won grant money, tailored my interests to projects that I was technically capable of executing, and got out of graduate school as fast as I could to beat the crowd. Many of us went into graduate school thinking that we wanted to be cosmologists studying general relativity and black holes. We wasted several valuable years spinning our wheels in an area that was badly overcrowded with physicists and *really smart people.* Getting out of graduate school as fast as you can is important. By the time you get your Ph.D., you will have spent all of your twenties working for less than $6,000 per year as a student in terms of nontuition income. Your friends in other fields will have gotten lucrative entry-level jobs at five times that income. Given the employment prospects in astronomy, you will probably not recover this loss of more than $100,000 before you retire. [936]

358 How many papers do astronomers publish each year?

A number of studies have been done on this subject over the years. The average number of papers published per year is about three per astronomer, with one of them being first-authored by the astronomer and the rest coauthored. First authoring means the astronomer's name comes first, as the originator of the idea or discovery who does most of the writing and research. Coauthoring means an astronomer's name appears somewhere in a list of authors and usually means the workload was significantly less. There is a popular misconception, even shared by some astronomers, that faculty members become unproductive researchers after they acquire tenure. A study by astronomers Helmut Abt and Honghan Zhou (*Publications of the Astronomical Society of the Pacific,* 1996) examined 214 tenured astronomers from 17 institutions, including colleges and laboratories. They found that 48 percent published more after tenure was granted, 33 percent published between 50 and 100 percent of their pretenure rate, and 19 percent published significantly less after tenure. Thus, it isn't true that when astronomers attain the security of tenure that they automatically become unproductive. Those that fall behind often are heavily committed to administrative duties, and the decision is not a personal but a required one. [960, 669, 668]

359 What has been the growth of astronomical knowledge over the years?

Table 15 is a very rough representation of the growth of astronomical research since 1970, based on measuring the shelf space taken up by four popular international research journals: *Astrophysical Journal, Astronomical Journal, Astronomy and Astrophysics,* and *Monthly Notices of the Royal Astronomical Society.* The table is not complete because there are dozens more research journals, but I think you can see the trends. Essentially, the more people you have working in a field, the more papers will be written and discoveries made. [160]

360 Do I have to be another Einstein to be an astronomer?

No, but it would help when you go for tenure! Seriously, you do not have to be an Einstein in absolute terms, but the catch is that, as viewed by nonscientists, you do have to *appear* to be nearly as brilliant. As for any career, your skill and competency are determined by how much raw information you have been able to accumulate and the skill that you have in manipulating this knowledge. In astronomy, you have to be fully competent with a vast body of basic facts. In addition, there are an equally

Table 15 **How productive is astronomical research and how many astronomers are there?** This table show the growth in the number of astronomers and the volume of papers and journal articles. Only four of the more than 1,000 journals are listed, in terms of the number of feet their journals take up on library shelves. The favored journal by U.S. astronomers is the *Astrophysical Journal,* for which one year's worth of volumes now takes up 41 feet of shelf space. Electronic publishing has arrived just in time!

Year	Astronomers (AAS members)	Papers (world)	Authors (world)	Shelf Length of Journals			
				ApJ	AJ	AA	MNRAS
1970	2,800	6,350	7,018	12	5	12	7
1975	3,300	12,700	10,900	20	3	12	9
1980	3,800	14,600	12,600	23	6	12	9
1985	4,400	18,800	16,500	26	7	12	15
1990	5,000	22,000	17,000	37	12	16	14
1995	5,800	24,000	16,100	41	17	21	17

Shelf length measured in feet. Journal abbreviations are: ApJ = *Astrophysical Journal*; AJ = *Astronomical Journal*; AA = *Astronomy and Astrophysics*; MNRAS = *Monthly Notices of the Royal Astronomical Society*.

vast array of tools you must have at your fingertips to enable you to figure out the physics of what you are observing. This latter resource can only be acquired via the textbook and lab approach as an undergraduate and graduate student. Sadly, there are lots of people out there in the world who think they can short-circuit this learning process and get right into crafting theories of the universe. They are wasting their time, just as they would be if, after reading one page of the business section of a newspaper, they thought they could run a bank or plot the economic future of an entire country. Good intentions and enthusiasm are simply not enough currency to become a competent, professional astronomer with a shot at a long-term career. [2041, 1082, 291]

361 Is it easy to discover something?

It's very easy. Astronomers collectively discover thousands of things every month, but only a few of these discoveries are spectacular or significant enough to merit writing them up in a research paper and having it published. This is an exciting time, because you never know what will turn up. Astronomers have assembled hundreds of catalogs of objects in the universe, but only a small percentage of them have been looked at carefully. I am still making discoveries in a catalog of 300,000 infrared sources in the sky that was put together in 1984. In another five years, there will be a catalog listing more than 100 million galaxies and several billion stars. No astronomer will ever look at every one of them in detail. Instead, we will comb through these catalogs and search for objects that have the characteristics we are interested in studying. Still, no matter how you do the study, you will end up with hundreds of objects matching some specific set of characteristics. It will take years for you to look at each one, if that even turns out to be important to your study at all. Instead, you will probably only look at the few dozen oddballs and examine them carefully. Most of the objects we already know about in our catalogs will remain anonymous and unstudied, unless some feature of them is deemed unusual by some future survey. [170]

362 Is what you are now doing what you expected to do when you first became interested in astronomy?

Not at all, but that's what makes life so interesting. When I started thinking about a career in astronomy in elementary school, I had no idea what astronomers actually do. I just wanted to study the stars and outer space. By high school I was still just in love with being in touch with the stars and galaxies and cosmology. I still didn't know what astronomers really did. I had never come across a single research article in astronomy, and what I read in *Sky and Telescope* seemed easy enough to learn. It wasn't until I met my first astronomer, Professor Stuart Bowyer, while a freshman at the University of California, Berkeley, that I began to realize just what the profession was all about. By 1971 I loved cosmology, and black holes were not yet in vogue, but general relativity fascinated me because it sounded like something straight out of science fiction. During my undergraduate years, I studied what I could on general relativity and decided I wanted to be a cosmologist. By my senior year, I had taken a graduate-level cosmology course and a general relativity course and had also begun to size up just what my competency was in physics and mathematics. Even with nearly a straight-A average in these areas, I realized one day that being a theoretician was not comfortable. I felt like I was working at my limits, with no creativity left over to work in an area of astronomy that would be highly competitive.

Once I was in graduate school at Harvard, I worked my way toward a Ph.D., but I mostly thought I would spend my first few years being a postdoctoral student and then land a job in the academic world doing my own research and teaching undergraduates. I had no thought that there would be other possibilities. Nor did I anticipate just how difficult it would be to get a faculty position. During the 1980s and part of the 1990s, I applied for more than 50 faculty positions. I was offered an assistant professorship at Rensselaer Polytechnic Institute in Troy, New York, but despite the support of the Department of Astronomy, the new dean of physical science at the college refused to confirm the appointment. I also made the so-called short lists at four other colleges but never won faculty appointments.

Today, I still do my own research whenever I can get grant money from NASA, but I never got the call from academia to become a professor, which is my biggest frustration professionally. I have taught at adult education centers at the Smithsonian Institution and John's Hopkins University, and, occasionally, an article of mine is accepted at one of the popular astronomy magazines, but that's it. But to teach others about astronomy I run a web site, a technological development that I had not counted on in the past! Thus, my dreams for what I would be doing as a professional astronomer never materialized in the way I had hoped they would, but if you keep your eyes open, new opportunities may arise that are equally satisfying. [2998]

363 What is the future job outlook for careers in astronomy?

It is hard to know or even imagine—so much can happen. There will be many astronomers retiring from the baby boom cohort in the next 20 years, which will make room for the astronomers in Generation X. We will never reach a point, however, where everyone that wants to become an astronomer and makes it through graduate school with a Ph.D. will be able to find long-term employment. Astronomy is just too popular compared to the number of stable, tenured jobs available in government labs and academia. Right now, there are about three times more Ph.D. astronomers than there are stable jobs. I see this perhaps shrinking slightly but not much in the next few decades. Thus, young Ph.D.s will always have some hard decisions to make after they have gotten their degrees, 10 years after high school. That's a long time to stay in school while your nonastronomy friends are out there making big bucks. [2996, 2658, 2356, 1671, 865, 555, 158, 139, 138]

364 While I study astronomy, should I study law or something related to astronomy?

Yikes! By all means study anything other than law! Actually, as long as the population continues to increase, there should always be a market for one more lawyer. As for astronomy, we are already experiencing a glut of astronomers compared to the number of high quality jobs available. I think we have at least twice as many astronomers as the market can support, and, as a consequence, there are a lot of one- and two-year positions out there. I would strongly recommend seeing your education in astronomy as a stepping stone to professions in computers and applied physics, although applied physicists are becoming ubiquitous too!

Learn a skill (computer programming, statistical analysis, engineering) while you are learning cosmology and astrophysics. This is your best insurance that you will have something to fall back on just in case you are not one of the lucky few to secure a stable job in astronomy. [2559, 2530, 2025, 1937, 1926, 1478, 1217, 752, 707, 470, 211]

365 Do you have any optimistic words for a 17-year-old student interested in astronomy?

First, don't listen to advice from astronomers. Our experiences will not be yours in a decade. By the time you get your Ph.D. and are looking for a job, the climate will be completely different, and no one can tell you for certain what things will be like in 10 years. I would say, follow your heart and your mind, but make sure you pick up some concrete skills as you go, the easiest being computer programming and statistical analysis. When I was an undergraduate, the Apollo Program had been shut down and things looked bleak. In 10 years, there will be lots happening in planetary astronomy, because of all of the missions being planned and built. Also, those pesky baby boomer astronomers will be retiring, so in the next 15 years there will be more opportunities for the next generation.

As a lifelong hobby, astronomy is an excellent choice because there are so many ways you can enjoy studying the sky. You can buy or build your own telescope, use binoculars, photograph the constellations, surf the Internet space sites, and much more. I would recommend that you become familiar with the terminology of astronomy. Every hobby has its own language and requires some time to master. Once you understand the various terms, subscribe to a magazine like *Astronomy* or *Sky and Telescope* and read it carefully each month. The articles will keep you up to date on what professional astronomers have discovered and how it all fits together. Eventually, you will find yourself drawn to a particular area in astronomy and then you can seek out more information on that topic.

Depending on how badly the astronomy bug has bitten you, you can either remain a generalist, just reading everything you can get your hands on, or you can really dig deeply into a particular topic, including learning something about the mathematics and physics that are used to explore the subject. Many people remain generalists all their lives and their astronomy experience is perfectly satisfying. If you remain a nonprofessional astronomer, there is no law that says you have to learn math and physics, but for many of the discussions you will be reading, it helps to have an accurate understanding of how gravity operates, how energy is transformed from one form to another, and how light interacts with matter.

If you feel you might eventually want to become a professional astronomer, you must take all of the math and physics courses you can. All astronomers have a solid and advanced understanding of physics because, after all, everything in the physical universe is governed by the laws of physics. You have to thoroughly understand physics in order to understand virtually every aspect of astronomy. There are no shortcuts. Astronomy as a career is a major challenge and bears no resemblance to what you experienced as an amateur astronomer. You will be lucky to look at the sky at night more than a few times a year, preferring to study digitized images on a computer screen or photographs and spectra obtained from an observing run at a major observatory. Astronomy has evolved into a very high-tech science, and you must develop computer-related skills, including fluency in computer languages, such as FORTRAN or C. You will be writing and giving talks almost constantly, so you had better have full mastery of the English language and be comfortable giving lectures and speaking publicly. You must also be comfortable with accepting challenges about your research under very public circumstances and able to keep your cool and not take any comments personally. If you don't like being criticized, even with an IQ of 150, then astronomy is not your career. [2951, 2797, 2445, 1814, 1517, 935, 933, 878, 292, 297, 301, 243, 196]

acceleration The motion produced by changing speed or direction of motion. The statement "My car can do zero to 60 in 10 seconds" means an acceleration of 60 miles per hour in 10 seconds or a paltry 8.8 feet/sec/sec. Gravity produces an acceleration of 32 feet/sec/sec on the surface of Earth every day.

accretion disk A flattened, rotating gas cloud usually found around a black hole or neutron star. The gas has been accreted from some outside source, such as a nearby companion star.

apogee The farthest point in the elliptical orbit of a body around Earth.

arc second There are 360 degrees in a full circle. If you take one of these degrees and divide it by 60 you get intervals of 60 arc minutes. If you divide each of these arc minutes by 60 you get arc seconds. There are 3,600 arc seconds per degree. An arc second is about what a toothpick's width looks like at 400 meters. It is also about how fat the image of a star looks like from the surface of Earth, thanks to the turbulence in the atmosphere.

astronomical unit (AU) The distance between Earth and the Sun defined as 149,598,000 kilometers. It is a standard of measure for distances in the solar system. It also forms the basis for determining astronomical distances. At a distance of 3.26 light years, 1 astronomical unit corresponds to an angular distance of 1 arc second.

asymptotic The state of a system that you get when you take it to its limit in either time or space. Asymptotically, a star will turn into an inert cinder. The force of gravity from any body will fall to zero. A stretched piece of chewing gum will snap into two pieces.

barycenter The point in space around which two or more orbiting bodies in a multiple-body system orbit. The Moon does not really orbit around the center of Earth. Instead, both Earth and the Moon orbit around a geometric point located a few thousand kilometers from the center of Earth. As seen from the Sun, the Earth-Moon system looks like a concentrated point of mass at the barycenter position, and it is that point that makes an elliptical orbit around the Sun every year.

blue shift The shift in the emitted frequency of a body to higher frequencies. As the siren of a fire truck approaches, the pitch of the siren is higher because its frequency of oscillation is blue shifted as heard by your ears.

Bose-Einstein condensate A new state of matter discovered near absolute zero in which groups of atoms that are nearly motionless begin to merge together into a new system.

conjunction When a planet passes at its closest point in the sky to another planet or the Sun.

constant, cosmological A factor added to some cosmological models to account for a possible repulsive force exerted on matter by the physical vacuum. Also known as Einstein's "biggest blunder." I sure wish I made mistakes like that.

constant, Hubble The observable rate of increase of a galaxy's apparent velocity relative to Earth with distance, expressed in units of kilometers/sec/mpc. Its unit is actually 1/time, and cosmologists often refer to the reciprocal of the Hubble constant as the Hubble time. If the universe has been expanding at this rate since the big bang, this would be the age of the universe today, but we know this is not the case, because the expansion has been slowing down, or perhaps even speeding up if the cosmological constant is not zero.

convection The boiling motion seen in some physical systems as heat energy attempts to pass through a viscous medium. What you see in a pot of boiling water or on the surface of the Sun.

coordinate A mathematical label used to define the location or state of a particle or a particular system. There are three coordinates for spatial position, one coordinate for time, and, depending on the application, coordinates denoting the spin axis of a body, forming what are called quaternions. In quantum mechanics, there are still other coordinates peculiar to subatomic systems.

correspondence principle In quantum mechanics, if you take a particular quantum number of a system and make the quantum number very large, you will end up with the corresponding "classical" value. This works for electric charge, angular momentum, and total energy but not for the intrinsic spin of a fundamental particle, because spin is not a feature of a system with an analogue in the macro world.

decay The physical transformation of one system into another system, as in the case of a heavy atomic nucleus or an unstable particle changing into a simpler and often lighter one with a lower energy. According to some theories, even the physical vacuum can decay.

dimension, hidden The theoretical possibility that there are more dimensions to space and that these dimensions are so small that they are hidden from direct observation. Fundamental particles experience them, and this determines their physical properties, if you trust the mathematics.

dimension, space The number of coordinates needed to define all the essential physical properties of a body's location in space.

Doppler shift The shift observed in the sound or light signals from a body as it moves closer or farther away from you.

ecliptic plane The band in the sky along which the planets and the Sun appear to move as viewed from Earth; a reflection of the fact that the orbits of the planets are confined to a very narrow range. Also the name given to the plane of the orbits of the planets.

equinox As viewed from Earth, the two times during the year when the Sun crosses the ecliptic plane, on March 21 and September 21. This is not the same as the date when the length of day and night are exactly the same.

exoplanet The name given to all of the new planets discovered to be orbiting other stars. Among these are the so-called epistellar jovians, which have about the mass of Jupiter and orbit their stars well within the size of the orbit of Mercury.

field The specification of the intensity or other magnitude of a system at each point in space and time. On a conventional weather map, plotting the local temperature across the United States results in a "scalar" temperature field. Plotting the arrows showing local wind speed gives you a "vector" velocity field.

field, electromagnetic The strength of the electromagnetic force at various points in space and time.

field, gravitational The strength of the gravitational force at various points in space and time. Actually, force is the rate at which the gravitational field changes in a particular region of space. Gravitational fields exist whether a force of gravity can be measured or not.

field theory The study of the nature and characteristics of the fundamental fields in nature, specifically, to construct a unified mathematical description of them.

fluorescence The process of emitting light by stimulating the electrons in atoms to make quantum mechanical jumps. This is what goes on in those long cylindrical light bulbs over your head at the office or in a classroom.

galactic nuclei The region of space at the center of spiral or elliptical galaxies where the density of stars is the highest. Typically, millions of stars can be found in a region of space only a few light years across.

galaxy A system containing more than 1 million stars that are independent of the Milky Way and are not the systems astronomers recognize as globular clusters. Some dwarf spheroidal galaxies look like globular clusters cut adrift in intergalactic space.

geodesic A curve in a space that represents the shortest distance between two points.

graviton A hypothetical particle whose exchange between bodies causes the phenomenon we see as the gravitational force. More properly, they generate the gravitational field itself.

greenhouse effect The trapping by the atmosphere of the infrared radiation emitted by a planet, causing the planet to heat up even more. When it gets completely out of balance, you end up with a planet like Venus. In limited form the greenhouse effect can heat a planet like Earth so that liquid water can exist on its surface, but too much of a good thing could make life on Earth very miserable in the next century.

Heisenberg's uncertainty principle A principle in modern quantum mechanics that states that you may not simultaneously make an infinitely accurate measurement of quantities, such as the speed of a particle and its location. Perfect knowledge of one means complete lack of knowledge of the other.

horizon, black hole Also called the "event horizon," this is the limiting surface surrounding the singularity of a black hole that represents a one-way entry, across which you may travel from an external space-time, but one for which you may not make the return trip, even traveling at the speed of light. For supermassive black holes, you would not experience anything unusual at this point in space, but a distant observer would see some strange things happen to you.

horizon, cosmological The limiting surface in three-dimensional space surrounding every observer defined by the distance light could have traveled toward the observer had it been emitted exactly at the instant of the big bang from a distant point in space. There is plenty of universe outside your local horizon, but you will not see the light signals from this distant matter until more time passes. This horizon expands at the rate of 1 light year per year.

hyperspace The hypothetical collection of space dimensions beyond the three that we know in the physical world.

incandescent The type of light emitted by a hot body, either from the surface of a star or the heating of a piece of matter or filament. The glow from your reading lamp is produced by incandescence.

insolation The sunlight and heat energy that strikes the surface of Earth at a particular latitude. (The stuff inside your jacket is insulation.)

interstellar medium The collection of gas particles, dust grains, and clouds that are found in the space between the stars (not someone versed in ESP or communicating telepathically with space aliens).

ionized A state of matter in which an atom has lost some or all of its electrons.

isotropic The condition in which some quantity appears to have the same value in all directions of the sky.

kinetic energy The energy a body has by virtue of only its speed of motion.

lepton Any of a class of particles that includes the electron, muon, and neutrino, which interacts only through the electromagnetic and weak forces.

linear scale A measuring scale in which the intervals are sequential and equal sized, like the markings on a tape measure.

local sidereal time The sky coordinates of the right ascension line, which is exactly at the north-south meridian of a local observer on Earth at a particular instant during the day or night.

luminosity The amount of energy per second emitted by a body. The sun has a luminosity of 3.9×10^{33} ergs per second, which astronomers often refer to as 1 solar luminosity. A light bulb has a luminosity of 60 watts.

mass A well-known but intrinsically mysterious property of matter that accounts for its resistance to being accelerated. In subatomic physics, some particles have zero rest mass, such as photons; others have a minuscule amount of mass, such as the neutrino, or enormous amounts, such as the W bosons. Most of the measurable mass of a proton is an artifact of the energy of the gluonic fields holding the three constituent quarks together, each of which has a rest mass of only a few percent of the total proton mass. Mass may be a property of the interaction of matter with a new field in nature called the Higgs field. Mass, by the way, is not the same as weight. Weight is the force produced by a specific amount of mass under acceleration usually by gravity at the surface of the Earth.

matter, baryonic Matter in the form of particles, such as protons and neutrons.

matter, dark Matter that may exist in very large quantities in the halos of galaxies or in intergalactic space, which contributes to the gravitational mass of a system but not to the amount of light present in the system. Dark matter was referred to as missing matter by astronomers prior to the 1980s, it may be in either baryonic or non-baryonic forms in the universe.

meridian The line on the sky that connects the north and south celestial poles and passes through your local zenith directly overhead.

metallicity The amount of elements heavier than helium that an object is composed of relative to its total mass. The metallicity of the sun is about 1.7 percent by mass.

meteor A body entering the atmosphere that produces a bright trail.

meteorite A body recovered from the ground not found in a cemetery.

millirad A unit of radiation dosage for living systems. Seventy millirads is about what you get from a standard chest X ray; 350 millirads is about what you get from all natural background sources.

nebula A cloud of gas in space that may be illuminated by a star or be seen as a dark spot because no stars are nearby.

neutrino A very light, possibly massless particle that only interacts with matter via the so-called weak nuclear force. Neutrinos can pass through many light years of lead and only suffer a 50–50 chance of being absorbed.

neutron star The remains of a massive star that has become a supernova. It represents the compressed core of the star and has about the mass of the sun but in a region only 20 kilometers in radius.

nova The detonation of the surface of a collapsed object, such as a white dwarf or neutron star, due to mass flow from a companion star. The ignition of the fresh infalling fuel produces a millionfold increase in the electromagnetic output from the star.

nucleosynthesis The process by which the heavy elements are created from the lighter elements, usually in the interior of massive stars, or were created in the first few minutes after the big bang.

omega The ratio of the observable density of the universe from all sources, compared to the critical density determined from the Hubble constant. If omega is greater than 1.0, the universe is likely to collapse in the future. Current best estimates show values less than 0.5 routinely, but dark matter may be present in large enough quantities to make omega very close to 1.0, as predicted by inflationary cosmology. The cosmological constant also contributes to the measurable value of omega.

organic Compounds composed primarily of carbon, hydrogen, and oxygen.

paradox A condition that can occur when two logically consistent outcomes are possible at the same time.

perigee The position in the elliptical orbit of a body around Earth where the distance from Earth is at its minimum.

perturbation The influence that one body has on another that causes the bodies to alter their previous motions. In most communities, this phenomenon is only a misdemeanor.

photon The name given to the packet of energy of the electromagnetic field.

plasma A gas composed of atoms that have had some of their electrons stripped. This "fourth" state of matter has nothing to do with the plasma in your blood or other fluids.

polarity Opposing conditions such as positive and negative, north and south, up and down, and manic and depressive.

potential energy The energy that a body has by virtue of its location within a field.

pulsar A neutron star that is spinning and emitting pulses of electromagnetic energy at well-defined time intervals.

quantum An irreducible packet of energy that has well-definable properties.

quantum field A field consisting of individual particles whose interactions or properties lead either to specific forces or types of matter particles. Each field has its own unique quantum particle, for example, the electromagnetic field quantum is the photon, and the gravitational field quantum is the hypothetical graviton. The exchange of these particles gives you the sensation of a force.

quantum fluctuation A spontaneous, acausal change in some physical properties of a system.

quantum indeterminacy The quantum mechanical condition in which the properties of a system are not localized in time or space.

quantum jump The change in a system from one stable state to another. Electrons can jump up or down in energy inside an atom if they are excited to do so by external influences. Not related to the TV series *Quantum Leap.*

quantum spin A fundamental property of a particle that has no analogue in the macro world but is very loosely related to the rotation of the particle about some axis in space.

quantum state A configuration for a system defined by a specific and unique set of values for its energy, angular momentum, and spin.

quark Any of the six fundamental particles that combine to make protons, neutrons, and other heavy nuclear particles that primarily interact via the strong nuclear force.

quasar A class of distant galaxies that have a central energy source, probably a supermassive black hole, which is emitting tremendous amounts of electromagnetic energy.

radiation A loose term used to describe the flow of energy in space from a source. It can be a stream of particles, but astronomers generally reserve the moniker "radiation" for electromagnetic energy or gravitational energy. Cosmic rays are actually particles, not radiation.

radioactive A term used to describe certain types of elements that are unstable and emit fragments such as alpha particles or electrons.

red shift The shifting of a sound or light signal to longer, red wavelengths. In cosmology, it refers to the phenomenon in which the space between galaxies has expanded, and this expansion has stretched the wavelength of light emitted by distant galaxies so that they now are longer than at the time of emission.

resolution The ability of an instrument to distinguish between two nearby values of intensity or some other measured parameter.

solstice The time during the planetary year when the Sun is at its greatest distance from the ecliptic plane as seen from the surface of the planet. For Earth, these dates are near June 21 and December 21.

space The property of the physical world embodied in the separations between objects. It may also be a physical field related to gravity.

sunspot A region of the Sun in which magnetic fields are concentrated, which provides sufficient pressure so that the trapped gas may be cooler than the surrounding solar surface, thereby making the region appear darker by contrast.

supernova The detonation of a massive star, which typically produces a luminosity increase equal to several billion times that of the Sun for a period of several months.

symmetry A property of a physical system that remains unchanged after some transformation has been applied. For example, if you translate a system in time, the property that stays the same is its total energy; if you rotate it by a specific distance, the property that remains unchanged is its angular momentum.

thermal energy The energy of a system contained in the random motions of its constituents measured by the system's temperature.

thermonuclear fusion The fusion of matter by the collision of particles as determined by their thermal energy.

tidal effects The many effects on a body due to the gravitational influences on it by a nearby body. Usually expressed in terms of a deformation in shape.

topological structure A component of the shape of a system. For example, the handle of a coffee cup is a topological structure on a basic cylindrical form closed at one end.

topology The basic shape or form of a system. A donut has a different topology than a basketball. Think about it.

tunneling The quantum mechanical ability of a system to change from one state to another in a way that is expressly forbidden by macroscopic particles and systems. Often expressed by the statement that an electron can escape from any box, or it can escape from any confining energy potential. It has nothing to do with digging with a shovel.

universal time The local civil time measured at an Earth longitude of zero degrees, located in Greenwich, England.

vacuum A poorly understood physical condition in which no physical object appears to be present but in which virtual particles abound and can produce some astounding phenomena, despite the fact that they are not directly observable. According to physicists these come in three types—true, false, and Hoover.

velocity The speed of a body in a particular direction in space.

wave function A mathematical quantity that when multiplied by itself results in the probability that a particle of a system will be in a particular state at a particular location in space-time.

white dwarf The remains of a low-mass star less than about five times the mass of the Sun. Supported entirely by so-called degeneracy pressure, it contains nearly the full mass of the original star in a region of space no larger than Earth.

wobble The motion of the axis of a planet due to external forces or torques or due to the constant redistribution of mass in the planet because of atmospheric motion.

world line The track or geodesic curve that a particle or system takes in four-dimensional space-time. It represents the history of a particle as it wiggles its way through space. Slices through the world line at constant time intervals reveal the location of the particle in three-dimensional space.

Illustration Credits

Figure 3 Courtesy of Dr. Jun Chen, University of Hawaii. **Figure 7** Courtesy of Dr. Geoff Marcy and Paul Butler, San Francisco State University. **Figure 9** Compton Gamma Ray Observatory, BATSE, NASA.

Plate 1 *Yohkoh* mission of Institute of Space and Astronautical Science (ISAS), Japan. The X-ray telescope was prepared by the Lockheed Palo Alto Research Laboratory, the National Astronomy Observatory of Japan, and the University of Tokyo with support from NASA and ISAS. **Plate 2a** AP/Wide World Photos. **Plate 2b** *Pathfinder,* Jet Propulsion Laboratory, NASA. **Plate 3** PRC96-07, January 6, 1996, B. Sahi and J. Trauger, NASA/AURA (Associated Universities for Research in Astronomy). **Plate 4** NASA. **Plate 5** The Peekskill car is owned by R. A. Langheinrich Meteorites and Fossils, Ilion, New York. **Plate 6** Courtesy of Dr. Louis Frank and Dr. J. B. Sigwarth, The University of Iowa. The underlying image is a subset of the Face of the Earth™, copyright © 1996 by ARC Science Simulations. **Plate 7** PRC96-13a, April 15, 1996, Robert O'Dell, Kerry P. Handron, Rice University, Houston, Texas and NASA. **Plate 8** Space Telescope Science Institute/NASA. **Plates 9a and 9b** NASA Goddard Space Flight Center and the COBE Science Working Group, images provided by NSSDC. **Plate 10** PRC96-29a, September 4, 1996, R. Windhorst, Arizona State University and NASA. **Plate 11** PRC96-35a, November 19, 1996, John Bahcall, Institute for Advanced Study, Princeton University and Mike Disney, University of Wales and NASA. **Plate 12** PRC96-10, April 24, 1996, W. N. Colley and E. Turner, Princeton University and J. A. Tyson, Bell Labs, Lucent Technologies and NASA. **Plate 13** PRC97-20, June 10, 1997, K. Sahu, M. Livio, L. Petro, D. Macchetto, Space Telescope Science Institute and NASA. **Plate 14** DMSP data from the U.S. Air Force, processing by NOAA National Geophysical Data Center.

Index